Looking Ahead

Learning About Academic Writing

LINDA ROBINSON FELLAG

Community College of Philadelphia

SERIES EDITORS

PATRICIA BYRD
Georgia State University

JOY M. REID
University of Wyoming

Video notes in Instructor's Manual by
Elizabeth Mejia
Washington State University

Heinle & Heinle Publishers
I(T)P An International Thomson Publishing Company

Pacific Grove • Albany • Bonn • Boston • Cincinnati • Detroit • London
Madrid • Melbourne • Mexico City • New York • Paris
San Francisco • Tokyo • Toronto • Washington

The publication of *Looking Ahead: Learning About Academic Writing* was directed by members of the Newbury House ESL/EFL at Heinle & Heinle:

Erik Gundersen, Editorial Director
Jonathan Boggs, Market Development Director
Kristin M. Thalheimer, Senior Production Services Coordinator
Nancy Mann Jordan, Senior Developmental Editor
Stanley J. Galek, Vice President and Publisher

Also participating in the publication of this program were:
Project Manager/Desktop Pagination: Thompson Steele, Inc.
Managing Developmental Editor: Amy Lawler
Manufacturing Coordinator: Mary Beth Hennebury
Associate Editor: Ken Pratt
Associate Market Development Director: Mary Sutton
Photo/video Specialist: Jonathan Stark
Media Services Coordinator: Jerry Christopher
Interior Designer: Sally Steele
Cover Designer: Ha Nguyen
Cover Artist: Katherine Stuart

ISBN 08384-7911-1
10 9 8 7 6 5 4 3 2 1

To my daughters, Nora and Nadia,

and all others who treasure reading

and writing

Thank You

The author and publisher would like to thank the following individuals who offered many helpful insights, ideas, and suggestions for change during the development of *Looking Ahead: Learning About Academic Writing:*

Victoria Badalamenti, *LaGuardia Community College, New York*
Karen Batchelor, *City College of San Francisco*
Cheryl Benz, *Miami Dade Community College*
Pam Butterfield, *Palomar College, California*
Lisa Camp, *Hunter College, New York*
Marvin Coates, *El Paso Community College, Valle Verde Campus*
Carol Culver, *San Francisco State University*
Kathleen Flynn, *Glendale Community College, California*
Barbara Foley, *Union County College, New Jersey*
Byrun Hauser, *Miami Dade Community College*
Gayle Henrotte, *Mt. San Antonio Community College, California*
Mary Hill-Shinn, *El Paso Community College*
Cynthia Howe, *Seattle Central Community College*
Sheila McKee, *University of North Texas*
Lynne Nickerson, *DeKalb College, Georgia*
Norman Prange, *Cuyahoga Community College, Ohio*
Jennifer Ross, *LaGuardia Community College, New York*
Dawn Schmid, *California State University at San Marcos*
Catherine Sessions, *Hunter College, New York*
Bob Shiel, *St. Augustine College, Illinois*
Joe Starr, *Houston Community College*
Christine Tierney, *Houston Community College*
Patricia Weyland, *Ohio State University*

ONTENTS

• • • • • • • •
Chapter 1

Chapter 4   Remembering   88

Chapter 6   Observing   142

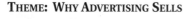

Chapter 7 Analyzing 170

*W*ill your students be ready to meet the academic writing expectations of their instructors and professors when they leave your ESL program? *T*hey will if they use *Looking Ahead,* Heinle & Heinle's new 4-level academic writing/grammar series.

SUCCESSFUL WRITING WITH *LOOKING AHEAD*!

Chapter 7
*A*nalyzing
Why Advertising Sells

GOALS

Will your students be ready . . . to perform various types of academic writing?

Looking Ahead focuses on the various types of writing that successful students must learn to employ: *investigating, explaining, evaluating, summarizing, organizing, describing, analyzing,* and others. In practicing these various forms of academic writing, students call upon a host of rhetorical modes such as *definition, classification,* and *contrast* to support their ideas and opinions. They also develop facility in using a host of academic writing formats such as *paragraphs, essays, reports,* and *memos.*

Will your students be ready . . . to understand and meet challenging academic expectations?

Each chapter begins with authentic academic assignments from across the disciplines (e.g. sociology, history) for the students to analyze and discuss. These assignments show how writing tasks are used in the "real world" of academic course work.

Will your students be ready . . . to apply their own writing skills to academic situations?

Each chapter contains several short writing activities and most contain at least one longer writing assignment designed to prepare students for the writing tasks they will encounter in college classes. Throughout the chapters, students practice writing activities that are appropriate for a specific academic setting (e.g. writing a science lab report). The writing activities in each chapter end with a writing assignment that guides students step-by-step through the process.

Sample Authentic College/University Remembering Assignments

In a college or university classroom, you will use the skills you learn in this chapter to complete assignments like the ones below:

Freshman Composition
Assignment: Diagnostic Essay
Write an essay about your birthplace, the place where you grew up, and the special events that helped to shape your early life. Try to remember and write as many details as possible about the early part of your life.

PUTTING IT ALL TOGETHER
FINAL WRITING ASSIGNMENT: STEPS TOWARD SELF-ESTEEM

Reading 3 suggests four steps for changing your life. Write a paragraph in which you give your opinion about **one** of the four steps. Begin by introducing the step with a sentence containing a reporting verb that identifies the source (by title and author). Then give your opinion about the step. Use your own experience, facts, or examples as support.

Once you have written your interview questions, you will need to develop a method for writing down the interviewee's responses. You may want to use a tape recorder to record the conversation. However, you should also take notes in case your recorder doesn't work properly or the person you interview doesn't want you to record him or her. Here are some suggested strategies:

Notetaking Tips

1. Write the ten questions on paper, leaving several lines between each question.
2. Ask the question slowly and clearly.
3. Listen carefully to the interviewee's answer. Write down important words.
4. Ask the person to repeat if you are not sure what was said.
5. Ask the person to read over the answers you wrote down.

    Before you interview, practice with a classmate. Take turns being the interviewer and interviewee. Practice with a tape recorder if you will use one in the real interview.
    Ask each other a few of the questions. Listen and take notes. Ask your partner to repeat if you do not understand or remember what was said. Then ask your partner to check your notes. If you used a tape recorder, play the tape to check the accuracy of your notes.
    Now you are ready to set up the interview.

Will your students be ready . . . to exercise key vocabulary acquisition skills?

Special focus is given to developing vocabulary acquisition skills necessary for success in a variety of academic fields. Students gain strategies for learning new vocabulary and the relevant grammar associated with these vocabulary items.

Will your students be ready . . . to exploit a variety of academic skills in writing?

Being a successful student means being a successful academic writer. In *Looking Ahead*, students learn essential academic writing skills like *brainstorming*, *seeking* and *using input from peers, gathering ideas from various sources, giving recognition to sources*, and *editing*.

Activity 5-1   Understanding Key Terms in Education

The following activity contains key terms taken from college catalogs and brochures. Notice that key terms may consist of a single *noun* or a *noun phrase* (*noun* + other word or words). With a partner, discuss the differences in meanings between these pairs of words. Discuss your ideas with your class.

1. a college major   *and*   a college course
2. an academic department   *and*   an academic discipline or field
3. a credit hour   *and*   a course
4. a required course   *and*   a prerequisite course
5. a core course   *and*   an elective course
6. a degree plan   *and*   a degree
7. an associate's degree   *and*   a bachelor's degree
8. admission   *and*   transfer
9. a college catalog   *and*   a program or department brochure

LEARNER'S NOTEBOOK

Looking Ahead to Your Future

Think back about the job that you wrote about previously in your notebook. Add another entry to describe the education and skills you will need to get this job. What skills, training, or degree will you need? How do you plan to get those skills? If you are undecided, write about an educational program and job you may want to pursue.

Will your students be ready . . . to apply the reflective skills necessary for fluency in academic writing?

Each chapter contains several *Learner's Notebook* activities that accomplish two purposes. First, *Notebook* activities give students an opportunity to gain fluency through reflective writing that will not be evaluated. Second, this type of free-writing helps students generate ideas for the academic writing tasks to come later in the unit.

Will your students be ready . . . to look ahead to their academic future?

Chapters end as they begin—with information about authentic academic tasks and assignments. Students can analyze these assignments to learn more about the work that will be required of them when they enter degree programs. These sample assignments motivate students by showing them that they will apply the skills they are learning with their work in *Looking Ahead*.

LOOKING AHEAD

Authentic Academic Assignments

Read the following academic assignments which relate to organizing. In a small group, answer the discussion questions that follow.

Data Processing 103

Internet Career Research: For this project, you will be conducting research on one possible career in data processing via the Internet. Using the resources you have accessed on the World Wide Web and through other parts of the Internet, find out the following information about a career in data processing.

1. The job title and description
2. Starting salary
3. Outlook for job availability

SUCCESSFUL GRAMMAR ACQUISITION WITH *LOOKING AHEAD*!

Will your students be ready . . . to recognize the different discourse types found in academic writing?
Authentic readings and writing assignments in *Looking Ahead* were selected based on the academic discourse types that students most often need to read and produce in academic settings. These authentic materials give students many opportunities to see and analyze how English grammar and rhetoric "work."

> **GOALS**
>
> **WRITING**
> ◆ develop analyzing skills
>
> **GRAMMAR**
> ◆ examine and practice several of the features of interactive communication and persuasion: *you* and *we*, questions, contractions, and *if* sentences
>
> **CONTENT**
> ◆ learn about and examine advertising techniques

> **Grammar Preview**
>
> In previous chapters, you have read and produced informational writing that *informs* an audience about a subject. This type of writing appears not only in academic course work, but also in publications that describe a college or university and its programs: course catalogs, brochures, application forms, for example.
>
> In the grammar activities in this chapter, you will examine and practice several of the important grammatical features of informational writing in the context of college publications so that you can better read and write these types of informational texts.

Will your students be ready . . . to apply the grammar of academic writing?
Recent research has shown that specific grammar structures appear in clusters within types of discourse. By concentrating exclusively on one grammar cluster in each chapter, *Looking Ahead* focuses only on the grammar that is essential for the writing typical of a specific discourse type.

Will your students be ready . . . to easily access important academic grammar information?
The *Grammar and Language Reference (GLR)* section at the back of the book pulls together all of the grammar explanations and authentic examples for easy student access. An icon  tells students when to refer to the *GLR*. Successful Academic Reading with *Looking Ahead*!

PASSIVE SENTENCES IN ACADEMIC WRITING	
Passive sentences occur in different academic disciplines. Science and social science textbooks contain have many uses of the passive, as in the following passages.	A shiny plastic balloon **is taken** into a warm room and filled with helium. It **is** then **taken** into a cold room. When the balloon **is moved** from the warm room into the cold room it becomes smaller. This happens because when helium **is cooled** it contracts, or shrinks.
	Isaac Newton **was born** in England in 1652. During his extensive career in science, he made scientific discoveries in areas such as light, color, and planetary orbits, in addition to gravity. Newton **is** also **credited** with the invention of the mathematical branch called calculus. His most famous book **was called** Principia. Because of his many contributions to science and mathematics, Newton **was knighted** in 1705. He died in 1727.
	For example, we **are** all **shaped** by our culture and **must be understood** in that context. Culture **is defined** as the patterns of behavior, beliefs, and values that **are shared** by a group of people.

SUCCESSFUL ACADEMIC READING WITH *LOOKING AHEAD*!

> **ON DOWN THE ROAD**
>
> The National Road was about to begin a second life. By the late 1800s, bicycles were becoming popular, and soon after, the automobile was invented. Once again, Americans took to the road for fun and travel. As traffic on the National Road increased in the early 1900s, cries for improved road surfaces arose.
>
> Roads gradually improved due to motorists' continued demands. In 1916, Congress 5 passed the Federal-Aid Road Act and established the Bureau of Public Roads. By 1923, new surfacing covered most of the National Road from Cumberland, Maryland, to Indianapolis.
>
> By the end of the nineteenth century, buses provided public transportation along the National Road. Later, buses ran from one city to another at scheduled times. Trucks hauled freight along the National Road. As travelers used the road to go greater distances, road 10 signs, gas stations, and motels became part of the roadside landscape.

Will your students be ready . . . to apply essential reading skills for successful writing preparation?
Simply stated, effective reading skills are essential for success as an academic writer. Academic writing requires that you draw on reading sources in a variety of ways—to get ideas for writing, to get background information on a topic, and to use the information you find to support your ideas. Given this, each chapter in *Looking Ahead* has a "reading theme," which allows students to become familiar with the vocabulary, ideas, and issues within that topic. In both content and style, readings reflect the types of selections that students encounter in their academic classes.

CNN VIDEO
WITH
LOOKING AHEAD!

Will your students be ready . . . to use a variety of authentic media to prepare for their academic future?
Each chapter in the *Looking Ahead* series has a CNN video clip related to the chapter theme and designed to further stimulate authentic discussion and writing. Appealing to the learning style preferences of auditory and visual students, the videos connect the content of *Looking Ahead* to the real world. An introduction to video use in the ESL classroom by Elizabeth Mejia (see the Instructor's Manual) provides the foundation for sound teaching strategies with video.

The CNN videos are provided free of charge for teachers who adopt one or more of the *Looking Ahead* textbooks for their classes.

THE WORLD WIDE WEB
WITH
LOOKING AHEAD!

Are you ready . . . to provide all you can for your students' academic preparation?
The authors and editors of *Looking Ahead* have created an on-line system

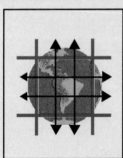

of support for teachers using the series. At **http://lookingahead.heinle.com**, teachers can find expanded versions of the Instructor's Manuals, lesson plans provided by teachers who are using the books, additional materials to supplement the books, and other support materials. In addition, the site offers opportunities to communicate with the editors and authors—to ask questions, share ideas, and make suggestions for improvements in the *Looking Ahead* series and its support materials.

GET READY WITH *LOOKING AHEAD*!

The four textbooks in the *Looking Ahead* series are designed to prepare students to be successful in their academic courses in U.S. colleges and universities. Specifically, *Looking Ahead* teaches students to read academic texts and materials, understand academic assignments, apply effective study skills, and respond appropriately to writing assignments. Each book "looks ahead" to the next in the series, and together as a group they look ahead to the writing students will do in their degree programs.

To the Teacher

Looking Ahead: Learning about Academic Writing is an intermediate-level writing and grammar textbook. It is divided into the following sections:

Goals: Writing, grammar, and content objectives for each chapter.

Authentic Academic Assignments: Real assignments from college courses that illustrate the chapter writing focus.

Getting Ready: The introductory section of each chapter.
    Chapter Introductions: Introductory statements explaining the grammar and writing highlighted in the chapter.
    Learner's Notebook: A writing and language learning journal.

Focusing: The "hands-on" section of each chapter.
    Readings: Authentic readings that tie together writing assignment activities.
    Writing Assignments: Two or three writing assignments per chapter. Students develop and improve short pieces of writing. Peer-revising and self-editing are included.
    Grammar Activities: Student exercises for the grammatical features of major types of academic writing keyed to readings and writing in each chapter.

Putting It All Together: Students apply their knowledge in writing activities that build on the materials presented in the *Focusing* section as well as their work in previous chapters.

Final Writing Assignment: Writing assignments that begin with paragraph length and by the end of the book culminate in multiple paragraph compositions. These prepare students for essay-length writing in *Looking Ahead: Developing Skills for Academic Writing,* Book 3 in the series.

Looking Ahead Assignments: Authentic college writing tasks that give students the opportunity to strategize about how they would handle future college writing.

The Grammar and Language Reference: A quick and easy reference that supplies additional explanations and examples of the grammar features discussed within the chapters. The GLR is a good way to individualize grammar instruction for students who need extra work on particular structures.

$\mathcal{T}$o the Student

Are You "Looking Ahead"?

What are your goals for the future? Are you looking ahead to a college degree and a profession? If your college education is in English, then you will need to write well. You will be required to write in many forms in college: summaries, reports, research papers, letters, and more. Improving your writing will help you to finish college and reach your goals.

How Will This Book Help You?

For many ESL students, writing is more challenging than speaking or listening. It's difficult to remember all the grammar rules when you write, and you leave your errors on paper for everyone to see. This book helps you build accuracy in your writing. Accuracy means that you apply the rules of written English grammar correctly. You also develop fluency (being able to understand and use the language easily) through the many readings and writing assignments in the book. In addition, *Looking Ahead* helps you "look ahead" to future college/university writing by learning about major kinds of college writing.

What Will You Find Inside?

Each chapter has three main sections: *Getting Ready, Focusing,* and *Putting It All Together. Getting Ready* introduces the chapter's writing and grammar points and gives you samples of real academic assignments. In the *Focusing* section, you develop writing skills like Summarizing, Organizing, and Describing. You also recognize and practice the grammar of academic writing, such as informational writing (writing that informs) or past time narrative (writing that tells a past story). This section includes one or two writing assignments and *Learner's Notebook* (learning journal) writing. The *Putting It All Together* section contains a *Final Writing Assignment* as well as the opportunity to study and discuss authentic writing assignments from college courses.

Where Can You Get More Help with Grammar?

At the end of the book, the *Grammar and Language Reference* (*GLR*) section contains explanations with specific examples of the grammar of academic writing. This section is a good reference for your questions about the grammar of written English.

*A*cknowledgments

A book represents the labor of many people. Patricia Byrd and Joy Reid, two of ESL's foremost professionals, conceived of an innovative way to prepare ESL learners for academic writing (in their teacher resource book, *Grammar in the Composition Classroom*), then creatively and carefully helped the authors of the *Looking Ahead* series to implement their new methods.

Pat and Joy guided us with patience and humor as we embarked on the extraordinary process of communicating daily through an e-mail group to develop our books. The editors at Heinle & Heinle Publishers, in particular Ken Pratt, Nancy Jordan, Amy Lawler, and Nancy Siddens, continually engaged in this dialogue, further facilitating the continuity and integrity of the series. In the process, my *Looking Ahead* author colleagues, Sharon Cavusgil of Georgia State University, Elizabeth Byleen of the University of Kansas, and Christine Holten and Judy Marasco of the University of California at Los Angeles, freely shared ideas.

The following ESL professionals also gave helpful comments during the development of this text: Kristin Thalheimer, Heinle & Heinle production director; and Joanne Lowry of Thompson Steele, Inc., ably guided the book through the production process.

Finally, I thank my family, Fodil, Nadia, and Nora Fellag, for respecting the fact that writing a book meant that they couldn't always enjoy my undivided attention—and my home-cooked meals.

Linda Robinson Fellag
Community College of Philadelphia
Philadelphia, Pennsylvania

Chapter 1

Summarizing

The Concept of Self

GOALS

WRITING
◆ identify and use the skills of summarizing

GRAMMAR
◆ examine and practice several of
the features of academic writing:
nouns and *noun phrases, complete
sentences, present tense verbs,*
and *reporting verbs.*

CONTENT
◆ learn about the concept of *self*

ACADEMIC FIELD
Psychology

Sample Authentic College/University Summarizing Assignments

At the beginning of each chapter of *Looking Ahead*, you will find samples of *real* writing assignments from college and university courses. The purpose of these samples is to give you an idea of the types of academic writing that lie ahead. Each textbook chapter focuses on one area of academic writing illustrated in sample assignments. You may wish to discuss the assignments with your classmates.

In a college or university classroom, you will use the summarizing skills you learn in this chapter to complete assignments like this:

Introduction to American Sign Language

Write a summary of one of the personal experience essays on deafness that your instructor has asked you to read. Your one- to two-page summary should inform classmates about three main aspects of the deaf person's experiences: his or her personal history, the effects of deafness on his or her life, and his or her opinions about the deaf and non-deaf cultures in general.

Cultural Traditions

Read and summarize a book dealing with a hero in a Western or non-Western culture. Choose a book from the list of titles suggested by the instructor, if desired. Your typed summary should include the name, title, and publisher of the book, the book's main thesis, an introduction to the heroic figure, a brief account of key events in his or her life, and the chief impact(s) of the hero on his or her culture and/or other cultures. Be sure to include enough background so that your classmates understand the place of the hero in his or her culture.

 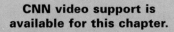

GETTING READY

LEARNER'S NOTEBOOK

Warm-up Activity

In this course, you will use a learner's notebook to record your thoughts and opinions. In your notebook you may write about your language learning or about the content of reading and writing in the course. When you make a notebook entry, do not worry about grammar, organization, or spelling. Just put down your ideas as they come to you. Later, you may use some of your ideas in an assignment or you may review your learner's notebook to track your progress.

Think about how you feel about yourself. In your learner's notebook, write down 20 things about yourself. For each characteristic, write a complete sentence. You may want to start your sentences in these ways:

I am usually   *My parents say that I*
I know a lot about   *I think that I am*
People tell me that I

Grammar Preview

Academic writing is the type of writing used in colleges and universities and other research institutions. Writing in textbooks, scholarly journals, and research reports conveys *academic* information, that is, information gained through *studying* and *learning*.

In a chemistry course, you read and write reports about the properties of chemicals. In a computer literacy course, you read textbooks about the history of computers. In an English composition course, you read and respond in writing to essays, poetry, and other literary works.

Academic writing contains the grammatical features that you will learn and practice throughout this book. These features include specialized vocabulary, complete sentences, and other structures you need to understand so you are better prepared to read and produce academic writing. The Grammar and Language Reference GLR section defines basic grammar terminology on pages 239–250 to help you study and discuss grammar.

The Grammar of Nouns and Noun Phrases in Academic Writing: Learning and Using Key Terms

In your first two years as a student in a U.S. college or university, you must learn a lot of new terminology. You learn the *key terms* in biology, computer science, sociology, psychology, and of the other areas that you study in your freshman and sophomore courses. In all of these courses, the terminology uses the same basic grammar. If you understand that grammar, you can learn these new words more easily and use them more accurately in your tests and writing.

The following chart shows examples of key terms taken from academic texts excerpted in this chapter. Notice that a key term may consist of a single *noun* or a noun phrase, *noun + other word(s)*.

The Grammar of Key Terms: Nouns and Noun Phrases

Noun	Noun Phrase
self	the ideal self
self-esteem	
psychology	

GLR   See pages 244–245 of the GLR for information on nouns and noun phrases.

Activity 1-1 Defining Key Terms

1. With a partner or a small group of classmates, look at the words in the list below. These key terms in the field of psychology describe personal characteristics. What does *self* mean in these words? Beside each word, make a check mark to indicate if the word has a *positive, negative,* or *neutral* (neither positive nor negative) meaning. Then, look up each word in a dictionary, discuss the definitions, and move any check marks that you may have put in the wrong place. Which of the words have very similar meanings? Which of these key terms are single nouns? Noun phrases?

Key Terms	Positive	Negative	Neutral
self-concept	_____	_____	_____
self-esteem	_____	_____	_____
self-confidence	_____	_____	_____
high self-esteem	_____	_____	_____
low self-esteem	_____	_____	_____

2. Read the following paragraphs, each of which briefly defines *self-esteem*. Then answer the discussion questions with your classmates.

Self-esteem is the feeling of appreciating your own inner value as a human being, independently of your accomplishments or standing in the world. Many people who are rich and famous are still unable to appreciate fully their own inner value. But a slave may be able to feel it, even as he sees others looking at him as if he were nothing.

Peter Michaelson, See Your Way to Self-Esteem (Prospect Books, 1993).

Self-esteem is the experience of being competent to cope with the basic challenges of life and of being worthy of happiness.

Nathaniel Branden, The Power of Self-Esteem (Bantam, 1994).

   a. Is the word *self-esteem* similar in meaning to any of the other words in the list in Activity 1-1 on page 5?

   b. Are the definitions of *self-esteem* in the two texts similar? If so, how?

   c. Are the definitions of *self-esteem* in the two texts different? If so, how?

LEARNER'S NOTEBOOK

Experiences through Reading

Find one sentence in either of the texts in Activity 1-1, question 2, that you agree with. Explain why in your learner's notebook. Tell how your experience(s) or the experiences of others "prove" that this sentence is true. Then share your ideas with a classmate.

Introduction to Summarizing: Academic Reading

Reading lies at the heart of academic study. As a matter of fact, researchers believe 70 percent of your academic success depends on how well you read. In other words, in order to pass college courses and get a degree, you must be able to read effectively.

Reading college-level material in a second language can be challenging. As you progress in college, reading assignments will become more difficult and more extensive. In all your courses, you can expect to read texts, discuss them in class, take examinations based on reading material, and/or write summaries, reports, or research papers based on written material. Indeed, reading and writing are central to all academic disciplines.

To be successful, you will need effective strategies to master the variety of tasks involved in academic reading:

- preparing yourself to read
- finding, understanding, and remembering important ideas and terms
- scheduling time to read
- communicating your knowledge of reading through discussion and writing

This textbook will help you discover strategies for these tasks.

Activity 1-2   Discussion

With a small group of classmates, discuss the courses you are presently taking or plan to take in your college or university. If you have them, share the textbooks from the classes or examine college textbooks your instructor has brought to class. Answer these questions about textbooks and classes:

1. What college courses are you taking (or will take in a coming term)?

2. How difficult are the course textbooks?

3. If you are taking college courses now, how much reading do you do every week? If you will take courses in a coming semester, how much reading do you think you will do every week?

4. What ideas do you have about how to manage the amount and the difficulty of the reading in these classes?

Reading Strategies

Every reader uses different strategies to help him or her read more effectively. One reader may write down main ideas or new vocabulary in a notebook to remember them. Another reader may learn best by listening to ideas or words and talking about them. Some may benefit from discussing readings in study groups, while others may prefer to study a reading text alone.

Which reading strategies work best for you? Practice different ones and see for yourself. Here are ten basic strategies to try:

Ten Basic Reading Strategies

1. Preview a text before you read it.
2. Read the text quickly (also called "skimming") without a dictionary.
3. Try to understand the main ideas.
4. Distinguish between important ideas and less important details.
5. Mark a text while you read.
6. Discuss a text after you read.
7. Make a chart or drawing of the organization and main ideas of the text.
8. List important ideas or key terms on notecards or in a notebook.
9. Test a classmate's understanding of a reading by asking questions.
10. Write a summary of the main ideas of a reading.

FOCUSING

READING 1   THE CONCEPT OF SELF
            (EXCERPT FROM A PSYCHOLOGY TEXTBOOK)

Activity 1-3   Previewing a Reading

1. Reading 1, "The Concept of Self," is from a textbook for an introductory college psychology course. Begin by *previewing* (looking at the title, headings, art, boldfaced words, and glossary before you read). Discuss the parts of the reading with a small group of classmates. What should each part tell you about the content?

PREVIEWING A READING

Title	the name of the reading
Headings	chapter names and other titles within the reading
Art	photographs, drawings, charts, or other graphics in the reading
Bold-faced Words	important terms or ideas emphasized by dark letters
Glossary	definitions of important terms in the reading

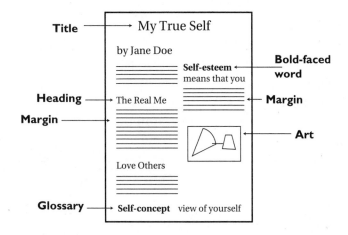

2. List the results of your preview in the space below. Discuss any unfamiliar words. Look them up in a dictionary and write in their meanings.

Part of Reading	Words or Description	Definitions
Title		
Headings		
Art		
Bold-faced Words		

3. Preview the following Glossary for Reading 1. Use a dictionary to check the meanings of the words. Discuss the words in your group.

Glossary

concept	idea
psychology	the study of mental processes and behavior
distinguish	show the differences between one thing and another
qualities	characteristics
personality	the characteristics, traits of a person
factor	something that contributes to a result
interact	act with others
stimulate	excite
unrealistically	not using practical sense
determine	learn, find out
discrepancies	differences
aspect	a way to view something
anxious	nervous

4. Based on your preview lists and the glossary, what do you think the reading will be about?

5. Read the following passage quickly without a dictionary, and think about the main idea. Concentrate on completing this sentence: "This reading is about _____." Even if some vocabulary is unclear, try to understand the "big picture." Then, read the passage a second time with a dictionary and do the exercises that follow.

THE CONCEPT OF SELF

One of the basic concepts in the field of psychology is the idea of **"self,"** which can be defined as your whole person, the qualities that distinguish you from everyone else. Psychologists have offered a number of different explanations about the concept of self. One well-known psychologist, Carl Rogers, believed that **self-concept**—your own view of who you are and what kind of person you are—is the most important factor in the develop-   5
ment of your personality.

According to Rogers, you slowly build an opinion of yourself as you interact with other people, beginning with your family. Benjamin B. Lahey explains in *Psychology: An Introduction*: "You might learn that you are a good athlete by seeing that you run faster than most other people or by your parents telling you that you are a good athlete."   10

Every person has two types of self. "There is the **self**—the person I think I am—and the **ideal self**—the person I wish I were," Lahey writes. "For example, I am pretty sure I can never be better than a "C" class racquetball player (self), but I would *love* to win tournaments in the "A" class (ideal self)."

Is it possible to live with two selves inside you, the self and the ideal self? You can, but 15 it may be difficult at times. First, you may feel very uncomfortable if there is a great difference between the person you *are* and the person you *wish* to be. "It's okay for the ideal self to be slightly out of reach—that can stimulate us to improve ourselves," Lahey explains, "but if the ideal self is so unrealistically perfect that we know it can never be reached, then we feel like failures." 20

Lahey reports that a recent study by Timothy Strauman (1992) at the University of Wisconsin proved Rogers' ideas. "Students in introductory psychology classes were interviewed and tested to determine if there were discrepancies between the way they view themselves (their concept of self) and the way that they think they would like to be or ought to be (two aspects of the ideal self)." The result of the study was that the students who saw 25 big differences between their selves and their ideal selves were sadder and more anxious than the students who did not see big differences.

Adapted from Benjamin B. Lahey, *Psychology: An Introduction*, 5th Ed. (Brown & Benchmark, 1995).

Activity 1-4 Post-reading Questions

With a small group of classmates, complete the following activities related to Reading 1.

1. *Main Idea*

   a. Complete this sentence by writing the main idea of the reading:

      _____ is about _____. It says

         Title of Reading   General Topic of Reading

      _____.

                    What the Reading Says about the Topic

   b. In which paragraph(s) do you find the main idea? Does one sentence in the reading tell the main idea? If so, write that sentence here.

      _____

2. *Marking the Text*

   a. In one margin of the reading, put stars next to the part of the reading that contains the main idea. With your classmates, restate this idea in a few simple words. Try to use your own words. Write your summary in the margin under the stars.

   b. Reread the text. When you read a part that you do not understand, put a question mark [?] in the margin. Be ready to discuss this part with other classmates and your instructor so you can understand it.

   c. Find a sentence that contains an important idea. Mark this sentence within the text with a highlighting pen. Why did you select this sentence? Did anyone in your group choose a different sentence? If so, why?

   d. In your group, use one or more of these three ways to mark the rest of the reading:

      - put stars in the margin
      - make notes in the margin
      - highlight important ideas within the text

   Share your marked texts with your group.

3. *Bold-faced Words*

   a. Look again at the bold-faced words in Reading 1. Why are these words in bold type? What do you think the instructor in this course expects students to do with these words?

   b. Test your understanding of these words by trying to explain each word to a classmate. Then, listen as your partner gives his or her explanation of the word. Do you have the same ideas about what the words mean? Share your definitions and questions with your group.

4. *Discussion*

a. Reread the following two sentences from Reading 1. Let each person in your group explain what the sentences mean. Then, share your opinions about the main idea(s) of each sentence. Do you agree with the idea(s) in the sentences? Why or why not?

> According to Rogers, you slowly build an opinion of yourself as you inter-act with other people.

> First, you may feel very uncomfortable if there is a great difference between the person you *are* and the person you *wish* to be.

LEARNER'S NOTEBOOK

Responding to a Reading

In your notebook, write answers to these questions: How difficult did you find Reading 1? What was the most difficult thing about it? How much did you under-stand when you read without a dictionary? Which of the ten reading strategies on page 8 do you think would best help you to understand and remember this read-ing if it were part of a course you were taking?

Activity 1-5   Writing Assignment 1: Writing about Self-Concept

Choose one of the two sentences from Activity 1-4, section 4. Write the sentence at the top of a piece of paper. Then, write a paragraph to connect your own experience to the main idea(s) in the sentence. Does your experience show that the idea(s) is true or false? Explain why.

Activity 1-6   Peer Response

Find a person in the class (or your instructor), with whom you feel comfortable sharing your paragraph. Exchange paragraphs and answer these questions about each other's writing:

1. Does the writer relate the ideas in Reading 1 to his or her life?

2. Does the writer think the idea(s) in the sentence is true or false? Why?

3. What is the best part of the writer's paragraph? Why? Tell your partner.

The Grammar of Complete Sentences in Academic Writing

When you talk with your friends, you generally speak in short answers rather than in complete sentences. Academic writing differs from conversational English—both in its special vocabulary and in its use of complete sentences rather than fragments. In your college courses you will need to read and write complete sentences in the four basic types used in English: *simple sentences, compound sentences, complex sentences,* and *compound-complex sentences.*

Throughout this book, you will have opportunities to observe how other writers use these sentence types and to practice using them yourself.

GLR	See pages 204–207 in the GLR.

Activity 1-7   Recognizing and Writing the Four Sentence Types

Examples of the four sentence types are provided in the GLR 🔘. Turn to pages 204–207 and study the examples. Working with another student, write additional examples of each type. Try to have all of them be on the same subject—for example, all about the city where you are living or about the school where you are studying.

Activity 1-8   Writing Simple Sentences

Complete the following *simple sentences* by adding a *subject* or a *verb* to complete the thought. Use the words that follow to complete the sentences. Pay attention to the pronouns in each sentence as you choose the correct word from the list.

• we   • people   • give   • consider   • want

1. You _____ yourself a nice person.

2. _____ learn about ourselves from others.

3. We often _____ to be better than others.

4. _____ can have problems with their self-concept.

5. Parents also _____ us a feeling of self-worth.

Activity 1-9   Completing Compound Sentences

Complete these *compound sentences* by adding your own ideas or ideas from Reading 1.

1. We may want to do something, but we _____.

2. People can have different concepts of their self and their ideal self, or they _____.

3. We interact with others, and _____.

4. You can learn to love yourself, or _____.

Activity 1-10   Using Complex Sentences

Complete the following *complex sentences* by adding your own ideas or ideas from Reading 1.

1. When a person feels like a failure, _____.

2. I could become a better person if _____.

3. Parents who _____ make their children feel worthy.

4. We must learn to accept ourselves because _____.

Activity 1-11   Analyzing Sentences in Reading 1

Divide your class into five teams. Assign one paragraph from the reading, "The Concept of Self," to each team. Analyze the sentences. What types of sentences are used in each paragraph? What types are used in the entire reading?

READING 2   MY ACADEMIC READING (SAMPLE STUDENT PARAGRAPH)

MY ACADEMIC READING

   This semester, I have to take English 072 (Speaking), English 082/092 (Reading and Writing), and Data Processing 103 (Computer Applications). I need to spend my time reading the books for all my classes. I know reading is difficult for me because English is my second language. I don't understand the meaning and pronunciation of the words. I know I have to try now because ESL is the basis for my later English studies. If I don't try now, I 5 think I can't try when I start to study English 101. It will be too late because this will be the time when I start to study my major. I want to study nursing for my career, and I know this major will require more reading in biology, history, psychology, medical language, writing, etc. I think I will need even more time then to read the books than I need in the classes I am taking this semester. I heard some teachers and some friends tell me that if I want my read- 10 ing to get better, the first way is to read more books, articles and stories, and try to understand them without a dictionary. I tried that already, but it did not work for me because when I read a story or article, it has a lot of words that I don't understand. If I stop on the words I don't understand and look their meanings up in the dictionary, I forget what I was reading before. I hope I can get better at this in the future. 15

Dung Nguyen
Vietnam

Activity 1-12   Post-reading Questions

1. The student paragraph, "My Academic Reading," is similar to your next writing assignment. To prepare for your writing, read that paragraph again. Discuss your reaction to the paragraph with a partner. Do you have similar problems or fears about reading? Do you agree with this student's ideas about how to become a better reader? What else could she do?

2. Also notice that the student's paragraph contains these essential features of an academic paragraph:

Features of an Academic Paragraph

Title: Presents the main idea of the writing in a word or brief phrase.

Main Idea: Tells the main point of the paragraph in a sentence.

Form: Indent the first line and allow margins (space) at the top, bottom, and left and right sides of the page.

The drawing that follows illustrates the form of a paragraph:

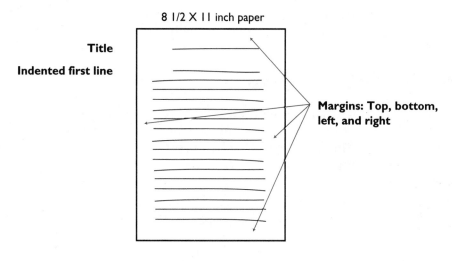

The Form of a Paragraph

Activity 1-13   Identifying Features of a Paragraph

Fill in the list below to identify these features in the student paragraph, "My Academic Reading." Review your answers in a small group of classmates.

Features of "My Academic Reading"

Title: _____

Main Idea: _____

_____

The Grammar of Generalizations in Academic Writing: Present Tense Verbs

In academic writing, you will find many present tense verbs. College textbooks, course descriptions, scholarly articles, and other academic writing are filled with *generalizations*. They give facts, theories, and other general statements; usually these generalizations use present tense verbs.

GLR   For an overview of present tense verbs. see the GLR, especially page 223.

Activity 1-14   Verbs in Generalizations

Underline the main verb in the first sentence of each paragraph in Reading 1, "The Concept of Self." What verb tenses are used? Which sentences are generalizations?

Activity 1-15   Writing about Habits

Generalizations are not just about facts and theories. They can also be about our habits. Fill in these sentences to make them complete. Give true information about yourself. After you have written the sentences, check the verbs to be sure that you have used the correct form and spelling.

EXAMPLES

My parents think that I am very hard-working.
I have a lot of artistic talent.

1. My friends believe that _____.

2. I think that _____.

3. In my opinion, I _____.

4. I _____ very well.

5. My favorite _____.

Activity 1-16   Writing Assignment 2: Writing about Academic Reading

Write a paragraph to describe your academic reading habits and goals. Answer some of these questions in your writing:

- What is one goal that relates to your reading? How can you achieve it?
- How do you manage the reading in your current classes?
- Where and when do you read? Do you study alone or with others?
- Do you mark the text in English or in another language? What do you mark?
- How do you use a dictionary?
- Do you think you may change the way you read in the future? If so, how?

To get ideas, reread your learner's notebook entry on your experience with Reading 1. Then review Reading 2 to see what another student wrote for a similar assignment.

Activity 1-17   Self-editing

1. Read your paragraph again. Does it say what you want it to say? Is it organized in the best way for your meaning and this particular writing task? Make any changes needed to improve the meaning of your writing.

2. Edit your individual sentences for the following, and correct any errors you find. After editing, check (✓) each box below to remind yourself that you have done that task.

    ☐ complete sentences

    ☐ correct punctuation

    ☐ correct verb tense

3. Rewrite your paragraph to make the corrections you identified while editing your sentences.

Activity 1-18   Peer Response

With a partner, share your paragraph, "My Academic Reading." As you read, think about the following questions. After reading the paper, discuss your responses to the questions with your partner.

1. Does your partner's composition answer all the questions in the assignment?

2. Does it have a main idea sentence?

3. What is the most interesting part of the paragraph? Why? Tell your partner.

Revise your paragraph and submit it to your instructor.

Introduction to Summarizing

Another important tool for academic success is *summarizing*. Summarizing helps you understand and remember important ideas in a reading. College teachers often assign summary writing to test your knowledge of a subject. Summaries are also used within larger writing assignments, such as reports or research papers.

According to *The Newbury House Dictionary of American English*, a summary is "a brief statement of the most important features (ideas, facts, actions, etc.) of an event or a work." In other words, a summary presents the main ideas of a reading in shortened form. To write a summary, you have to examine a reading closely and write your own account of its main ideas. You must first understand what you have read, so you should use the reading strategies on page 8.

Audience and Purpose

When you write a summary, you first think about the topic. Then, you consider the *audience* (readers) and *purpose* (reason or goal) for your writing. The audience for this type of writing may be your instructor, other students, or yourself.

Characteristics of a Summary

In every case, you make sure your summary includes these basic characteristics:

- It identifies the source being summarized.
- It presents the main ideas and main supporting points—not all the ideas.
- It is shorter than the original.
- It keeps the meaning of the original text.
- It does not contain your opinions about the text.

Summarizing for Others

Your instructor will need to know the name and author of the text you are summarizing because other students may be summarizing different texts. Other students will also need to know the title and author since they may want to read the original text themselves.

Here is an example of a beginning sentence for a summary:

The article, "The Concept of Self," explains the personality theory of Carl Rogers.

If your audience is another person or persons, write as if they have not read the original text, even if you know they have. This means you should state the main idea and main supporting points clearly so that a reader can easily follow your summary. Your *purpose* in writing is to inform your readers and/or to show how well you understand the reading.

Summarizing for Yourself

If you are writing a summary to use as a study tool for yourself, the audience, of course, is you. You have read the original text, so you may not feel that you need to include the title and author or that you may not need to write as clearly as if you were writing for someone else. However, remember that you may read this summary when you begin to study for an examination a month or more after you read the original text. Will you remember the name, author, and main ideas about the reading? Be careful to include these elements in a summary written as your study guide, so you can use the summary effectively.

Activity 1-19 Evaluating Summaries

Read the following brief summaries of Reading 1, "The Concept of Self." With your class, discuss which is the best summary.

1. In "The Concept of Self," Benjamin Lahey writes about the ideas of Carl Rogers. Rogers believes that our self-concept affects our personality very much. We have two self-concepts: the real self and the ideal (make-believe) self. Both are important, but they can cause us psychological problems. In summary, Rogers believes that we must know all our feelings well.

2. If your parents say you are a good athlete, it makes you believe that you are. You may think that you are nice, but you want to be less selfish. It's not realistic to think that you can be perfect.

3. A recent study at the University of Wisconsin shows that if your ideas of your "real" self and your "ideal" self are very different, you may have psychological problems. Students may be more nervous. You need to symbolize your feelings. Your parents can also affect how you think of yourself.

Organizing a Summary

The length of a summary depends on the length of the original text, but a good summary is organized in typical academic writing style:

Introduction: Begin with the title and author of the original work. Introduce the main idea of the original text.

Body: Present the ideas in the order in which they occur. Include some important supporting points.

Conclusion: Restate the author's overall idea, results, or conclusion.

Taking Notes for a Summary

A simple way to write a summary begins with note-taking.

- For each paragraph in the reading, put a number on a piece of paper.
- Read paragraph 1 and on your paper write a sentence to express the main idea of the paragraph.
- Do the same for all the paragraphs in the reading. When you finish, you should be able to put your sentences together into a summary. Follow academic writing organization.

Sometimes you may find that successive paragraphs (two or more paragraphs *in a row*) contain only one idea. In this case, you may need to write only one sentence to express the main idea of a group of paragraphs.

On the other hand, sometimes one paragraph will contain more than one important idea, so you may need to write more than one sentence about this paragraph.

Activity 1-20   Organizing a Summary

The following sentences can be put together to make a summary, but they are in the wrong order. Working with a partner, put the sentences in the correct order using the previous explanation of the characteristics of summaries. Write the appropriate number in the blank in front of each sentence. Discuss your results with your classmates.

Positive Plus: The Practical Plan for Liking Yourself Better

By Dr. Joyce Brothers

_____ **1.** Parts Three and Four of the book identify negative qualities that you might have, such as spending too much money, working too much, being too anxious, or lying.

_____ **2.** In her book, Brothers, who is a well-known American psychologist, helps you decide whether change is really necessary in your life.

_____ **3.** Finally, Brothers explains how you can become a better person even if you have crises in your life.

_____ **4.** *Positive Plus* by Dr. Joyce Brothers is a guidebook for changing your negative qualities into positive ones.

_____ 5. In Part One, "Second Chances," she shows you how to identify the person you would like to be.

_____ 6. In Part Two, "Your Psychological Tool Kit," Brothers explains techniques you can use to change yourself.

The Grammar of Writing Summaries: Reporting Other People's Words and Ideas

Summaries can include sentences such as this:

Carl Rogers, a well-known psychologist, said that the concept of self is important to our personality.

> **GLR**   See page 228 in the GLR for sentences that make use of reporting verbs.

Activity 1-21   Identifying and Using Reporting Verbs

1. Read the sentences in Activity 1-19 again and circle each verb. Compare your answers to those of another student and make changes if you need to. What types of verbs are used in those sentences? Which sentences use reporting verbs?

2. Fill in the blanks in the following sentences with an appropriate reporting verb from the following list. More than one word will work in each sentence, but choose the one that you like the best. The sentences report on ideas you will find in Reading 3, "Building Self-Esteem."

   - writes   • tells   • says   • points out   • states   • adds

   a. In *Say Goodbye to Shy*, Jean Ann Stevens _____ that in order to change yourself you must believe you can change.

   b. Stevens also _____ that you must be willing to spend time to change your behavior.

   c. In *Coping through Self-Esteem*, Rhoda McFarland _____ about how to use positive statements to build your self-confidence.

d. McFarland _____ that if you repeat these statements to yourself enough, you will believe they are true.

Activity 1-22   Using Reporting Verbs

Use the reporting verbs in the list in Activity 1-21 to write your own original sentences about the chapter introduction, "Reading and Summarizing." Write five sentences to report about ideas from this short reading. Try to use your own words.

EXAMPLES

The book states that college reading is difficult.

The author writes about reading strategies.

READING 3   BUILDING SELF-ESTEEM
(EXCERPT FROM A POPULAR PSYCHOLOGY BOOK)

Activity 1-23   Pre-reading Discussion

Reading 3 is a short selection that gives you advice about how to become more self-confident. In a group, answer these questions to help prepare you for the reading.

1. Preview the title ("Building Self-Esteem"). What does the title tell you about the content of the reading? Do the glossary words below give you clues about what ideas will appear the reading?

Glossary	
enhance	improve
priority	task or belief that is most important
adopt	copy, imitate
reprogramming	giving new instructions
miserable	sad, heartbroken

2. Reading 3 says that you should first identify the things about yourself you would like to change. Here are three methods for identifying negative qualities:

a. Make a list of the things you don't like about yourself.

b. Ask your friends to tell you about your negative qualities.

c. Ask your parents or other family members to point out your negative qualities.

Which of the methods would work best for you? Why?

3. Many "self-help" books have been written to help people build self-confidence and self-esteem. As you read this passage from one such book, think about this question: Do you agree with the advice that the writer gives?

BUILDING SELF-ESTEEM

The following four essential elements are necessary before starting a program to enhance your self-esteem and develop a stronger, more confident you. If cultivating a positive self-image is important to you—high on your priority list—adopting these four steps will start you on the road to changing your life forever.

1. Believe that you *can* change. Only believing in yourself by reprogramming your mind   5
   to build a more self-confident you, will make it happen.
2. Really *want* to change the negative behavior pattern that has made you miserable for
   so long.
3. Be willing to devote the necessary time and energy to making these changes.
4. Practice positive behavior by taking risks, allowing for short-term failures and disap-   10
   pointments in order to reach your long-term success goals. *Practice* is the basis of all
   effective methods of improving self-esteem.

Jean Ann Stevens, *Say Goodbye to Shy: Change Your Thinking, Change Your Life*
(Newport Beach, CA: SandPiper Press, 1995).

Activity 1-24   A Sample Learner's Notebook

Read the sample learner's notebook entry that follows. With a group of classmates, discuss how the writer feels about his writing ability and his language learning ability. Do you share any of his feelings?

SAMPLE LEARNER'S NOTEBOOK

I am a student at Community College of Philadelphia. It is now almost the end of the semester. Last month I took my English 092 midterm. I know I didn't do well on the midterm. I like my writing class a lot. The teacher explains very clearly, and she also helps all the students to work on the computer to correct their assignments. I come to class very often, except when I am sick or I get lost. Sometimes our teacher tells us to change classrooms. I always get lost. Sometimes I look at my classmates' assignments. I feel bad because they did well in their assignments and I didn't. Well, I told myself I should not feel bad about it because most of them graduated from high school and some of them have been studying grammar for two or three years. If I think about it, I feel proud of myself because my grammar is not very good like others, but I am still sitting in the same class as them. I tell myself a lot of times, "No matter how good they are, I will be two steps behind them."

Tuan Anh Huynh
Vietnam

LEARNER'S NOTEBOOK

Reflecting about Language Learning

Write about these questions in your learner's notebook: Do you share some of the feelings about your language learning that Tuan Anh Huynh has? Are you self-confident about writing in English? About reading? About speaking and listening? Why or why not?

PUTTING IT ALL TOGETHER

FINAL WRITING ASSIGNMENT: STEPS TOWARD SELF-ESTEEM

Reading 3 suggests four steps for changing your life. Write a paragraph in which you give your opinion about **one** of the four steps. Begin by introducing the step with a sentence containing a reporting verb that identifies the source (by title and author). Then give your opinion about the step. Use your own experience, facts, or examples as support.

EXAMPLE

In the article, "Building Self-Esteem," Jean Ann Stevens states that you must believe in yourself before you can change.

Use the organization suggestions on page 26. Follow the standard paragraph form illustrated on page 17.

Self-editing

1. Read your paragraph again. Does it say what you want it to say? Is it organized in the best way for your meaning and this particular writing task? Make any changes needed to improve the meaning of your writing.

2. Edit your individual sentences for the following, and correct any errors you find. After editing, check (✓) each box as a reminder that you have done each task.

   ❑ complete sentences

   ❑ correct punctuation

   ❑ correct verb tense

   ❑ correct use of reporting verbs

   ❑ correct use of key terms

3. Rewrite your paragraph to make the corrections you decided on while you were editing your sentences.

Peer Response

Share your paragraph with a partner. Discuss the following questions:

1. Does the writer introduce one of the four steps from Reading 3? Does he or she use a reporting verb and include the title and author? Underline this sentence.

2. Does the writer state his or her opinion about the step? Circle this sentence.

3. Does the writer use details to support his or her opinion? Underline the details.

4. Does the paragraph have a conclusion?

5. What do you like most about the paragraph? Tell your partner.

Revise your paragraph and submit it to your instructor.

LEARNER'S NOTEBOOK

Your Writing Habits

After you have turned in your revised paragraph to your instructor, write about your written assignments for this course. Have they been difficult? What do you find the most difficult part about writing? Do you make major changes when you revise? Is it easier to write now that you have written three paragraphs for this course?

LOOKING AHEAD Authentic Academic Assignment

The activities in this textbook encourage you to "look ahead" to your academic and professional future. What kinds of reading will you be doing? What types of writing will be required?

At the end of each chapter, you will find *real* assignments from college and university courses. You are not expected to *do* these assignments. They are presented here so you can read them and get an idea of the writing assignments you will face in the future. You can discuss, plan and practice how you *could complete* these assignments so that when you face a similar task, you will be better prepared.

With a partner or a small group of classmates, carefully read the academic assignment that follows. Then do the discussion activity after the assignment.

Introduction to Psychology

The objective of this broad course is to familiarize students with these general topics: 1) the field of psychology and its goals, 2) the origins and history of psychology; 3) current theories and issues in the field; 4) the contrast between psychology and related fields; 5) scientific methods of research; 6) the nature of human behavior; and 7) applications of psychology.

(To accomplish goal 7, students read a chapter on personality and then receive the following assignment.)

Writing Assignment

From the Suggested Readings at the end of Chapter 11, choose one book that interests you. *Read* and *summarize* the gist of the book into a three- to five-page typed paper. Your summary should include the source of your material, an explanation of the historical context of the author's theory in the field of psychology, and a clearly written summary of the main ideas presented. Write your paper to inform a beginning psychology student about an important development in the field.

Requirements

In order to write the assignment, you must (1) understand the material in the source book; (2) be familiar with the theories and theorists referred to in the source book; and (3) be able to effectively present the major points found in the source book.

Evaluative Criteria

Your instructor will evaluate your essay with these criteria in mind: (1) Did you clearly understand the material that you read? (2) Did you clearly *summarize* the material? (3) Did you provide an ample amount of background about prior perspectives in this area of psychology? (4) Did you state your ideas in understandable, grammatically correct language?

DISCUSSION

With a small group of classmates, answer these questions and complete the tasks:

1. What is the purpose of this assignment? State the purpose in a sentence.

2. What is not clear about this assignment? Make a list of what you would need to know in order to complete the assignment successfully.

Chapter 2

*D*etail
and Support

On the Road

GOALS

WRITING
◆ identify and use main ideas
  and support in writing

GRAMMAR
◆ examine and practice several of
  the features of past time narrative
  writing and informational writing

CONTENT
◆ explore the history of
  transportation and places

A C A D E M I C   F I E L D
History

Sample Authentic College/University Activities Requiring Detail and Support

In your college or university courses, you will use the skills in this chapter to complete assignments like the following:

Women's Literature
Assignment: Character Analysis

Analyze Louise Mallard in Kate Chopin's "The Story of An Hour." Describe two or three major strengths or weaknesses in her personality. Use *supporting details* from the story to show that she possesses these qualities. Your three- to five-page paper should be typed double-spaced.

Art History 2
Assignment: Art Description

Write a brief report in which you describe the characteristic techniques of one painter's work from either the Expressionist, Cubist, or Impressionist period. Confine your report to two or three major pieces by the artist. Include *details* about each work in order to *support* your conclusions about the artist's techniques. Your report should be two to three pages long, preferably typed. Photocopies or reproductions of the pieces described may be attached.

GETTING READY

LEARNER'S NOTEBOOK

Warm-up Activity

The title of this chapter, "On the Road," is an idiom in English. Being "on the road" can mean that one is traveling. Traveling salesmen often live "on the road," meaning that they drive (or fly) from one state to another, sleep in different hotels, and eat at many restaurants. In general, how do you feel about traveling? Would you enjoy being "on the road"? Or do you prefer to stay at home? Explain why in your notebook.

Grammar Preview

Past time narrative writing relates events in the past. This type of writing appears in college and university textbooks as well as in personal narratives. For example, you may read and write about the history of the United States as well as various academic disciplines in your introductory courses. A textbook on accounting could include a chapter on the history and development of accounting.

In addition to using past tense verbs, past time narratives often include proper nouns and chronological organizers ("in 1492," "next," and many others). Passive verbs can be found when a narrative focuses on processes and events rather than on the actions of people.

Writers also include general truth statements in past time narratives. These statements give explanations and point out the meanings of events. If a generalization was true in the past, but is no longer true, the writer will use a past tense verb. If the generalization is still true now, the writer will probably use a present tense verb.

In the grammar activities in this chapter, you will observe and practice several of these important grammatical features so you can be a better reader and writer of academic past time narratives.

Introduction to Detail and Support

In academic reading, not only "the big picture" (the main idea), but also the main supporting points and details are important. In courses such as American History or Chemistry, you will be expected to remember small pieces of information *and* larger concepts.

The *main idea* of a reading usually appears in the beginning *paragraph* or paragraphs. A paragraph usually contains information about one idea. Each subsequent paragraph presents ideas to explain, illustrate, show, or prove the main idea. These ideas are called *support* because they support the main idea. A reading may contain two main types of support: *supporting points* and *details*. As the chart below shows, supporting points introduce the most important parts of the main idea. Details give specific information about each supporting point.

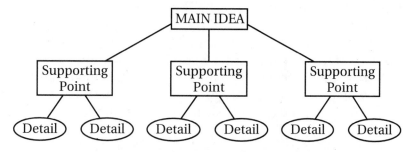

Supporting Points and Details of an Academic Reading

For instance, in a paragraph entitled "The Ways We Move," the main idea is the major methods of transportation we use. Each supporting point describes one transportation method: automobiles, trains, or buses. Details tell more about each transportation mode, such as speed and cost. The following chart illustrates this organization:

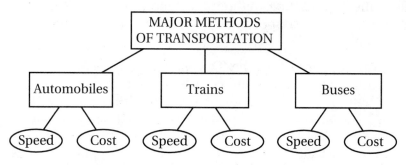

Supporting Points and Details of "The Ways We Move"

Activity 2-1   Finding the Main Idea

With a partner, identify and underline the main idea sentence in the following paragraphs. Discuss whether the paragraphs follow the charts on the previous page.

1. The technology for building modern American highways started with roads made of wood or broken stone. In the late 18th century, engineers built "corduroy" roads. These dirt roads were covered with tree trunks laid across the width of the road. At the same time, plank roads were popular. These were roads covered with split logs. However, a great advancement in highway technology came with the advent of stone roads. European engineers built these roads by placing broken stone in layers packed into the soil. These technological advances greatly influenced road construction in the United States.

2. Early canoes, the first boats built by man, came in three main forms. In North America, the most common type was the bark canoe. Native Americans used the bark of birch and other trees to build their canoes. Later, the first Europeans used bark canoes to explore North America. In Africa, canoes traditionally were made from the skins of animals. Large skins were dried and stretched over a long, slim wooden frame to form the canoe. The third type of traditional canoe was a dugout. These canoes, which were "dug out" of large logs, were most commonly used in South America and Asia. The canoe, in one form or another, existed in every part of the world.

Activity 2-2   Identifying the Main Idea and Support

The paragraphs in Activity 2-1 follow the organization shown in the two charts on the previous page. Each paragraph contains a main idea, supporting points, and details.

In this activity, read each of the following sample paragraphs. Working with a partner, identify and mark the main idea. Then, using the charts on the previous page as resources, fill in the organization outline that follows each paragraph to show which sentences tell the main idea, supporting points, and details. Paragraph 1 has been done for you as an example.

1. The Appian Way has been called the "Queen of Roads" because of its length, its construction, and its long life. The project was a large one because the road was to extend the length of Italy. Eventually it stretched from Rome to the "heel" of the Italian "boot." The road is also remarkable in construction. It was made of stone blocks covered with lava slabs. Also, it was "crowned," which means the center was higher than the sides, allowing rain to drain off. The Appian Way has survived the

test of time. It has outlived the Roman Empire and was widely used until the 6th century. Some of its bridges still carry traffic today.

Main Idea Sentence: The Appian Way has been called the "Queen of Roads" because of its length, its construction, and its long life.

Supporting Point 1: The project was a large one because the road was to extend the length of Italy.

Detail(s) for 1: Eventually it stretched from Rome to the "heel" of the Italian "boot."

Supporting Point 2: The road is also remarkable in construction.

Detail(s) for 2: It was made of stone blocks covered with lava slabs. Also, it was "crowned," which means the center was higher than the sides, allowing rain to drain off.

Supporting Point 3: The Appian Way has also survived the test of time.

Detail(s) for 3: It has outlived the Roman Empire and was widely used until the 6th century. Some of its bridges still carry traffic today.

---

2. Fifth Avenue in New York City is an interesting street filled with people, shops, and museums. Huge crowds of New Yorkers and visitors make this an interesting "people-watching" street. Every time I walk there, people are out in great numbers, walking their dogs, skating on the ice rink in Rockefeller Plaza, taking photographs, or looking in store windows. People also come to Fifth Avenue for the great shopping. All the largest department stores are here, as well as specialty shops selling designer clothing, books, souvenirs, and just about everything else. Fifth Avenue is also noted for its museums. The largest one is the Metropolitan Museum of Art, which is well-known for Egyptian, Roman, European, and Asian art. There is so much to see and do that I always enjoy visiting Fifth Avenue.

Main Idea Sentence: _____

Supporting Point 1: _____

Detail(s) for 1: _____

_____

Supporting Point 2: _____

Detail(s) for 2: _____

_____

Supporting Point 3: _____

Detail(s) for 3: _____

_____

3. In bad weather, travelers sometimes leave their automobiles at home. In wintertime, city dwellers might even use skis or sleds to travel if the roads are too icy. During snow storms in some parts of the northeastern United States, for example, workers may use skis to get to work. In addition, some parents pull their small children to school on sleds. Workers and students also take public transportation when snow or sleet make driving dangerous. Traveling by train or subway is faster and safer than automobile travel when roads are snow- or ice-covered. Moreover, when rain falls so heavily that floods cover roads and cars, people travel by boats. Residents ride in boats along neighborhood roads to get in and out of flooded homes. Police also use motor boats to rescue people from flooded areas. Bad weather forces people to find alternative methods for traveling when automobiles cannot transport them.

Main Idea Sentence: _____

Supporting Point 1: _____

Detail(s) for 1: _____

_____

Supporting Point 2: _____

Detail(s) for 2: _____

_____

Supporting Point 3: _____

Detail(s) for 3: _____

_____

Using Details in Writing

Writers use many types of details to explain the supporting ideas in their writing, often in the *same* piece of writing. Below are some commonly used types of details, their meanings, and a brief description of their features. Sentences from Activity 2-2, pages 34–36, illustrate these types.

TYPE OF DETAILS	MEANING
Factual	Tell facts about the topic
Personal experience	Tell the writer's experience
Examples	Illustrate an idea
Description	Tell how something looks, feels, sounds, tastes, or other characteristics

---

USING DETAILS IN WRITING

• Factual	The road was made of stone blocks. (Act. 2-2, no. 1)
• Personal experience	Every time I walk there, people are out in great numbers.... (Act. 2-2, no. 2)
• Examples	During snow storms in some parts of the northeastern United States, for example, workers may use skis to get to work. (Act. 2-2, no. 2)
• Description	Also, it was "crowned," which means the center was higher than the sides, allowing rain to drain off. (Act. 2-2, no. 1)

FOCUSING

Activity 2-3   Writing Assignment: A Paragraph about Transportation

Write a paragraph that describes one method of transportation. Use one of the suggested main idea sentences that follow, or make up your own main idea sentence. Be sure that your paragraph includes a main idea sentence, main supporting points, and details. Refer to the "Getting Ready" section of this chapter for ideas about organization.

Suggested Main Idea Sentences:

1. A bicycle is an excellent form of transportation for a college student.

2. The most convenient way to travel is by _____ (examples: car, foot, subway, bus, roller blades).

3. Traveling by automobile has several disadvantages.

Activity 2-4   Peer Response

After you have written your paragraph, exchange it with a classmate. Read each other's paragraphs, answer the following questions, and discuss your paragraphs.

1. Does your partner's paragraph have a main idea sentence? Underline it.

2. Does the paragraph include main supporting points and details?

3. What types of details does the paragraph include? Note each type in the margin of your partner's paper.

4. What is the most interesting part of the paragraph? Why?

READING 1   THE NATIONAL ROAD (EXCERPT FROM MAGAZINE ARTICLE)

Activity 2-5   Pre-reading Discussion

The article "The National Road" tells the history of an important road in the United States. Before you read, discuss these questions with classmates in a small group:

1. Read the title of the article. Where do you think the National Road started and ended?

2. Read the first paragraph. What does it mean when the senator said he wanted to "*bind* the *republic* together with a perfect system of roads"? (You may want to look up the italicized words in the dictionary.) Why do you think he wanted to do this?

3. Before you read, define each of the words in the list. Use your knowledge, your class-mates' knowledge, a dictionary, or the article below. Discuss how these words could relate to roads.

   - settlers   - settlements   - frontier   - extend   - wilderness
   - territory   - prosper   - freight   - surveyors   - network

THE NATIONAL ROAD

"Let us, then, bind the republic together with a perfect system of roads and canals. Let us conquer space," Senator John C. Calhoun told Congress in 1816.

Settlers had been moving west since the early 1700s. By 1802, so many farms and towns had been settled in the Ohio Valley that people living in the territory were calling for statehood. But the area was a long way from the Eastern cities and towns where most of 5 the nation's business took place. It took weeks of travel over rough wilderness tracks to reach the western outposts that wanted to be part of the nation.

A road was what the nation needed—a well-built road to carry its people and goods westward and to link its established cities and towns with the growing settlements on its new frontier. A road would help the nation prosper. Along it, business would grow and news and 10 important communications could be carried to keep the growing nation working together.

In 1805, a proposal was put before Congress for a road to connect East with West—"a road from Cumberland ... within the state of Maryland, to the river Ohio." A year later, Congress passed the bill, and President Thomas Jefferson appointed surveyors to lay out the route that would open the rugged Allegheny Mountains of Pennsylvania and the lands 15 beyond them to travelers and business.

Officially, this road was called the Cumberland Road, but it soon was known as the National Pike, the Great Turnpike, and the Old Pike. The name that stuck, however, was the National Road. True to this name, it is the only road ever built directly by the federal government. 20

By the time the road reached the Ohio River in 1818, many knew that it did not go far enough. The call went up to extend the road across Ohio, Indiana, and Illinois to the Mississippi River. By 1839, the road had reached Vandalia, Illinois, where lack of money and political disputes stopped it.

In its best years, the National Road was the busiest in the land. Most of America's pio- 25 neers followed its six hundred miles across six states to settle the lands along it and those farther west. Stagecoaches, carriages, Conestoga wagons loaded with freight, and droves of cattle and sheep traveled the road. Inns, taverns, and towns grew up along its length. It was the only good route connecting East and West.

But by mid-century, there was another way to travel: the railroad. Trains were faster, 30 more comfortable, and cheaper than stagecoaches and wagons. As the railroad moved west, the National Road grew quiet. It was used mostly by local traffic, so little effort was made to keep it repaired.

Early in the 1900s, however, another new vehicle—the automobile—brought the road back to life. Good roads were needed again as Americans began traveling by car and trucks 35 carried goods to market. The Old Pike soon became part of a national network of roads. America's National Road, created to connect East with West, is now part of U.S. Route 40, a highway that stretches all the way from the East to the West Coast.

Cobblestone magazine, June 1991, Vol. 12, No. 6, 4–5.

Activity 2-6   Identifying Main Idea and Support

1. In your group, discuss the main idea of "The National Road." Identify and underline the sentence that best expresses this idea.

2. Paragraph 7 shows how a main idea is developed with a main supporting point and details. Reread the paragraph and mark the main supporting point and the detail in the paragraph reprinted here.

Main Idea Sentence

In its best years, the National Road was the busiest in the land. Most of America's pioneers followed its six hundred miles across six states to settle the lands along it and those farther west. Stagecoaches, carriages, Conestoga wagons loaded with freight, and droves of cattle and sheep traveled the road. Inns, taverns, and towns grew up along its length. It was the only good route connecting East and West.

3. Identify and write in the following chart one example of each type of detail that you find in the article. Discuss with your group which type of detail is used most in the article and which type(s) do not appear here.

Type of Detail	Line #	Example Detail Sentence
a. Fact	____	_____
b. Personal Experience	____	_____
c. Example	____	_____
d. Description	____	_____

Activity 2-7 Post-reading Discussion

In a group, draw the route of the National Road on the following map. Mark the location where you are, if you are in the United States. Compare your route with other classmates'.

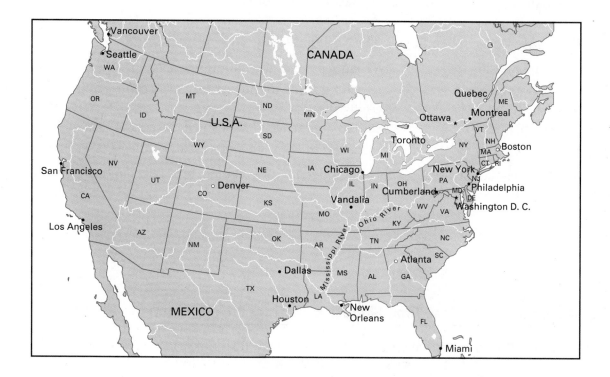

LEARNER'S NOTEBOOK

Responding to a Reading

Write answers to one of these questions in your learner's notebook:

1. A New Road

Did you ever see a new road being built? How long did the work take? What happened first, second, third, and so on in the work?

2. The National Road

What do you think were the most difficult parts of building this road? What do you think it was like for the workers? What part of this story most interested you? Why?

The Grammar of Past Time Narrative Writing: Past Tense Verbs

"The National Road" is a past time narrative text. It contains details that use past tense verbs (*simple past, past progressive*, and *past perfect verbs*). Present tense verbs such as simple present and present perfect verbs can also be found in these narratives, especially in sentences that tie the past to the present.

Past Tense Verbs in Reading 1: The National Road

Simple past	A road *was* what the nation *needed* ...
Past progressive	... people living in the territory *were calling* for statehood.
Past perfect	Settlers *had reached* west since the early 1700s.
Past perfect progressive	Settlers *had been moving* west since the early 1700s.

A list of irregular past verb forms is included in the Irregular Verbs chart in the Appendix found on pages 251–254.

GLR   Refer to pages 214–215 of the GLR for more information.

The Grammar of Past Time Narrative Writing: Proper Nouns

You will find narrative writing in introductory textbooks. In college courses, you might read about the development of computers, the invention of engineering processes, the discoveries of vaccines, or the stories of famous mathematicians.

All of these narratives will contain many *proper nouns*: names of specific people, places, dates, and things. The first letters of proper names of people and places are always capitalized. Proper nouns may consist of single nouns or of noun phrases. In academic classes such as history, you will often be expected to learn and remember these names for examinations.

Proper Nouns in Reading 1: The National Road

> *Senator John C. Calhoun*
> *Congress*
> *Ohio Valley*

GLR   Review page 216 of the GLR for more information.

Activity 2-8   Identifying Proper Nouns

Scan (read quickly for specific information) Reading 1 to find five more examples of proper nouns. Discuss with your class how you know that the words and phrases you have found are proper nouns.

Activity 2-9   Identifying Past Tense Verbs and Proper Nouns

In a small group, reread the following passages from Reading 1. Underline the past tense verbs. Read the GLR ⬤ on "verb tense and form" to review different past time verbs. Then circle the proper nouns. Check your answers with classmates.

1. Early in the 1900s, however, another new vehicle—the automobile—brought the road back to life. Good roads were needed again as Americans began traveling by car and trucks carried goods to market. The Old Pike soon became part of a national network of roads. America's National Road, created to connect East with West, is now part of U.S. Route 40, a highway that stretches all the way from the East to the West Coast.

2. Settlers had been moving west since the early 1700s. By 1802, so many farms and towns had been settled in the Ohio Valley that people living in the territory were calling for statehood. But the area was a long way from the Eastern cities and towns where most of the nation's business took place.

Activity 2-10   Using Past Tense Verbs

With a partner, fill in the blanks of the passage below with the correct past tense forms of the verbs in the list. Some of the verbs may be used more than once in the paragraph. Remember that many past tense verbs are irregular, so check the Irregular Verb chart on page 251-254. Then, check your verb choices by rereading the passage on page 39.

- be • stop • travel • grow • follow • know • reach • go

By the time the road _____ the Ohio River in 1818, many _____ that it did not go far enough. The call _____ up to extend the road across Ohio, Indiana, and Illinois to the Mississippi River. By 1839, the road _____ Vandalia, Illinois, where lack of money and political disputes _____ it.

In its best years, the National Road _____ the busiest in the land. Most of America's pioneers _____ its six hundred miles across six states to settle the lands along it and those farther west. Stagecoaches, carriages, Conestoga wagons loaded with freight, and droves of cattle and sheep _____ the road. Inns, taverns, and towns _____ up along its length. It _____ the only good route connecting East and West.

The Grammar of Past Time Narrative Writing: Recognizing Passive Voice Verbs

Although passive voice is more common in scientific and technical writing, past time narratives in all academic disciplines can include passive voice verbs. In this chapter, you will learn how passive voice verbs are used.

EXAMPLE

It *was used* mostly by local traffic ...

The verb phrase is called *passive* because the subject of the sentence is not the *doer* of the action, but the *receiver* of the action. The writer begins with "it" because the *road* is more important to his story than the *people* who went on it. This is an important reason why the passive voice verb is used.

> **GLR** Refer to pages 222–223 of the GLR for more information on passive sentences.

Activity 2-11   Identifying Passive Voice Verbs

With a partner, identify the three passive voice verbs in this passage from Reading 1. Discuss who or what did the action in each of these passive voice sentences.

> In 1805, a proposal was put before Congress for a road to connect East with West—"a road from Cumberland ... within the state of Maryland, to the river Ohio." A year later, Congress passed the bill, and President Thomas Jefferson appointed surveyors to lay out the route that would open the rugged Allegheny Mountains of Pennsylvania and the lands beyond them to travelers and business.
>
> Officially, this road was called the Cumberland Road, but it soon was known as the National Pike, the Great Turnpike, and the Old Pike. The name that stuck, however, was the National Road.

Activity 2-12   Using Past Tense Verbs

Complete the following paragraph with the past tense forms of verbs in the list. Compare your answers with your class.

• leave • cause • want • abandon • bring • introduce • see • run

During the mid-1800s an interesting means of transportation _____ in the American West: the "American Camel Express." In 1850, the U.S. Army _____ camels to the Southwestern U.S. to haul salt among several California and Nevada towns. The Army _____ to use the camels to carry goods in the deserts, but the Army later _____ its experiments and _____ the camels in the desert. Using camels _____ complaints by stagecoach drivers because stagecoach horses often _____ away in panic when they _____ the camels. The camels _____ in the Southwestern U.S. deserts as late as 1912.

Adapted from *Compton's Interactive Encyclopedia*, 1996.

Activity 2-13   Writing Assignment 2: A Place in the Past

For this assignment, you will write a paragraph about a familiar place from your past. You may want to write about a place in an old neighborhood, a room in a home where you once lived, or a memorable place you visited.

In a small group, discuss the following topics. Then decide which topic is the best for you.

1. My Childhood Street

   Do you remember the neighborhood where you lived as a child? Could you describe the street? What was on either side of the street? What do you remember most about it? How did it make you feel? Who lived there? What sounds and smells do you remember?

2. Special Place

   Is there one special place you loved to visit when you were younger? Where was it? What did it look like? Why did you like it? What did you do there?

3. Memorable Place

Did you and your family or friends take a trip to a memorable place? Where was it? With whom did you travel? When? What was special about the place? What did you do there? What did it look like?

When you have selected your topic, remember what you saw, heard, smelled, and felt at this place so that you can include details of description in your writing.

Include a main idea sentence, supporting points, and details in your paragraph.

Activity 2-14   Self-editing

1. Read your paragraph again. Does it say what you want it to say? Is it organized in the best way for your meaning and this particular writing task? Make any changes needed to improve the meaning of your writing.

2. Edit your paragraph for the following, and correct any errors that you find. After you have reviewed each of these features, check (✓) the box as a reminder that you have done that task.

   ☐ complete sentences

   ☐ correct punctuation

   ☐ correct verb tenses

   ☐ correct capitalization of proper nouns

3. Rewrite your paragraph making the corrections you decided on while you were editing your sentences.

Activity 2-15   Peer Response

With a partner, exchange paragraphs. Read the questions that follow. When you read each other's paragraphs, keep these questions in mind. Make suggestions to your partner in answer to the questions. Help each other with any changes or additions to your paragraphs before you turn them in.

1. Does the paragraph have a main idea sentence? Underline the sentence. Show it to your partner.

2. Does the writer seem to remember all of the important details about the place? If you have questions, write them in the margin of the paragraph at each place where the writer needs to add more or better details.

3. Does the writer include enough description of what he or she saw, heard, smelled, or felt? Write questions or notes in the margin of the paragraph near each place where you would like to see more sensory details.

4. What do you like the most about the paragraph? Why?

READING 2   ON DOWN THE ROAD (EXCERPT FROM A MAGAZINE ARTICLE)

Activity 2-16   Pre-reading Discussion

Reading 2 continues the story of the National Road. Before you read it, reread Reading 1 and answer these questions with a small group of classmates:

1. Skim Reading 1. Look for the names of types of vehicles that traveled on the National Road.

2. In Reading 1, what effects did the railroad and the automobile have on the National Road?

3. What were the advantages and disadvantages of these different modes of transportation?

4. Before you read Reading 2, match these transportation-related words with the meanings on the right. Put the appropriate number in each blank. Discuss the words with the students in your group.

_____ a. surfacing   1. transported goods, cargo

_____ b. freight   2. a number for a type of road that passes through more than one state

_____ c. bypassing   3. material used to cover roads

_____ d. motorists   4. a group of intersecting horizontal and vertical lines

_____ e. grid   5. drivers

_____ f. Interstate 70 6. passing by or going around

5. More vocabulary words are included in the glossary that appears before Reading 2. Study the words and their meanings before you begin to read. Discuss with a classmate what you expect the reading to be about, based on the words in Activity 2-16 and in the glossary.

Glossary

arose	rose up, emerged
hauled	carried, transported
roadside landscape	scenery beside a road
tombstone	grave marker
outgrew	became too large for

ON DOWN THE ROAD

The National Road was about to begin a second life. By the late 1800s, bicycles were becoming popular, and soon after, the automobile was invented. Once again, Americans took to the road for fun and travel. As traffic on the National Road increased in the early 1900s, cries for improved road surfaces arose.

Roads gradually improved due to motorists' continued demands. In 1916, Congress 5 passed the Federal-Aid Road Act and established the Bureau of Public Roads. By 1923, new surfacing covered most of the National Road from Cumberland, Maryland, to Indianapolis.

By the end of the nineteenth century, buses provided public transportation along the National Road. Later, buses ran from one city to another at scheduled times. Trucks hauled freight along the National Road. As travelers used the road to go greater distances, road 10 signs, gas stations, and motels became part of the roadside landscape.

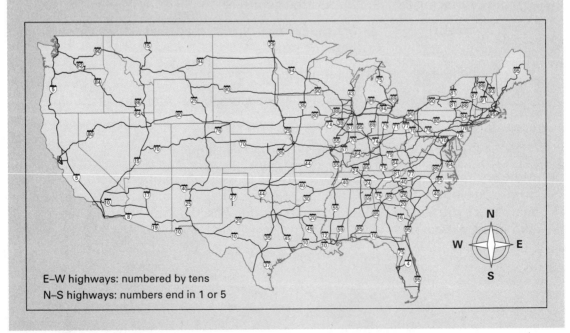

E–W highways: numbered by tens
N–S highways: numbers end in 1 or 5

In 1925, the Joint Board on Interstate Highways recommended a national grid system for numbering highways. Under this system, east-west routes were assigned even numbers by tens, and north-south highways were given numbers ending in one or five. The National Road became part of U.S. Route 40 in 1926. 15

Some cars rushed along the highway at the then frightening speed of fifty miles per hour. Accidents were common. In Ohio, large signs along the National Road cautioned motorists: "Keep your name in a city directory, not on a tombstone." White crosses marked the sites of fatal accidents.

Although automobile traffic decreased for a few years during World War II, the use of 20 the road continued to grow into the 1950s. Then, once again, the demands of travel outgrew the old road. By the mid-1960s, a superhighway, Interstate 70, ran parallel to the National Road and drained it of much of its cross-country traffic. Bypassing cities and towns, Interstate 70 allows motorists to cover more miles in less time.

Today, though it may not be the fastest route, the six-hundred-mile stretch of U.S. 40 25 between Cumberland, Maryland, and Vandalia, Illinois, offers a drive past much of the National Road's history.

Source: *Cobblestone* magazine, June 1991, Vol. 12, No. 6, 36–40.

Activity 2-17   Post-reading Discussion

Discuss these questions about Reading 2 with a small group of classmates.

1. "On Down the Road" lists four types of vehicles that traveled on the National Road from the late 1800s to the present. Skim the reading, then put these vehicles in order according to when they were used on the road.

   _____ buses

   _____ automobiles

   _____ bicycles

   _____ trucks

2. What types of businesses and other sites developed along the National Road? What kinds do you think exist there today? (Compare your ideas with the information given in "On Down the Road.")

Activity 2-18   Remembering Proper Nouns

Specific dates are one type of proper noun. The dates that follow have been used to construct a timeline of the early major events on the National Road. Under each date, a brief sentence summarizes the major event that occurred at that date. Discuss which words in each sentence are proper nouns. Be sure to capitalize proper nouns.

Early Events on the National Road

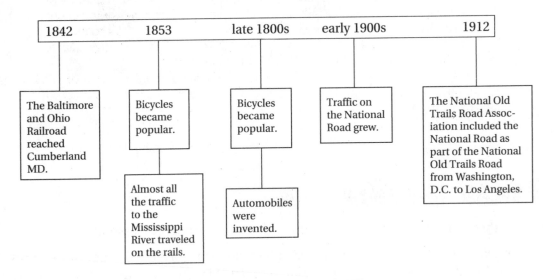

Activity 2-19   Dates as Proper Nouns

Use the dates that follow to create your own timeline of later major events on the National Road. You can find the information in Reading 2. Working individually or in a group, write a brief sentence under each date telling what happened at that time. Discuss your sentences with the class. Discuss which words in the sentences are proper nouns.

Later Events on the National Road

1916   1923   1925   1926   1950s   mid-1960s

The Grammar of Past Time Narratives: Using Chronological Organizers

Writers use chronological organizers—*adverbs, adverb phrases,* and *adverb clauses* that show time—to indicate time relationships among events in a past time narrative. Notice how chronological organizers show the order of events in the final paragraphs of Reading 2:

> adverb adverb phrase
> **Then**, **once again**, the demands of travel outgrew the old road.
> adverb phrase
> **By the mid-1960s**, a superhighway, Interstate 70, ran parallel to the National Road and drained it of much of its cross-country traffic. Bypassing cities and towns, Interstate 70 allows motorists to cover more miles in less time.
> adverb
> **Today**, though it may not be the fastest route, the six-hundred-mile stretch of U.S. 40 between Cumberland, Maryland, and Vandalia, Illinois, offers a drive past much of the National Road's history.

> **GLR**   Refer to page 215 of the GLR for more information on chronological organizers.

Activity 2-20   Identifying Chronological Organizers

Reread the following paragraphs from Readings 1 and 2. With a partner or group of classmates, identify and circle the chronological organizers (*adverbs, adverb phrases,* and *adverb clauses*). Discuss your answers with your class.

1. By the time the road reached the Ohio River in 1818, many knew that it did not go far enough. The call went up to extend the road across Ohio, Indiana, and Illinois to the Mississippi River. By 1839, the road had reached Vandalia, Illinois, where lack of money and political disputes stopped it.

2. By the end of the nineteenth century, buses provided public transportation along the National Road. Later, buses ran from one city to another at scheduled times. Trucks hauled freight along the National Road. As travelers used the road to go greater distances, road signs, gas stations, and motels became part of the roadside landscape.

LEARNER'S NOTEBOOK

Remembering a Highway

In your learner's notebook, write about one highway you have traveled on. What is the name or number of the highway? Where is it? By what means of transportation did you travel on it? What did the landscape look like alongside the road?

READING 3   SAMPLE STUDENT PARAGRAPHS

Read the two sample paragraphs that follow. With a small group of classmates, answer the questions that follow the writing samples.

PARAGRAPH A: TRAVELING BY HORSE

One hundred years ago, horses provided the best way to travel. At that time, most people traveled from city to city in coaches or buggies. When someone was sick, a family member rode by horse to call the doctor, and the doctor came by buggy. Mailmen rode from door to door on their horses to deliver the mail. It was a fast and efficient way to get from place to place. But this way of traveling was both good and bad. It was good because 5 people didn't pollute the air. Cars, trains, and other means of transportation today leave gases behind when they move. But it was bad because riding on a horse damaged the horse's back and legs. And traveling by horse could be dangerous, especially on bad roads, in bad weather, and at night. It was also much slower than transportation today. The ways of transportation today are better than travel by horse 100 years ago because they are safer 10 and faster.

Malavika Mangeshkumar
India

PARAGRAPH B: THE ADVANTAGES OF SPACE TRAVEL

What do you think about space travel? Of course, there are both advantages and disadvantages. Space travel is a good idea because if we had not explored space, we would not have satellites. Satellites have helped us to know what is happening around the world. They have helped us predict weather. We have also learned a lot about the moon and other planets. When Neil Armstrong became famous by walking on the moon, he helped us to realize that we can explore other bodies in space. Because of the invention of rockets and space exploration, scientists have been able to make medicine that we can only make from special ingredients that can only be made in outer space. The disadvantage of traveling in space is that astronauts take a big risk. Several astronauts, including a schoolteacher, were killed when the space shuttle *Challenger* exploded in 1989 because of mechanical problems. Astronauts also face cold temperatures and the chance that they could run out of oxygen. The Apollo 13 astronauts almost died from lack of oxygen. Space travel is a scary, fun and interesting adventure.

5

10

Vaishnavi Mangeshkumar
India

Activity 2-21   Post-reading Discussion

Discuss these questions in a small group:

1. What is the main idea of each paragraph? What does it say about travel?

2. Put a check mark (✓) next to each type of detail that you find in each paragraph. Mark one example of each type of detail sentence in the paragraphs.

   Paragraph A

   _____ example   _____ personal experience

   _____ fact   _____ description

   Paragraph B:

   _____ example   _____ personal experience

   _____ fact   _____ description

3. Mark one or more places in each paragraph where the writer could add more detail. Indicate which type of detail the writer might add.

4. Both paragraphs present advantages and disadvantages of one type of transportation. In Paragraph A, what does the writer compare "Traveling by Horse" to? In "The Advantages of Space Travel," does the writer compare space travel to another type of transportation?

5. Make a list of the advantages and disadvantages of traveling by horse and space travel using the following chart as a guide.

Topic: Traveling by Horse

Advantages: Disadvantages:

a. _____   a. _____

b. _____   b. _____

c. _____   c. _____

6. Which of the paragraphs appeals to you the most? Why?

LEARNER'S NOTEBOOK

Remembering Details from a Reading

In your notebook, write what you remember about Paragraph A or about Paragraph B. Do not look back at the reading. Write about historical and sensory (relating to sight, hearing, smell, or touch) details from one of the paragraphs. After reviewing your work, write about why you think you were you able to remember those details.

The Grammar of Past Narrative Writing: Past and Present Tense Verbs

"Traveling by Horse," the first student sample composition, described a past mode of transportation. The writing is narrative because it tells a story about life in the past. However, like many past time narratives, part of the writing also refers to the present. These present time sentences tell about present events, about facts, or about *general truths* (statements of beliefs or ideas). The writer has to remember to use past time verbs to tell past events and present time verbs to tell about general truths or present activities.

EXAMPLES OF GENERAL TRUTH STATEMENTS

The ways of transportation today are better than travel by horse 100 years ago because they are safer and faster.

The disadvantage of traveling in space is that astronauts take a big risk.

GLR   Refer to page 250 of the GLR for more information on verb forms and verb tenses and page 223 for more information on present tense verbs.

Activity 2-22   Identifying Past Tense and General Truth Verbs

With a partner, reread the following passages from readings in this chapter. In each passage, the verbs are bold and underlined. Discuss where and why past tense and present tense verbs are used. The first paragraph is marked as a model.

1. Early in the 1900s, however, another new vehicle—the automobile—**brought** the
    road back to life. Good roads **were needed** again as Americans **began** traveling by car
    and trucks carried goods to market. The Old Pike soon **became** part of a national
    network of roads. America's National Road, **created** to connect East with West,
    is now part of U.S. Route 40, a highway that **stretches** all the way from the East to the
    West Coast.

2. By the mid-1960s, a superhighway, Interstate 70, **ran** parallel to the National Road
    and **drained** it of much of its cross-country traffic. Bypassing cities and towns,
    Interstate 70 **allows** motorists to cover more miles in less time.

    Today, though it **is** not the fastest route, the six-hundred-mile stretch of U.S. 40
    between Cumberland, Maryland, and Vandalia, Illinois, **offers** a drive past much of
    the National Road's history.

3. Several astronauts, including a school teacher, **were killed** when the space shuttle
    Challenger **exploded** in 1989 because of mechanical problems. Astronauts also **face**
    cold temperatures and the chance that they **could run out** of oxygen and **die**. The
    Apollo 13 astronauts almost **died** from lack of oxygen. Space travel **is** a scary, fun,
    and interesting adventure.

4. But this way of traveling **was** both good and bad. It **was** good because people **didn't**
    pollute the air. Cars, trains, and other means of transportation today **leave** gases
    behind when they **move**. But it **was** bad because it **hurt** the horse's legs. And traveling by horse **was** not safe. It **was** also much slower than transportation today.

PUTTING IT ALL TOGETHER

FINAL WRITING ASSIGNMENT: METHODS OF TRANSPORTATION

For this assignment, think about one method of transportation that you know from experience or have read about in this chapter (for example, bus, horse, automobile, or railroad). Choose a method that you think has definite advantages and/or disadvantages and explain what they are. Tell about an experience in which you used this mode of transportation and explain why you liked or disliked it.

Use facts, examples, personal experience, and description to support your ideas. Try to include sensory and historical details in your writing.

Read the sample paragraphs on pages 52–53 again to see how other writing students completed this assignment.

Self-editing

1. Read your paragraph again. Does it say what you want it to say? Is it organized in the best way for your meaning and this particular writing task? Make any changes needed to improve the meaning of your writing.

2. Edit your paragraph for the following, and correct any errors that you find. After you have reviewed each of these features, check (✓) the box as a reminder that you have done that task.

   ☐ complete sentences
   ☐ correct punctuation
   ☐ correct verb tenses
   ☐ correct capitalization of proper nouns
   ☐ clear chronological organization through use of chronological organizers

3. Rewrite your paragraph to make the corrections you identified while you were editing your sentences.

Peer Response

Exchange your writing assignment with a new partner. Read each other's papers and share ideas relating to the following questions. Then, revise your writing as necessary.

1. Does the writer tell about a method of transportation? Does he or she tell about its advantages and disadvantages?

2. Does the writer include enough details? Mark places in the paragraph margin where the writer could add details. Suggest which types of details to add.

3. What is the most interesting part of the composition? Why?

LEARNER'S NOTEBOOK

Looking Ahead to College

Write answers to these questions in your learner's notebook.

Which subjects do you think will have the most challenging readings in your college courses? Why? Which subjects will be the most interesting? Which subjects will be the hardest for you to write about? Why? Which will be the most interesting writing subjects? Why?

L
O
O
K
I
N
G

A
H
E
A
D

• •
Authentic Academic Assignment

Urban studies

Philadelphia: City of Neighborhoods Project

Assignment: Philadelphia is a city of distinct urban neighborhoods. In order to learn more about the city's diverse areas, you will visit, observe, and take notes about five contiguous city blocks in your neighborhood and describe three salient features of the street: types of businesses, residence types, and general appearance of the area.

Audience/Purpose: Your report will be distributed to every member of the class. The purpose of your field research report is to orient a classmate about an area of the city that he or she may not know about. In turn, you will gain information about the city from reading the reports of your classmates.

Report: Prepare a three-part report: a description of the neighborhood street that includes the name of the neighborhood and specific street identification, supported by a neighborhood map and photographs and/or drawings, and lists of detailed notes that describe each of the features.

Tasks: Be prepared to visit the street on several occasions in order to examine the features carefully from different vantage points and to take field notes. You may need to return to the site in order to checked notes previously taken. Use the college's Internet-connected computers in the Educational Resource Center or in the Student Academic Computer Center to access the Lykos city map site. Photographs or drawings should support the written data about one of the street's features.

DISCUSSION

1. What questions would you ask the instructor of this course before starting this assignment?

2. Which part of the assignment would you find the most difficult? The most interesting? Why?

3. How would you begin?

4. Explain in steps how you would complete this assignment.

5. Who might you use as a resource person in helping you do the assignment or check your work?

*O*rganizing

Do's and Don'ts

GOALS

WRITING
◆ recognize and use standard English academic organization in writing

GRAMMAR
◆ examine and practice several of the features of informational and persuasive writing: *nouns* and *noun phrases, definition structures, present tense verbs, adverbs of frequency and modal verbs to limit generalizations,* and *modal verbs to state rules*

CONTENT
◆ explore cultural taboos (tabus) and rules

ACADEMIC FIELD
Anthropology

Sample Authentic College/University Organizing Assignments

In a college or university classroom, you will use the skills you learn in this chapter to complete assignments like this:

Introduction to Psychology

Prepare a three- to five-page written report about one of the topics presented on page 520 in Chapter 5 ("Basic Principles of Learning"). Organize your report to include a brief introduction, support, and conclusion with your analysis of the principle.

Intermediate German

Write a two- to four-page composition about the German educational system. In your paper, use chronological organization, tracing elementary to college educational structures.

CNN video support is available for this chapter.

Turner Le@rning
A Time Warner Company

GETTING READY

Warm-up Activity

Look at the photograph on the first page of this chapter. Does the picture show behavior that is different from your native culture or the culture in which you now live? Write about this photograph in your learner's notebook. What does the photograph depict? If the behavior shown in the photograph is unacceptable or unusual in your culture, explain what is different. How does the action in the photograph make you feel? How do people in this situation act in your culture? Which way is better? Why?

Grammar Preview

Informational writing *informs* you about subjects. In college and university courses, you will encounter this type of writing in textbooks and other sources. For instance, you will read write about different kinds of family groups in an introductory sociology or anthropology textbook. Textbooks on chemistry and biology will inform you about the composition of matter and living things.

This type of writing generally contains many nouns and noun phrases. Informational writing often uses present tense verbs and generic (general) nouns to relate statements of general truth (*A nuclear family consists of parents and children*). Writers also use structures such as modal auxiliary verbs, adverbs of frequency, quantifiers, and opinion structures to reduce the strength of general truth statements. Informational texts can include past tense verbs if the text relates a generalization that was true in the past, but is no longer true. Also, informational writing may include past narrative sections that tell about the history of an academic subject.

In the grammar activities in this chapter, you will examine and practice several of these important grammatical features so you can effectively read and write informational texts.

The Grammar of Nouns and Noun Phrases in Informational Writing: Learning and Using Key Terms

The field of anthropology ("ology," *the study of* + "anthro," *man*) has many key terms that relate to cultures and societies. One of these terms is *taboo* or *tabu*, which *The Newbury House Dictionary of American English* defines as "a forbidden act, especially one that goes against social customs or religious practices." Reading 1 explains that *tabu* comes from a Tongan word. In a college anthropology course, you would be expected to understand the concept of *tabu* and be able to relate it to different cultural groups.

Activity 3-1   Identifying and Practicing Key Terms

1. Read the following paragraph, taken from Reading 1. It defines the main key term in this chapter:

   Tabu is something we *shouldn't* do. It isn't something we don't like to do, nor is it something we don't want to do. Tabu is something shameful. It isn't something that is silly to do, nor is it something dangerous. Instead, it is something that would make us feel guilty if we did it. By telling us what we shouldn't do, tabu helps us to know what we ought to do.

2. With a small group of students, identify the phrases below that follows as *Tabu* or *Not Tabu* in U.S. culture today. Are any of these practices changing in this culture? Does the acceptability of the practices depend on certain situations? Discuss your answers with the class.

   ### Tabu (T) or Not Tabu (N) in the U.S.?

   ☐ drinking beer   ☐ wearing shorts in public

   ☐ living together before marriage   ☐ kissing in public

   ☐ eating dog meat   ☐ cursing in class

   ☐ wearing white clothing to a funeral   ☐ eating while walking

   ☐ eating cheese   ☐ interracial marriage

   ☐ marrying your brother or sister

3. If your native culture is not the U.S. culture, tell your group members whether the phrases are tabu or not tabu. Tell about whether the rules about these behaviors are changing, or if the rules differ depending on the circumstances.

4. Discuss the difference in meaning of these words: *tabu* and *crime*. Who decides whether an action is a *tabu*? Who decides whether an action is a *crime*? Can an action be both a *tabu* and a *crime*? Discuss your ideas with the class.

LEARNER'S NOTEBOOK

Previewing a Topic

Write about three tabus from other cultures that you have heard about. For example, you may write about food, clothing, marriage, or behavior tabus.

The Grammar of Defining: Present Tense Verbs

Defining key terms and other important words involves complete sentences, nouns, and verbs. The verb form is usually the simple present tense; it expresses a general truth.

EXAMPLES

Tabu *is* something we shouldn't do.

Tabu *is* something shameful.

Self-esteem *is* the feeling of appreciating your own inner value as a human being ...

GLR   See page 223 in the GLR for more information on present tense verbs.

Activity 3-2   Using Present Tense Verbs in Definitions

Complete the following definition sentences by choosing one of the verbs in the list. Change the forms of the verbs as necessary to make simple present tense verbs.

• be   • refer to   • mean   • indicate

1. Zaire _____ a country in central Africa.

2. The Koran _____ the religious book of Muslims.

3. Orthodox Jews _____ Jews who follow strict religious laws.

4. Kosher food _____ proper food in the Jewish religion.

5. Tonga _____ an island in the South Seas.

6. Wearing a *burkha*, or head veil, in India _____ that a young woman is engaged to be married.

7. Old Order Amish people _____ religious people who live in small communities in Pennsylvania, New York, the Midwest, and parts of Canada.

The Grammar of Defining: Using Articles and Nouns for Generic Meaning

A *definition* is a statement of general truth, so defining uses articles and nouns that show *generic* (general) meaning. Decide if your noun is singular, plural, or noncount in order to determine the correct article to use. Study these examples and their use of articles and nouns:

EXAMPLES

Singular	A *chadri* is a face covering that is worn by women in Muslim countries.
Plural	*Tabu foods* are ones that we *shouldn't* eat.
Noncount	*Culture* refers to the ideas, activities, and ways of behaving that are special to a country, people, or region.

> **GLR** See pages 220 and 240 of the GLR for additional explanations, examples, and practice in the use of articles and nouns in defining.

Activity 3-3   Identifying Types of Nouns

1. Mark each noun as singular count (SC), plural count (PC), or noncount (NC). Use a dictionary, such as the *Newbury House Dictionary of American English*, to identify nouns as singular, plural, or noncount.

   a. _____ behavior   g. _____ information
   b. _____ societies   h. _____ child
   c. _____ parents   i. _____ food
   d. _____ example   j. _____ clothing
   e. _____ education   k. _____ belief
   f. _____ relationship   l. _____ laws

2. For each of the singular count nouns, insert the appropriate article (*a* or *an*).

   EXAMPLES

   a rule   *an* order

The Grammar of Defining: Classifying Nouns

When you write a definition of a noun, you *classify* the noun. That is, you put the word into a category. The word that you are defining is *detailed and exact*. The classifying term is *general and broad*. The remainder of the sentence contains details that complete the concept of the word.

EXAMPLES

detailed and exact   general and broad
Haggis is *a type of food* that is made from sheep's parts.

detailed and exact   general and broad
A *monk* is a *religious leader* who follows strict rules of behavior.

Activity 3-4   Identifying Classifying Terms

1. Return to Activity 3-2. For each sentence, circle the classifying term.

2. Encyclopedias and dictionaries often use the format of a formal definition.

EXAMPLES

WORD	IS/ARE	CLASSIFYING TERM	DEFINING DETAILS
A society	is	a wide, non-specific group of people	who share some of the same background and culture.
A mixed marriage	is	a marriage	between two people of different races, religions, or cultures.

Activity 3-5   Examining Dictionary Definitions

1. With a partner, use a dictionary to find the definitions of these words that relate to anthropology. Fill in the chart that follows with the definitions:

Word	Dictionary Definition
tabu	*a forbidden act*, especially one that goes against social customs or religious practices
community	_____
	_____
relationship	_____
	_____
custom	_____
	_____

2. With your partner, underline the *classifying term* and circle the *defining details* in each definition.

Introduction to Organizing Paragraphs

In academic writing, paragraphs begin with a main idea and develop that idea by adding supporting points and details. The following box expresses this organization:

Paragraph Organization

Topic sentence: In one sentence, introduce the main idea and tell what you want to say about the topic. This introductory sentence controls or limits what you write in the paragraph.

Body: One or more sentences use main supporting points to explain the *topic sentence* more fully. Each supporting point uses details to tell more about that point. Generally, a paragraph should include at least two main supporting points plus details.

Conclusion: One sentence restates or comments about the main idea.

Activity 3-6   Finding the Parts of a Paragraph

With a partner, reread paragraphs 2 and 3 in Chapter 2, Activity 2-2 on pages 35–36. For each paragraph, mark the topic sentence, the body (support sentences), and the conclusion. Discuss your answers with the class.

Audience and Purpose in Writing

Your audience (your readers) and your purpose (your aim or goal) are important when you write. In this chapter, your audience will be your classmates and your instructor. Your purpose in writing about a cultural topic will be to inform your audience about it, and, in part, to express your opinion about it.

Especially when you write about cultural rules or customs that may not be familiar to your audience, you will need to explain the topic clearly, stating from which culture they come and how they are followed. You will need to define culturally related terms clearly and in enough detail that readers can understand what you are writing about.

LEARNER'S NOTEBOOK

Considering Your Audience

In your notebook, write about your audience for this chapter. What will interest your classmates and your instructor? What do they already know about tabus? What don't they know? How can you write what will interest them?

FOCUSING

READING 1   TABU: HEY, DON'T DO THAT! (MAGAZINE ARTICLE)

Activity 3-7   Pre-reading Discussion

1. With a partner or group of classmates, match the following words from Reading 1 with the definitions in the opposite column. Put the appropriate number of the definition in the blank. Then, discuss with classmates how these words relate to cultural rules such as *tabu*.

   _____ a. turns off   1. offends

   _____ b. shameful   2. modest, not proud

   _____ c. awkwardness   3. holy, hallowed

   _____ d. sacred   4. being uncomfortable

   _____ e. humble   5. fertile

   _____ f. fruitful   6. dishonorable

2. Before you begin Reading 1, read the glossary. Discuss the words you are not sure about with your classmates. Which words may be key terms in anthropology that you would need to remember for an examination?

> **Glossary**
>
> **termites**   wood-eating insects
> **street vendors**   outdoor salespersons
> **suit (verb)**   satisfy or please
> **Torah and Koran** holy books of Jews and Muslims, respectively
> **orthodox**   following traditional customs and teachings
> **bonnets**   soft hats for women

Activity 3-8   Focused Reading

1. Read the first paragraph of Reading 1. Then read the second paragraph and the first line of the third paragraph. Answer these questions about the writer, the audience, and the purpose of his writing:

   a. Which culture do you think the writer comes from? How do you know?

   b. When the writer refers to "*you*" in paragraph 2, who is he addressing? Which cultural group does *he* think his audience is from?

   c. In the first line of paragraph 3, who does "*our*" refer to?

   d. What do you think is the writer's purpose in writing this essay?

2. Reading 1, an *essay*, follows the standard rules for academic organization. As you read "Tabu: Hey, Don't Do That!" pay attention not only to the content, but to the organization as well. Think about these questions as you read:

   a. Where is the introduction and main idea sentence?

   b. Which part of the article supports the main idea?

   c. Which part is the conclusion?

TABU: HEY, DON'T DO THAT!

Tabu is something we *shouldn't* do. It isn't something we don't like to do, nor is it something we don't want to do. Tabu is something shameful. It isn't something that is silly to do, nor is it something dangerous to do. Instead, it is something that would make us feel guilty if we did it. By telling us what we shouldn't do, tabu helps us to know what we ought to do.

Let's start with food. Lots of Japanese people love to eat raw fish. Many French people 5 adore horse meat. Zairean children in central Africa enjoy eating flying termites and catch huge handfuls of them. A Scottish national dish is haggis, made from minced sheep's heart, lung, liver, and fat cooked with onions and savory herbs in the stomach of the slaughtered animal. Street vendors in Turkey make pita-bread sandwiches from the half head of a goat, eyeball and all. Many Americans love mushrooms, but if a mushroom so much as tries to 10 get on the plate of my five-year-old son, he acts as if the world is about to end. Now, some or all of these delicacies may not be *your* cup of tea, but they are not tabu to you.

Our foods may not suit people of other cultures, either. I have had long talks with Zairean friends about cheese, for instance. To them, cheese is rotten milk, and they cannot understand why I like it, nor can they imagine eating it themselves. Cheese turns these 15 friends off, but it is not tabu to them.

Tabu foods are ones that we *shouldn't* eat. Many Jews and Muslims never eat pork because it is against their religions to do so. It says so in the Bible and the Koran. One time a good friend of mine, who is a Muslim, and I were having a delicious dinner at some people's house. We were both enjoying some meat loaf when he discovered there was ground 20 pork in it. Although he was very polite and said nothing to our hostess, who was innocently unaware that he is a Muslim and cannot eat pork, he told me later that he had felt sick to his stomach from shame after having eaten something he knew he was not supposed to eat. In such circumstances, many people ask for God's forgiveness, even when the mistake is no one's fault.   25

Tabu also can indirectly refer to what one *should* eat. Orthodox Jews and Muslims may follow very strict dietary laws, for example. In both cases, animals must be slaughtered and meat prepared in special ways by religious officials. Food that is kosher (from a Hebrew word meaning "proper") is carefully prepared in factories, restaurants, and homes. Different dishes and utensils are used for different foods and may not be mixed. It would be tabu to do otherwise.   30

Tabu comes from a South Sea islands word meaning "forbidden." When Captain James Cook visited Tonga in 1777, he wrote in his diary about what people told him they shouldn't do and how they used the word *tapu* to describe these activities. Tongans were talking about marriage and other social relations, and they listed people one should not look at, talk to, or wed. Captain Cook brought the word home with him, and it has become part of the 35 English language as "tabu" or "taboo."

Other tabus have to do with language. Every once in a while, we hear someone say something we know is not polite or that might be OK in some situations but not others. Cussing (cursing or swearing) is an example. Sometimes we hear cussing on TV and in some kinds of music. In newspaper comics, if an artist wants to make someone appear to be 40 cussing, he or she places a string of symbols like this *#*! in a balloon above the character's head. It is tabu to write them in the paper. People may cuss when they get angry. When I am doing carpentry around the house and hit my thumb with a hammer, I may say things that don't ordinarily leave my lips. But none of us would ever cuss like that in a synagogue, church, mosque, temple, or shrine. Nor would we cuss around our mothers, children, or 45 elderly people. It is tabu to do so. It would be disrespectful, and we would feel ashamed.

Still other tabus have to do with dress. Old Order Amish people, who live in small communities in New York, Pennsylvania, the Midwest, and a few parts of Canada, cannot wear clothing that is pretty, fashionable, vain, or proud. It is tabu to wear buttons or zippers, and so shirts and blouses are fastened with straight pins. Men do not wear clothes with collars 50 or pockets. Colorful or patterned cloth is never worn. Both men and women are expected to wear hats or bonnets. Men should have an untrimmed beard, but never a mustache. Shoes must be black and tall. And it is tabu to be noisy, to use electricity, and to own or run gasoline engines. Horse-drawn buggies must be black, closed up, and without seats that lean back. 55

Now, that is a lot *not* to do. Why do people have so many tabus? Tabus are a bit like a frame around a picture (something else, by the way, that it is tabu for Old Order Amish to own): They let us know what we *should* do by telling us what we *shouldn't* do. People who share a tabu feel that they have something very important in common: They know what is "proper" behavior—what is kosher. Often rules for what is tabu and what is proper are writ- 60 ten in sacred books like the Bible or the Koran, or they are recited from memory by a priest or another religious official. Following such rules makes people into a community. Living together by sharing such rules is its own joy.

It is not that Old Order Amish people do not know about electricity, gasoline engines, or buttons. They certainly do, because they see people all around them using such things and 65 having an easier life as a consequence. The point that Old Order Amish people would make is that it is good to live by the sweat of one's brow. They love the land and feel a sacred obligation to work it with their hands, not distance themselves from it with machines. Their interpretation of the Bible is that people should live humble and fruitful lives, full of the rewards of close-to-the-earth hard work. Amish people help each other and anyone else in 70 need without expecting or wanting thanks. It is tabu to do otherwise.

Tabu is following a rule *not* to do something. It is like a fence that keeps us away from what is wrong. A good life is a proper life, full of happiness gained by knowing that we are doing what we ought to be doing and what our parents and grandparents and other people we love would be proud to see us doing, even if they are not around to look. 75

Allen F. Roberts, *FACES* magazine, Fall 1996.

Activity 3-9   Post-reading Discussion

1. With a small group of students, answer the following questions. Discuss your answers with your class.

   a. Which part of the article is the introduction? Mark this part in the text.

   b. Underline the topic sentence of each paragraph.

   c. Mark where the conclusion begins in the text.

2. Reading 1 is an essay-length piece of writing, so it contains many types of details. Using the information from Chapter 2, find an example of each of these types of details in the reading. Write the example sentence in the space given. Also mark the paragraph number.

TYPE OF DETAILS	EXAMPLE SENTENCE (or sentence part)	Paragraph
Facts	_____	_____
	_____	_____
Personal Experience	_____	_____
	_____	_____
Examples	_____	_____
	_____	_____
Description	_____	_____
	_____	_____

Activity 4-10   Organizational Chart for Paragraphs in an Essay

The text, "Tabu: Hey, Don't Do That," contains many paragraphs. Examine two paragraphs and fill in the following chart to show how the ideas in these paragraphs are organized. When you fill in the chart, take sentences directly from the text or use your own words to express the ideas. Discuss your answers with your class.

ORGANIZATIONAL CHART
TABU: HEY, DON'T DO THAT!

Paragraph 4

Topic sentence: _____.

Main supporting point 1: _____

Detail 1: _____ It says so in the Bible and the Koran. _____

Detail 2: _____

Paragraph 9

Topic Sentence: _____ Still other tabus have to do with dress. _____

Main supporting point 1: _____

Detail 1: _____

Detail 2: _____

Detail 3: _____

Detail 4: _____

Main supporting point 2: *Men should have an untrimmed beard, but never a mustache.*

Detail 1: _____

Main supporting point 3: _____

Main supporting point 4: _____

LEARNER'S NOTEBOOK

Warm-up Activity

In Reading 1, the writer says "Following such [cultural] rules makes people into a community. Living together by sharing such rules is its own joy." Do you think this statement is true? Do you feel that you are part of a cultural community? Or do you feel that you are part of more than one cultural community? How does following cultural rules make you feel?

Activity 3-11   Preparing to Write about a Cultural Tabu

To prepare to write about a cultural tabu, begin by thinking about tabus in a culture you know well. Major cultural areas in which tabus exist are food, dress, marriage, family relationships, and language. You will need to explain the tabu by giving details, so think about a cultural tabu that you know well.

READING 2   SAMPLE STUDENT PARAGRAPHS

Activity 3-12   Focused Reading

Notice how student writers have organized the following paragraphs about cultural tabus. Think about this question as you are reading: Do the student paragraphs have the three main parts of a paragraph: introduction (with topic sentence), body (support), and conclusion?

PARAGRAPH A: A TABU FROM THE SOVIET UNION

A tabu is something which we should not do, according to our parents, our religion, or our society. There are tabus in food, in dress, in language, in marriage, etc. I would like to introduce to you one big tabu that existed during the Communist system in the Soviet Union. According to this tabu, people couldn't say and think bad things about the political system in the Soviet Union. The government was afraid of people's criticism. People were 5 afraid to criticize the government, too. When somebody said something improper or without respect about the political system, this person was arrested. There are many different tabus. Some of them are good, some not. I think that in time people will forget inappropriate or uncomfortable tabus. I am happy that I no longer have to live with this tabu.

Olga Povolotskaya
Ukraine

PARAGRAPH B: TABUS FOR BUDDHIST MONKS

There are many tabus for marriage, dress, food, and language in my Cambodian culture. Some of them relate to the food and the dress of Buddhist monks. Certain things are tabu for the Buddhist monk to eat or drink. For example, eating the flesh of people, elephants, monkeys, tigers, lions, leopards, snakes, and dogs, and drinking alcohol are forbidden because they are against my religion. Tabus also exist in the dress of Buddhist monks. If a monk 5 wears black, blue, or green colors, laypeople will never call him a monk and he will quit being a monk as soon as this happens. Monks always wear yellow, red, and brown clothing. There are three kinds of clothing: the 8-meter, 10-meter, and 12-meter robe. They are cut following the rules for monks' clothing. A tabu is something we should not do. But we sometimes hear and know that people do these things. It is improper for us to do this.   10

Phai Thach
Cambodia

Activity 3-13   Post-reading Discussion

With a partner or a small group of classmates, answer these questions about the sample student paragraphs.

1. Does the paragraph contain an introduction? Which is the topic sentence?

2. Which sentences make up the body?

3. Which sentence is the conclusion sentence?

4. Is the paragraph interesting? Why or why not?

LEARNER'S NOTEBOOK

Responding to a Reading

Think of the student paragraph you enjoyed the most. Write answers to the following questions in your learner's notebook: Why did you like this paragraph the best? If you could talk with the author, what questions would you ask?

Activity 3-14   Brainstorming for Writing

If you are unsure of a topic, you may want to "brainstorm" new ideas by discussing tabus in food, dress, marriage, family relationships, and language with a partner or a group of classmates.

Take notes about possible topics. Ask your partner or group members about your topic and help them brainstorm about their topics. Take notes about ideas you might use.

Activity 3-15   Writing Assignment: Writing about a Cultural Tabu

Write your paragraph about a tabu from a culture you know well. When you decide on a topic, be sure to explain it well. Identify the culture in which the tabu exists. Explain the tabu by giving details. Define any terms that your audience (your instructor and classmates) may be unfamiliar with. Be sure to follow the standard rules for paragraph organization.

The Grammar of Informational Writing: Present Tense Verbs

Informational writing uses present tense verbs to tell about general truths or beliefs, or to write about present time activities such as habits or regular actions. In writing about tabus, you tell about both general truths and present time activities, so your writing contains mainly present tense verbs.

> **GLR**   Refer to page 223 of the GLR for more information about the form, time, and meaning of present tense verbs.

Activity 3-16   Identifying Present Tense Verbs

Reread the two sample student compositions. With a partner, mark the present time verbs. Then answer these questions:

1. What is the predominant verb tense used in both paragraphs? Why?

2. In Paragraph A, the writer also uses past tense verbs. Why?

3. When you wrote about a tabu from your culture, which verb tense did you use? Why?

Activity 3-17   Using Present Tense Verbs

With a partner, complete the following paragraph with the correct forms of the verbs in the list. Discuss your answers with your class.

- be   • meet   • wear   • leave   • marry   • like   • want   • do   • talk

A Bride's Clothing

In my Cambodian culture, there _____ tabus about a bride's clothing. The bride never _____ black clothing because elderly people and her parents _____ her to display to everyone that she _____ a virgin. But when one _____ opposite that in a wedding, all guests _____ her alone. After that, they never _____ to her when they _____ her. The bride also never _____ sexy clothing after she _____, either, because no people _____ or _____ to see one who _____ sexy clothing. The bride always _____ yellow-colored clothing on the first day after the wedding. She _____ white on the second day after her marriage. These _____ some of the strict tabus about a bride's clothing.

Phai Thach
Cambodia

The Grammar of Writing Generalizations: Adverbs of Frequency

Informational writing contains generalizations, or general truth statements. In this type of writing, adverbs of frequency define the strength of the generalizations. Examine how the adverbs of frequency control the strength of these statements:

adverb of frequency
Monks *always* wear yellow, red, and brown clothing.

adverb of frequency
But we *sometimes* hear and know that people do these things.

GLR See page 230 of the GLR for more information on adverbs of frequency.

Activity 3-18 Examining Adverbs of Frequency

With a partner, read the following sentences. Circle the adverbs of frequency. Discuss how the adverb of frequency defines the strength of each general truth statement.

1. Every once in a while, we hear someone say something we know is not polite.

2. Sometimes we hear swearing on TV and in some kinds of music.

3. You may have heard some jokes about mothers-in-law, for example. These usually are not very nice.

4. The bride also never wears sexy clothing after she marries.

5. The bride always wears yellow-colored clothing on the first day after her wedding.

Activity 3-19 Peer Response

With a partner, exchange your paragraphs about tabus. Read each other's paragraphs and answer these questions. Discuss your answers with your partner.

1. Does the writer tell about a tabu from a culture he or she knows well?

2. Does a topic sentence introduce this tabu and say something about it?

3. Does the body of the paragraph contain enough detail to explain the tabu? If not, mark places in the margin where more detail is needed. Write questions you have about the content.

LEARNER'S NOTEBOOK

Responding to a Reading

Write in answer to these questions in your learner's notebook: What was the most interesting part of your partner's paragraph? What is your reaction to the tabu that your partner wrote about?

READING 3   CLOTHING DO'S AND DON'TS (MAGAZINE ARTICLE)

Activity 3-20   Pre-reading Discussion

1. The title of Reading 3 is "Clothing Do's and Don'ts." What do the words "do's" and "don'ts" refer to? What does the title suggest about the content of the essay?

2. Read the glossary before you begin reading the essay. Discuss unclear meanings with your class.

Glossary

display	show
interaction	communication with
baring	uncovering
reproductive	relating to having children
gourd	a fruit with a hard outer shell
torso	the human body from the neck to the hips
veiled	covered by a light cloth worn over the face

Activity 3-21   Focused Reading

As you read "Clothing Do's and Don'ts," pay attention to the content as well as the time of the verbs. Think about which verb tenses are used and why.

CLOTHING DO'S AND DON'TS

In many states in the United States, some stores have a summer sign on the door that says, "No shirts, no shoes, no service." Every society has rules about clothing, including some very strict rules that can be considered tabus. Clothing tabus reflect every society's most deeply valued ideas about display of the body and human interaction.

In almost all societies, covering certain areas of the body is considered essential. In 5
most groups, publicly baring the reproductive organs is tabu, and they must be covered, even if only by a small piece of cloth, a bundle of grass, a gourd, or a narrow string. Other societies go further, insisting that the entire torso and limbs be covered as well. In some regions, women are expected to cover their heads and sometimes even their faces.

Tabus about clothing differ so much from one society to another that people from dif- 10
ferent parts of the world can easily misunderstand each other's clothing rules. For example, people in Turkey who keep their body fully covered have been shocked at the sight of European tourists wearing shorts. American clothing rules allow us to bare much of our body in hot weather, and we may be puzzled by the sight of Middle Eastern visitors with a veiled head and face.   15

When we understand that clothing tabus express important and treasured values, it helps us appreciate the way others dress.

Doranne Jacobson, *FACES* magazine, Fall 1996.

Activity 3-22   Post-reading Discussion

Answer these questions about "Clothing Do's and Don'ts" in a small group.

1. Can you find one sentence that best represents the main idea? Underline it.

2. Find five clothing "do's and don'ts" from the story. Write them here, using your words or the words from the story:

_____

_____

_____

_____

_____

3. Circle each verb used in the story. Which verb tense is most often used here? Why?

4. What message does the writer give us in the conclusion? Do you agree? Why or why not?

The Grammar of Writing Generalizations: Using Generic Nouns

Generic nouns and generic noun phrases refer to a whole class of things or people. In other words, when you write *Americans* or *American college students,* you mean **all** *Americans* and **all** *American college students.* The word and phrase are generic; they represent all members of the class.

In readings about tabus and other subjects of anthropology, generic nouns often tell about cultural rules and cultural groups. Here is one example from "Clothing Do's and Don'ts," paragraph 1:

> *Clothing tabus* reflect every society's most deeply valued ideas about display of the body and human interaction.

The generic noun phrase *Clothing tabus* means the general class of things known as tabus about clothing. Note that the plural generic noun does not need an article such as *a, an,* or *the.* If the generic noun is singular, it will need an article.

> **GLR**   See page 220 of the GLR for more information on generic nouns and page 240 for the rules of article use with generic nouns.

Activity 3-23   Examining Generic Nouns

In this passage from "Clothing Do's and Don'ts," the generic noun phrases are printed in italics. With a partner, discuss the meaning of each noun phrase.

> *Tabus about clothing* differ so much from one society to another that *people from different parts of the world* can easily misunderstand each other's clothing rules. For example, *people in Turkey* who keep their body fully covered have been shocked at the sight of *European tourists* wearing shorts. *American clothing rules* allow us to bare much of our body in hot weather, and we may be puzzled by the sight of *Middle Eastern visitors* with a veiled head and face.

| Activity 3-24   Writing Generalizations Using Generic Nouns |

Write an original sentence using each of the generic nouns or generic noun phrases below. Write about your culture or another culture you know well.

college teachers   elderly people

young men   eating habits

a parent

The Grammar of Writing Generalizations: Quantifiers

Writers often control or limit the strength of generalizations. Instead of saying that *all* members of a group behave in a certain way, for example, they may want to limit their generalization by limiting the members to *most, many, some,* or a certain number of members. Quantifiers (words or phrases that tell the number of a group) control the strength of generalizations. Examine the quantifiers in these sentences:

quantifier
Lots of Japanese people love to eat raw fish.

quantifier
Many French people adore horse meat.

These generalizations are limited in strength. The statements do not say that *all* Japanese people love raw fish or *all* French people adore horse meat. The quantifier words *lots of* and *many* limit the number of the members of the group.

> **GLR**   Refer to page 231 of the GLR for more information on quantifiers.

| Activity 3-25   Evaluating Quantifiers in Generalizations |

With a partner, read the following pairs of generalizations. The first statement comes from a reading in this chapter. Compare the strength of this statement with the generalization that follows it. Underline any quantifier words or phrases that you find in either statement.

1. Many Americans love *mushrooms* ... (Reading 1)

    Americans love mushrooms.

2. In almost all societies, covering certain areas *of the body is considered essential.* (Reading 3)

    In all societies, covering certain areas of the body is considered essential.

3. In most groups, publicly baring the reproductive organs is tabu, and they must be covered, even if only by a small piece of cloth, a bundle of grass, a gourd, or a narrow string. (Reading 3)

    In social groups, publicly baring the reproductive organs is tabu.

4. In India, some Muslim women wear the burkha, a two-piece garment consisting of an overcoat and a separate head veil. (Reading 4)

    In India, Muslim women wear the burkha.

The Grammar of Writing Generalizations: Modal Verbs to Limit Generalizations

In writing generalizations, the modal auxiliary verbs *may, might,* or *can* may also be used to limit or control the strength of the general truth statement. Read this sentence from Reading 1:

modal verb
Orthodox Jews and Muslims *may follow* very strict dietary laws.

The modal auxiliary verb *may* limits the strength of the generalization so that it means that *it is possible* that Orthodox Jews and Muslims behave in this way. If the modal verb is omitted, the generalization means that *it is certain* that Orthodox Jews and Muslims behave in this way.

> GLR   See pages 231–233 of the GLR for more information on modal auxiliary verbs.

Activity 3-26   Examining Modal Verbs That Limit Generalizations

Discuss the differences in meaning between the following pairs of statements. Underline the modal auxiliary verbs.

1. Our foods may not suit people of other cultures, either.

    Our foods do not suit people of other cultures, either.

2. People may curse when they get angry.

    People curse when they get angry.

3. Elderly people may prefer to live independently.

    Elderly people prefer to live independently.

4. A French child might drink a glass a wine with dinner every night.

    A French child drinks a glass a wine with dinner every night.

5. People can disapprove of a mixed marriage couple in the United States.

    People disapprove of a mixed marriage couple in the United States.

The Grammar of Stating Rules or Values in Writing: Modal Verbs

In addition, the modal auxiliary verbs *should, can, may,* and *must* are often used to state rules or values, as in these examples:

modal verb
Tabu is something we *shouldn't* do.

modal verb
Muslims *cannot* eat pork.

modal verb
Old Amish Order men *must* grow a beard when they marry.

These modals differ in the strength of the requirement. *Should* means that the rule is a requirement and is highly recommended, but if the rule is broken the punishment is not severe. *Cannot* is often used to state forbidden actions or impossible actions. The strongest rule statements are with *must;* if these rules are broken, the penalties are severe.

> **GLR**   See pages 231—233 of the GLR for more information on different modal verbs.

Activity 3-27   Using Different Modal Verbs to Indicate the Strength of Rules

Different writers will use different modals because they have different ideas and interpretations of the rules and the punishment for breaking the rules. With a partner, discuss how you would write the following sentences:

1. Children should/must obey their parents.

2. Children cannot/should not/must not disobey their parents.

3. If you want to be healthy, you should/must exercise.

4. You must/should help your friends in order to be a good person.

5. You cannot/should not/must not drink alcohol and drive a car.

Activity 3-28   Recognizing Modal Verbs that State Rules or Values

Circle the modal verbs (modal auxiliaries + main verbs) used to state rules in the following sentences taken from "Tabu: Hey, Don't Do That." Check your answers with a partner.

1. Although he was very polite and said nothing to our hostess, who was innocently unaware that he is a Muslim and cannot eat pork, he told me later that he had felt sick to his stomach from shame after having eaten something he knew he was not supposed to eat.

2. Tongans were talking about marriage and other social relations, and they listed people one should not look at, talk to, or wed.

3. Old Order Amish people, who live in small communities in New York, Pennsylvania, the Midwest, and a few parts of Canada, cannot wear clothing that is pretty, fashionable, vain, or proud.

4. Men should have an untrimmed beard, but never a mustache.

READING 4   PHOTOGRAPHS AND CAPTIONS

The following photographs and accompanying descriptions (captions) illustrate some of the clothing rules that exist in cultures. Look over the photos, read the captions, and then answer the questions that follow with a partner or a small group of classmates. In your discussion, keep in mind that the clothing habits depicted in the photographs may differ from those in your culture, but they are acceptable in the culture from which they come.

Clothing Rules That Exist in Different Cultures

Top Left: Women in Uzbekistan appear in public wearing an all-covering *chadri*, which protects them from the gaze of men outside their families. They can see through the netting over the eyes. The covering expresses their modesty, personal virtue, and family honor.

Top Right: Scotsmen wear short skirts, called kilts, on special occasions.

Bottom: Young girls and women in Iran are expected to wear the *chador* over their other clothes. They hold the fabric in place by clutching it with one hand under the chin. The cloth is a reminder of the need to follow traditional female roles in Iran, where a fundamentalist Islamic government is in power. In Iran and some other countries governed by fundamentalists, women who appear in public with their head uncovered can be arrested or killed. Many Muslims object to such strict clothing rules for women.

Activity 3-29   Post-reading Discussion

With a partner or a small group of classmates, discuss the photographs on pages 82–83. Answer the following questions. Share your ideas with your class.

1. How do you feel about clothing rules in general?

2. Do any of the clothing rules illustrated in the photographs exist in a culture that you know well? Which ones?

3. Which clothing tabus (in the photos or in general) do you like the most? Why?

4. Which clothing tabus do you dislike the most? Why?

Activity 3-30   Writing about Rules and Values Using Modal Verbs

Look at the photographs in Reading 4 again. For each photograph, write a modal verb sentence to describe the clothing that is shown. Refer to pages 231–232 of the GLR for help with form and meaning. You may want to use these or other modal auxiliaries in your sentences:

can / cannot   must / have to / must not   should / should not   may / may not

EXAMPLE

In Scotland, men *may* wear skirts.

PUTTING IT ALL TOGETHER

FINAL WRITING ASSIGNMENT: A PARAGRAPH ABOUT CLOTHING RULES

Write a paragraph about a clothing tabu or rule in a culture that you know. Choose **one** of the following topics for your writing. You may use the photographs in Reading 4 as the basis of your writing or you may write about other clothing rules or tabus that you know about.

Your audience will be your instructor and those members of your class who come from different cultures than yours. You will need to define culturally-related terms clearly and explain them in detail.

1. Describe one clothing rule you think is appropriate. Explain the rule, where it is used and why you like it. Define any terms or items you think may be unfamiliar to your readers. If you have had personal experience with this clothing rule, tell about that, too.

2. Describe one clothing rule you think is inappropriate. Explain the rule, where it is used, and why you dislike it. Define culturally based terms or items that may be unfamiliar to your readers. If you have had personal experience with this clothing rule, tell about that, too.

3. Compare one category of clothing in a culture that you know well and the same category of clothing in another culture. How are they different? Which do you like more? Which have you used? Be sure to define any terms related to clothing that may be unfamiliar to that readers from other cultures.

Self-editing

1. Read your paragraph again. Does it say what you want it to say? Is it organized in the best way for your meaning and this particular writing task? Make any changes needed to improve the meaning of your writing. You are writing to *inform* readers about a tabu or rule in a culture, so check for the language of informational writing.

2. Edit your individual sentences for the following, and correct any errors you find. After you have edited for each of these features, check (✓) the box to remind yourself that you have done that task.

- ☐ complete sentences
- ☐ correct punctuation
- ☐ correct verb tenses
- ☐ correct capitalization of proper nouns
- ☐ correct use of articles with generic nouns in generalizations
- ☐ correct definition structures for any defined terms
- ☐ correct statement of generalizations—using modal auxiliaries, adverbs of frequency, and quantifiers for exactly the right meaning

3. Rewrite your paragraph to make the corrections you decided on while you were editing your sentences.

Peer Response

With a partner, exchange your final writing assignment paragraphs. Read each other's papers and answer these questions. Discuss your answers with your partner.

1. Does the writer write about one of the topics in the assignment? If not, what is the writer's topic?

2. Does a topic sentence introduce the writer's opinions?

3. Does the writer use enough detail from the photographs or his or her experience to explain his or her ideas? If not, mark places in the margin where more detail is needed. Write questions you have about the content.

4. Does the writer introduce any terms or items from his or her culture that are unfamiliar to you? Are these terms defined clearly? If not, mark places where the writer needs to clarify a culturally related term.

5. Is the paragraph interesting? Which part interests you the most? Why?

LEARNER'S NOTEBOOK

Responding to a Reading

In your learner's notebook, write about your partner's final writing assignment paragraph. Complete these ideas in your writing:

I like_____'s paragraph because _____.

The best detail is _____.

The most interesting part of the paragraph is _____ because

_____.

L
O
O
K
I
N
G

A
H
E
A
D

Authentic Academic Assignment

Read the following academic assignments which relate to organizing. In a small group, answer the discussion questions that follow.

Data Processing 103

Internet Career Research: For this project, you will be conducting research on one possible career in data processing via the Internet. Using the resources you have accessed on the World Wide Web and through other parts of the Internet, find out the following information about a career in data processing.

1. The job title and description
2. Starting salary
3. Outlook for job availability

4. Requirements: education and job experience
5. Opportunities for advancement
6. Types of companies that seek this type of professional
7. Related professional organizations
8. Address, phone number of local professional organization
9. Local and other educational institutions that offer degrees relevant to this profession
10. Advantages and disadvantages of working in this profession

When you write your paper, include parenthetical source information. Identify the Internet/WWW address from which you attained the information.

Write a five- to eight-page paper.

DISCUSSION

1. Before you discuss the assignment, read the list of 10 research areas in the introduction to the assignment. Look up unfamiliar words in the dictionary. Ask your classmates and your instructor to explain words that you do not understand.

2. What is the most difficult part of this assignment?

3. What questions would you ask the instructor to clarify the assignment?

4. How would you handle the work?

5. How long would it take you to do the work?

6. What do you think you could do in order to get an "A" on this assignment?

7. How could the organizing skills practiced in this chapter help you with this assignment?

Chapter 4

*R*emembering

Special Memories

GOALS

WRITING
◆ develop and practice remembering skills in writing

GRAMMAR
◆ examine and practice several of the features of past narrative and academic writing: *past tense and other verbs, chronological organizers, personal pronouns, punctuation,* and *word forms*

CONTENT
◆ explore past personal and academic events

ACADEMIC FIELDS
Psychology
Sociology

Sample Authentic
College/University
Remembering Assignments

In a college or university classroom, you will use the skills you learn in this chapter to complete assignments like the ones below:

Freshman Composition

Assignment: Diagnostic Essay

Write an essay about your birthplace, the place where you grew up, and the special events that helped to shape your early life. Try to remember and write as many details as possible about the early part of your life.

Introduction to Sociology

Assignment: Field Research Report

Write a three- to five-page report on one of the social topics that we have discussed in class so far, using information from an interview as the basis for your support. Your interview should consist of at least 15 questions. Follow the sample format distributed in class.

GETTING READY

LEARNER'S NOTEBOOK

Warm-up Activity

The title of this chapter is "Special Memories." Is there one special memory from your past which comes to your mind now? Write as much as you can about it. If you cannot remember some parts of the event, indicate this by beginning these parts of the story with "I cannot remember ..."

Grammar Preview

In Chapter 2, you examined academic past time narratives in the discipline of history. This type of writing is also used in other academic disciplines such as introductory psychology and biology courses, where students read and write about scientific studies and experiments.

Past time narratives use predominantly past tense verbs. Other verb tenses tie the past to the present and the future. Chronological organizers and proper nouns also appear. As in other types of writing, writers of past time narratives also use punctuation to indicate boundaries between and within complete sentences.

In the grammar activities in this chapter, you will continue to observe and practice several of these important grammatical features, and will write personal narratives, in order to better read and write academic past time narratives.

Introduction to Remembering: The Five Senses

When you write about past events, you need to remember these events accurately and in detail. Two particular strategies that can help you to gather information about past events are using the five senses and asking essential questions.

Asking questions that relate to the five senses of sight, hearing, smell, touch, and taste is a good way to begin to remember a past event.

Five Senses Questions

What did _____ look like?   What did _____ sound like?

How did _____ smell?   How did _____ feel (touch)?

How did _____ taste?

Reread your first learner's notebook entry from page 90. Then, use the Five Senses Questions from the chart above to ask yourself more questions about the event. Write your answers to the questions in the margins of your learner's notebook. Then, revise your entry, adding the new information generated from this activity.

Remembering: Essential Questions

Another way to write more accurately and in greater detail about a past event is to use essential questions as a trigger for remembering. These questions—*who, what, when, where, why,* and *how*—are used by journalists to make sure their news stories are complete.

You can use this strategy to add even more detail to your writing by asking a second question after each essential question. The second question can generate more specific details for your writing.

Essential Questions: The Five W's and the H

Who was involved?
   Can you recall any more details about the people involved?
What happened?
   Can you think of any more details about what happened?
When did it happen?
   Can you add any more details about the time?
Where did it happen?
   Can you add any more details about the place?
Why did it happen?
   Can you remember any more details about why it happened?
How did it happen?
   Can you remember any more details about how it happened?

Activity 4-2   Asking Essential Questions in Remembering

Exchange your revised learner's notebook activity with a partner. Read your partner's paper. Does your partner answer each of the essential questions and detail questions from the list on the previous page?

If not, in the margin of the paper, mark the place where your partner could add the answer to one of the questions. Explain your marks to your partner and see if he or she can recall more information about the past event described in the writing. As you ask the questions, have your partner make notes about added details in the margin. Then each of you can revise your paper once again to add more information.

LEARNER'S NOTEBOOK

Reflecting about Your Past

In your learner's notebook, write about your ability to remember past experiences. Do you remember things clearly that happened when you were a child? How far back are your earliest memories? Do you remember them in great detail or in general? Which events are you better able to remember? Why? Does asking yourself questions help you to remember better? Do you sit quietly and clear your mind to help you remember?

FOCUSING

READING 1   CULTURAL CIRCUMSTANCES AND MEMORY SKILLS
(EXCERPT FROM A PSYCHOLOGY TEXTBOOK)

Activity 4-3   Pre-reading Discussion

Reading 1 is an academic past time narrative from a psychology textbook. It relates a scientific study involving the memory skills of two groups of people. Before reading, answer these questions with a group of classmates:

1. Read the title of the text. What might be the relationship between culture and memory skills?

2. Paragraph 1 tells you that "Australian aboriginal people" are one of the groups involved in the scientific study about memory. What can you guess about the memory skills of this group of people?

3. Read over the glossary of words. Discuss any unclear definitions with your class-mates and your instructor. What do the words suggest the reading will be about?

GLOSSARY

intellectual	related to thinking	**seed pod**	case for a plant seed
impact	effect	**distinction**	difference
fundamental	basic	**methodical**	careful
aspects	features, parts	**fidget**	to move nervously
hypothesized	made a theory	**mutter**	to speak unclearly and quietly
aboriginal	native		
reasoned	thought logically	**hurriedly**	in a hurry
thrive	to grow strong and healthy	**speculated**	guessed
		subjects	persons who are examined or studied
adolescents	teenager		
twig	small branch		

CULTURAL CIRCUMSTANCES AND MEMORY SKILLS

Does culture influence even basic intellectual skills such as memory? Some psychologists believe that our cultural circumstances have a powerful impact on many fundamental aspects of intelligence. For example, psychologist Judith Kearins (1986) hypothesized that Australian aboriginal people possess better visual memory skills for objects than white Australian children. She reasoned that excellent visual memory skills have allowed the aboriginal people 5 to thrive in the different physical desert environments in which many of them live.

In Kearins' experiments, aboriginal and white adolescents were given 30 seconds to memorize the location of objects arranged on a rectangular grid. The experimenter then mixed the objects up and the subject was asked to replace them in their original positions. Two of the tasks involved manufactured objects (matchbox, ring, eraser) and two 10 involved natural objects (twig, seed pod, feather, bone, etc.). The aboriginal adoles-cents performed significantly better than white Australians on all of the tasks. White adolescents performed better when the task material was manufactured objects than they did when the objects were natural, but this distinction did not affect the performance of the aboriginal children.   15

Kearins found that aboriginal and white Australian subjects used different memory strategies to approach the task. The aboriginal adolescents sat very still, were silent, and appeared to concentrate deeply. They were slow and methodical in replacing the objects. Most of the white adolescents, on the other hand, tended to fidget and mutter, and replaced the first few objects hurriedly. Kearins speculated that the white children were muttering the 20 verbal labels of the objects in an effort to remember them, whereas the aboriginal children were more likely to memorize the arrangement of the objects in visual terms. Perhaps the different cultures emphasize verbal or visual approaches to memorization because of the importance of those skills in each culture.

Think about your own approach to memorization. How would you have approached the 25 memory task in Kearins' experiment? Would you have memorized the placement of the objects in visual terms, or would you have memorized verbal labels for the objects ("The feather in the top-left, then moving clockwise, the stick, the weird-looking bone . . .")? What type of information is most important for you to remember to survive in your ethnic group? What cultural differences have you noticed between your community and other ethnic com- 30 munities in terms of their approach to intellectual skills? Finally, has your ethnic community influenced your approach to memorization and other intellectual skills—and, if so, how has it done so?

Benjamin B. Lahey, *Psychology: An Introduction* (Brown & Benchmark, 1995).

Activity 4-4   Post-reading Discussion

With a small group of classmates, answers these questions about Reading 1:

1. In your words, what is the main idea of this text? Circle a sentence or sentences from paragraph 1 that best express the main idea. Discuss your answers with classmates.

2. Identify and underline one sentence from each remaining paragraph that contains the most important idea. Discuss your answers in your group and with your class.

3. In paragraph 4, the writer addresses comments and questions to *you.* Who is the writer speaking to? Why do you think the writer uses the pronouns *you* and *your?*

4. In your group, take turns answering each question in paragraph 4.

Reflecting on Memory Skills

In your notebook, answer the questions in paragraph 4 of Reading 1 that relate to your memorization skills. Based on your group discussion, do you think different cultures have different or similar ways to remember things? Explain the differences or similarities that you found in your group.

READING 2 SAMPLE STUDENT PARAGRAPHS

Activity 4-5 Focused Reading

Reading 2 presents two past time narratives written by students. As you read, think about the five senses and essential questions. Do the writers write about past events clearly and in great detail? Do any parts of the events need more detail?

PARAGRAPH A: A MAGIC DRUG

Twenty-four years ago when I was only five months old, my parents were invited to a party by their best friends who lived nearby. When they left the house, my mother told my oldest brother (who was nine years old) to look after me, and if something went wrong, if I cried or anything else, to call her. One hour later my brother was visited by his friends, who asked him to go out and play soccer. He said, "Okay, but I need to run home periodically 5 and check my baby brother." Outside it was late fall, and it was cold and rainy. When my brother ran home to look in on me, I had wet my diapers. Then he made two big mistakes.

First, he undressed me, and then he opened the windows in my room without calling mom to ask if he should. After this, he left me alone and went out to play soccer. When my parents got back home, they saw a strange sight. I was lying in the bed undressed and pale and 10 it was very cold inside the room. My mother was scared when she saw me. She took my temperature and it was high. My mother had a shock. When my parents brought me in the hospital, the doctors said that I had pneumonia, and maybe I wouldn't survive. The only thing that saved my life 24 years ago was the discovery of a new drug for pneumonia for children two years old and younger. Only this drug saved my life, and soon I felt better. My 15 parents said that was the first and last time they ever left me alone with my oldest brother or with anyone else.

Aleksandr Alksnis
Ukraine

PARAGRAPH B: THE LIFE OF MY MOTHER

I remember a long time ago, when I was four years old, every morning, I would get up and usually would ask my aunt, "Where is my mother?" She would tell me, "Your mom went to work." After I heard this answer, I would get very sad. Sometimes I would cry, but finally I would feel okay and play something with my aunt, because I knew my mom was a business person. She had a store and she was a wonderful tailor. My mother had a small 5 store in the supermarket. She sold everything from cloth, scissors, thimbles, and needles to notebooks and pencils for students. At 2 o'clock, she would close the store, and go to work at another place, which was a tailor school. She had about 25 students there. They studied sewing. She taught them sewing until 5 p.m. After that, they went home and my mom began to sew clothes for her customers. My mother sewed only one style. They called it an 10 "aodai." I don't know the English meaning, but I know that it is a dress only worn by Vietnamese women. My mother continued to work and work. She didn't have much time to spend at home. She usually got a hug and a kiss from me when she came home. My mother worked very hard. She had to take care of me, my father, my grandparents, my aunt, and my uncle because she was the oldest daughter in the family. My father didn't help my mom 15 because he was in jail after 1975. Then, in May 1978, my mother became sick. My aunt took her to the hospital, but the doctor could not cure her. One day, she told my aunt to tell the doctor to let her return home to visit for two days, and the doctor accepted. I was very happy when I saw my mother come home. I remember that afternoon. She picked me up and took me to the garden of my grandparents. We sat at the foot of a tree. She told me a lot of sto- 20 ries. Before it got dark, she took me home and told me to eat some food. At this time, I thought I was going to be very happy. But after that, my mom felt tired and went to bed. Two hours later, she died. I went to my mother's bed and talked to her. I told her that I loved her. I never blamed her for not coddling me like other children, and I understood her very much. However, I still feel a little guilty because I never told her how much I loved her 25 while she was still alive.

Anh Trang
Vietnam

Activity 4-6   Post-reading Discussion

In a small group, discuss the two sample student paragraphs, focusing on these questions.

1. Does the writer of Paragraph A include enough detail about his infant experience? If not, where would you like more information? Write your questions in the margins at points where more detail is needed.

2. Discuss your written questions with other members of the group and with your class.

3. Do the same for Paragraph B.

4. Which of the paragraphs appeals to you more? Why?

Activity 4-7   Writing Assignment 1: Childhood Event

Writing personal narratives will help you prepare to read and write academic past time narratives. For this assignment, remember and write about one special childhood event. Choose a different past event than the one you wrote about for the warm-up activity. As the writers of the sample paragraphs did, be sure to write about just one event.

Use your five senses and the "essential questions" for gathering ideas and remembering clearly and in detail before you write.

In your introduction, you may want to answer some of the essential questions like what happened, when, and where. The body of your paragraph should give details about the event. The conclusion may tell the final part of the story and also comment about the event.

For this assignment, you will prepare, write, and revise your paragraph. Then, before you turn it in, read the section on "Revising a Paragraph" below. Also, read and discuss the student sample paragraph and revision that follow.

Revising a Paragraph

When you write a paragraph for English class, how many times do you write it before you turn it in? Some students write their papers one time only; others write and revise their work several times before they turn it in.

You should always revise your writing at least once before you turn in the first draft to your instructor. Then, after you receive feedback from a classmate and your instructor, you can write a second draft in which you can add more details. You may think of new ideas you want to add. You can also correct grammatical or spelling mistakes. Sometimes you may need to write a third or fourth draft of a paper. As an old English saying goes, "Practice makes perfect."

READING 3   FIRST AND SECOND DRAFTS OF A SAMPLE STUDENT PARAGRAPH

Activity 4-8   Focused Reading

Read the following sample student paragraph, "My Broken Arm." This is a first draft. The student turned it in and his instructor marked the places where she thought he needed to add more details. Read the questions and notes that the instructor wrote in the margins. Then read the student's second draft, which is also printed here. Answer the questions that follow each version of the paragraph.

FIRST DRAFT

My Broken Arm

Why did you live there?

Why were you sad?

Who is your friend? Where does he live?

When I lived in a resettlement camp in Thailand, I always played soccer with my friends. We went to school together, and we walked around the camp every day. We always had fun in the camp. One day I had an accident because of the other soccer team. A member of the other team kicked my leg, and I fell down on the ground and broke my left arm. I was very sad because the next day, the American ambassador called my family to examine our health, and then we got ready to come to the United States. Later, my family received an announcement that we could emigrate to the United States, and I was very happy. My family and my friend's family came to the United States on the same day. Now, I never play soccer because I don't have a team. Also, my friend does not live near me. Sometimes I visit my friend's house.

Who did you play with?

Can you tell more about the accident?

When?

Can you add a conclusion?

5

10

15

Phon Quan N. Son
Vietnam

Activity 4-9   Post-reading Discussion

Answer these questions in your group after you have read the First Draft paragraph:

1. Read the questions in the margins of the paragraph. Do you understand them? Discuss their meanings.

2. For each question, discuss what types of details the student should add.

3. Mark other places where you think more details are needed. Write a question asking for more information.

SECOND DRAFT

My Broken Arm

When I was ten years old, I spent one year in a resettlement camp in Thailand **after I had left my country, Vietnam**. I had fun there because **there were many children to play with**. Every day I always played soccer **with my friends after school. About 10 to 15 boys played on the beach near our house**. One day a boy on the other team kicked my leg **while I was running next to him**, and I fell down on the ground. **My arm was aching and I was** 5 **crying**. My friend **Phong** helped me home, **and then, my parents were scared, so they took me to the hospital. The doctor and nurses examined me. They found that I had a broken arm. They gave me some medicine and put a cast on my arm. I remember that my arm hurt very much. The next day,** the American ambassador called my family and told us to have a health examination. This made me very sad **because I thought that they** 10 **would not accept me with my arm, but they did.** Then, we got ready to come to the United States. **Four months** later, my family received an announcement that we could emigrate to the United States, and I was very happy. My family and my friend Phong's family came to the United States on the same day. Now, I never play soccer because I don't have a team. **Also, Phong does not live near me although I sometimes visit him in Maryland.** 15 **We remember our days in the camp, especially the day that I broke my arm**.

Phon Quan N. Son
Vietnam

Activity 4-10   Post-reading Discussion

Answer these questions in your group:

1. Which of the two paragraphs—the first draft or second draft—do you prefer? Why?

2. Read the questions in the margins of the first draft. Then read the bold face sentences in the second draft. Did the writer add information in the second draft to answer all of his teacher's questions?

3. Is there additional information that you would like to see in a *third* draft? If so, mark the questions at the appropriate places in the margins.

Activity 4-11   Revising Your Paragraph

Using the technique that you applied to "My Broken Arm," reread your own paragraph. Mark places where you might add more information. Refer to the five senses questions and the essential questions discussed above for ideas about types of details to add.

Revise your paper before you turn it in to your instructor.

The Grammar of Past Time Narratives: Past Tense and Other Verbs

In past time narratives, writers use past tense verbs (simple past, past progressive, and past perfect tenses) to tell the basic story of a past event. Other verbs are used to comment on the story, give generalizations, give definitions, and make predictions. For example, you *remember* events that *happened* which you *will* never *forget*. Pay attention to the tenses of the verbs in these example sentences from past time narratives.

Past Tense Narrative Verbs

       simple past   past perfect

When my brother *ran* home to look in on me, I *had wet* my diapers.

        simple present   simple past   simple past

However, I still *feel* a little guilty because I never *told* her how much I *loved* her

   simple past

while she *was* still alive.

       past continuous   past continuous

My arm *was aching* and I *was crying*.

> **GLR**   See page 250 of the GLR for more information on verbs.

The Grammar of Past Time Narratives: Modal Auxiliary Verbs for Past Time Meanings

Some modal auxiliary verbs are used to communicate about past time events. *Could, would,* and *had to* have past time meanings when combined with a simple form of the verb.

Examples: Using Modals for Past Time Meanings	
could + verb for past time abilities	I *could* go to the beach when I was a child.
would + verb for past time habits	I *would* often play soccer in my old neighborhood.
had to + verb for rules and obligations	I *had to* walk to school in my country.

> **GLR**   See pages 231–233 of the GLR for more information on modal auxiliary verbs.

Activity 4-12   Identifying Verbs in Past Time Narrative

Read the following sample student paragraph. The verb tenses in the paragraph are bold face. With a partner or group of classmates, answer the following questions:

1. Find sentences in the paragraph that tell the basic story. Which past tense verbs are used in these sentences?

2. Find sentences in the paragraph that do not tell the basic story, but comment on the story, give generalizations, point to meanings, and make predictions. Which verb tenses are used in these sentences? Why?

MY FIRST DAY AT SCHOOL

I still **remember** a day in the beginning of the fall of 1978 when I **was** five years old. At that time, I **was living** in Vietnam. My mother **brought** me to school. The name of my school **was** Phu Dong. The first day at school, I **wore** a white shirt with blue shorts. I also **carried** a new book bag. I **was** joyful when I **saw** many children my same age standing with their parents in front of the school. I **thought** in my mind that I **could talk** or play games   5 with them in the next few hours. When the bell **rang,** I and all my little friends **came** in the class. At this time, I **was** afraid when I **saw** my teacher. She **was** a severe woman, about 36 years old. I **was** upset when she **called** my name. It **happened** suddenly, so I **cried.** Suddenly I **ran** off out of the classroom. I **didn't want** to come back to this class. My mother **was standing** outside of the classroom. When she **saw** me run off, she **held** me 10 back; then she **brought** me back in the class again. This time, I **had to obey** my mother, and I **followed** her into the class. From the beginning of that day, I really **became** a well-behaved student. I **obeyed** the teacher, and I **did not do** anything wrong in the class. I **think** my first day at school **is** my best memory. I **will remember** it forever. I **will keep** it for my whole life.   15

Nhon Ha
Vietnam

The Grammar of Past Time Narratives: Using Chronological Organizers

Chronological organizers help the reader to follow the order of events in a past time narrative. Notice how the student writer of Reading 2 has used a variety of

chronological organizers—an *adverb phrase, adverb clause,* and *single-word adverb*—
to show the order of events in his story:

> adverb phrase   adverb clause
> *One day* a boy on the other team kicked my leg *while I was running next to him,* and I
> fell down on the ground. My arm was aching and I was crying. My friend Phong helped
>
>   adverb
> me home, and *then* my parents were scared, so they took me to the hospital.

GLR   See page 215 of the GLR for more information on chronological organizers.

Activity 4-13   Identifying Chronological Organizers

Reread the paragraph in Activity 4-12. With a partner or group of classmates, identify
and circle the chronological organizers *(adverbs, adverb phrases,* or *adverb clauses).*
Discuss your answers with your class.

Activity 4-14   Peer Response

With a partner, exchange your writing assignment paragraphs. Read each other's paragraphs and answer these questions. Discuss your answers with your partner.

1. Does the writer tell about an event in his or her childhood?

2. Does a topic sentence introduce this event?

3. Does the body of the paragraph contain enough detail relating to the five senses and
   essential questions? If not, mark places in the margin where more detail is needed.
   Note any questions you have about the content.

4. Does the writer use past tense verbs to tell the story? Are they used correctly?

5. Does the writer use other time verbs correctly?

6. Is the story interesting? What is your reaction to this event?

LEARNER'S NOTEBOOK

Writing a Letter

Write a letter to your partner about the special memory he or she wrote about. Answer the following questions in your letter. What did you like best about the paper? Why? Did the story remind you of an event in your own life or someone you know? If so, tell your partner about this story. Begin your letter with a greeting and end it with a closing.

Greeting: *Dear* _____[your partner's name]_____

Closing: *Sincerely,*
_____[your name]_____

The Grammar of Past Time Narratives: Using Proper Nouns and Noun Phrases

Writers use proper nouns and noun phrases to identify specific places, dates, and persons involved in past events. In college and university classes, you will be expected to recall the meaning of proper nouns in academic past time narratives. Notice that the bold-faced proper nouns in this excerpt from the Activity 4-12 reading indicate important ideas in the passage:

At that time, I was living in **Vietnam**. My mother brought me to school when I was five years old. The name of my school was **Phu Dong**.

Activity 4-15 Identifying Proper Nouns

With a partner, read over the sample student paragraphs in Reading 3. Circle all the proper nouns. Share your answers with your class.

Using Sentence-End Punctuation: Structures and Forms Common to All Types of Writing

In English, punctuation marks separate sentences in writing. A period marks the end of a sentence.

Some writers have difficulty in using English punctuation marks because they differ from the punctuation in their native language. In fact, most errors in English punctuation occur at the end of a sentence, where writers either may put no punctuation, or put a comma.

The following chart summarizes the common errors with periods in English:

Common Errors with Periods

Error 1   **No punctuation between sentences**

NOT: *I love my mother she is my best friend.*

USE: I love my mother. She is my best friend.

Error 2   **Commas, instead of periods, between sentences**

NOT: *That car is expensive, it costs $20,000.*

USE: That car is expensive. It costs $20,000.

Error 3   **Periods with incomplete sentences**

NOT: *I like my blue jeans. Because they are old and comfortable.*

USE: I like my blue jeans because they are old and comfortable.

NOT: *My computer has many features. For example, a spell checker.*

USE: My computer has many features, for example, a spell checker.

GLR   See pages 207–212 in the GLR to learn more about how to use punctuation marks.

Activity 4-16   Using Punctuation Correctly

Correct the punctuation errors in the sentences that follow. Some sentences have no errors. Refer to the chart above.

1. I moved to the United States. Because I wanted more opportunity.

2. I had a good job in Vietnam, I was an accountant.

3. I graduated from college with honors I transferred to Temple University.

4. I made a big decision to come to the United States, but I do not regret it.

5. One of my most memorable visits was when my friends and I took a trip to the beach, I will never forget that day.

6. My life in Haiti was wonderful. Although my family was poor.

7. I was feeling angry, I decided to leave home and live by myself.

8. I have left behind many family members, for example, my grandparents, my aunts and uncles, and many cousins.

PUTTING IT ALL TOGETHER

FINAL WRITING ASSIGNMENT: AN INTERVIEW

Selecting an Interview Subject

For the Final Writing Assignment, you will use your remembering and past time narrative skills to interview someone about one special memory from his or her past. *Interviewing* means getting information by questioning. In an interview, you meet with a person to ask them questions, in this case, questions about a past event in his or her life. The most important steps in an interview are writing the questions and recording the answers. Usually, the person conducting the interview takes notes by hand or records the interview with an audio or video recorder.

You may interview a family member, a friend, a classmate, or an instructor. Begin by getting your subject's permission to be interviewed for your assignment.

Writing Interview Questions

Once you have chosen an interview subject, prepare by writing questions that you will ask. Remember that you will be interviewing the person about just *one past event* in his or her life, not about the person's entire life. Write at least ten questions that will relate to a single event. You may want to use the five senses and essential questions.

EXAMPLES

How old were you when you made a pair of shoes?
Why did you do it?

Show your questions to your instructor. Make sure that your questions are written in grammatically correct form.

GLR   See page 235 of the GLR for more information on question formation.

Notetaking Practice

Once you have written your interview questions, you will need to develop a method for writing down the interviewee's responses. You may want to use a tape recorder to record the conversation. However, you should also take notes in case your recorder doesn't work properly or the person you interview doesn't want you to record him or her. Here are some suggested strategies:

Notetaking Tips

1. Write the ten questions on paper, leaving several lines between each question.

2. Ask the question slowly and clearly.

3. Listen carefully to the interviewee's answer. Write down important words.

4. Ask the person to repeat if you are not sure what was said.

5. Ask the person to read over the answers you wrote down.

Before you interview, practice with a classmate. Take turns being the interviewer and interviewee. Practice with a tape recorder if you will use one in the real interview.

Ask each other a few of the questions. Listen and take notes. Ask your partner to repeat if you do not understand or remember what was said. Then ask your partner to check your notes. If you used a tape recorder, play the tape to check the accuracy of your notes.

Now you are ready to set up the interview.

READING 4   INTERVIEW TRANSCRIPT AND SAMPLE STUDENT PARAGRAPH

A. INTERVIEW ABOUT A SPECIAL MEMORY

Read the following transcript (record of questions and answers) from a student's interview with her grandmother.

Student: Grandma, tell me the story about when you made some shoes.

Grandmother: It was when I was 7 or 8. I was herding my sheep and cows.

Student: What happened?

Grandmother: I can't remember everything. I was walking up a hill. I saw two pieces of cork on the ground.   5

Student: Cork?

Grandmother: Yeah. Cork from cork trees.

Student: What's it look like?

Grandmother: Like bark, tree bark.

Student: So did it remind you of shoes?   10

Grandmother: Well, sort of. I picked it up and I looked at it and I thought … ummm … maybe I could make a pair of shoes.…

Student: Couldn't you just buy a pair of shoes?

Grandmother: No, we didn't have any money. Nobody had shoes back in the Depression.

Student: You didn't have shoes? How did you walk … I mean, in the mountains?   15 when it was cold?

Grandmother: It was pretty tough. We have a lot of stones on the ground around the village. And we didn't even have shoes in the winter when it snowed.

Student: Wow! That's terrible! So how did you make the shoes?

Grandmother: I took the pieces of cork and I tore 'em so they were long and flat, the size   20 of my feet.

Student: Was it hard?

Grandmother: No. Cork's pretty soft.

Student: Ah.

Grandmother: So I made the cork look kind of like the bottoms of shoes. Then, I looked   25 all around and found a stone. I used it to punch holes in the top of the cork. Then I made some straps, you know, like sandal straps, out of long strips of grass. I stuck the grass through the holes, tied 'em and made 'em go over the top of my foot.

Student: That must've taken a long time!   30

Grandmother: Yeah, well, I didn't have anything else better to do.

Student:	How'd you know how to make them?
Grandmother:	Well, I knew what shoes looked like … I mean, I'd never seen any, but I knew what they were.
Student:	So did they work? Did you walk in 'em?
Grandmother:	Well, sort of. I walked in 'em a little bit.
Student:	Bet they felt great!
Grandmother:	Yeah, they were great. I remember I was so excited … I told everyone. It felt like walking on air. I made believe I was rich.
Student:	So did you keep 'em?
Grandmother:	Not really. They fell apart after a few minutes. I knew they would.
Student:	I bet you felt bad.
Grandmother:	No, it was okay. I mean, you don't know how excited I felt when I took those few steps. I'll never forget it.
Student:	I'm glad you told me.

35

40

45

B. PARAGRAPH FROM AN INTERVIEW ABOUT A SPECIAL MEMORY

Read the following paragraph, based on a student's interview with her grandmother.

A POOR GIRL'S SHOES

When my grandmother was a child, she was living in a small mountain village in Algeria, which was then a French colony. When she was about seven or eight years old, it was the worst part of the "Great Depression." People were living in poor conditions all over the world, but they were especially miserable in the countryside of Algeria. In those conditions, most children had never even seen a pair of shoes or owned one. Almost everybody walked barefooted on the rough ground, in ice and snow. One time when my grandmother was herding her sheep and cows in the hills, she found two pieces of cork which were about the size and shape of shoe soles. She had an idea. She took them and punched some holes in them with a sharp piece of wood. Then she made strings with long pieces of grass, and made some very rough-looking sandals. She slipped her feet into them and took a few steps. The feeling was so strong for her. She felt like she was stepping on a cloud. She could not feel the sharp stones on the ground and the soft cork was so comfortable. She knew her "shoes" would only last a few moments before they would break, but she was very excited. For a few moments, she had an idea of how rich people must feel since they can afford to wear shoes all the time. The temporary shoes broke soon, but they had made her very happy that day.

Nora Fellag
U.S.A.

Post-reading Discussion

Discuss these questions about Reading 4 with a group of classmates:

1. Does the paragraph accurately reflect the information the student got from the interview? If not, point out any places where you think the information in the paragraph does not match the interview answers.

2. Does the paragraph have an introduction? What information do you find there? Is there any information in this part that is not reflected in the interview? Where do you think the writer got this information?

3. Did the writer put the information in the interview in the same order in her written paragraph? Why or why not?

4. Did the writer include all the essential question and five senses information in her interview paragraph? If not, did she leave any information out?

5. Is the story interesting? Why or why not?

The Grammar of Academic Writing: Differences Between Written and Spoken English

Writers use more formal grammar and vocabulary in academic writing than they do in speaking. Certain expressions that are used regularly in spoken English are not appropriate in academic writing. Examine these equivalent ideas in the spoken and in written versions of Reading 4:

Spoken		Written
Student:	So did it remind you of shoes?	*… she found two pieces of cork which were about the size and shape of shoe soles. She had an idea.*
Grandmother:	Well, sort of. *I picked it up and looked at it and I thought … ummm … maybe I could make a pair of shoes …*	
Student:	So did you keep 'em?	*She knew her "shoes" would only last a few moments before they would break …*
Grandmother:	*Not really. They fell apart in a few minutes. I knew they would.*	

Changing Spoken Answers to Written Statements

When you write statements that are based on spoken answers, you may need to change the language to make it more formal. Fill in the chart with written statements that contain the same information as the spoken answers to the questions given. The name of the person being interviewed appears in parentheses. The first two are done for you:

Spoken Questions	Spoken Answers	Written Statements
1. When did you leave Italy? (Serafina)	In 1980.	Serafina left Italy in 1980.
2. What do you remember most about your trip? (Chin)	A beautiful temple.	Chin remembers the beautiful temple that he visited during his trip.
3. Did all your family go with you? (Tri)	Yes.	
4. What did you do when you found out your sister's leg was broken? (Susan)	I cried and cried.	
5. What did the police do? (Mangesh)	They looked all around and searched for clues.	
6. Did you know that your boyfriend would come back? (Xiao)	I don't know. I really wasn't sure.	

Finding Written Equivalents for Spoken Expressions

The following sentences contain spoken expressions (in italics) that may not be appropriate in written academic English. With a partner, think of a more appropriate written equivalent that could be substituted for each spoken expression.

1. When I was a *kid*, I lived in a village in Cambodia.

2. My *mom* taught me how to ride a bicycle.

3. I was *a little bit* scared to go to school.

4. I *got* a job cleaning cars in 1980.

5. We took *lots of stuff* with us when we went on the trip.

6. I told the *guy* in the supermarket that I didn't steal the *lady's* wallet.

7. *Well,* then I said *bye* to all my friends.

8. *You know,* my father had to punish me because I was bad.

9. I felt *okay* on the first day of college.

Writing Your Interview Paragraph About a Special Memory

When you are ready to write your interview paragraph, include an introduction with the name of the interviewee or his or her relationship to you and a brief description of his or her background and the event. The body of your paragraph will include the events of the basic story, written mainly with past tense verbs. In the conclusion, you may want to comment on the story. Refer to the previous sample student paragraph for ideas about the organization of your paragraph.

Peer Response

With a partner, exchange your final writing assignment notes and paragraphs. Read each other's papers and answer these questions. Discuss your answers with your partner.

1. Does the writer include sentences that introduce the interviewee and the past event?

2. Does the body of the paragraph contain essential and five senses questions about the special event?

3. Are the questions in the notes grammatically correct?

4. Do the answers in the paragraph match the questions? Do you understand them?

5. Is the story interesting? What is your reaction to this event?

LEARNER'S NOTEBOOK

Reflecting on Your Interview

Write answers to these questions in your learner's notebook: Was your interview successful? Why or why not? Did you have any problems? Explain. How did you feel while you were conducting the interview? The next time you conduct an interview, what will you do differently?

● ●

L
O
O
K
I
N
G

A
H
E
A
D

Authentic Academic Assignments

Read the following academic assignment related to remembering. In a small group, answer the questions that follow. Then do the writing assignment on the next page.

Community Service (Social Work)

Assignment 1   Historical Interview: Using the community organization resources you have gained from this class, locate and interview someone who has lived in the city for at least 25 years. Write a three- to five-page report based on the interview.

Focus your questions on the community in which the person has lived. Include answers to the following questions and any others you choose in your interview report.

1. What is the interviewee's name, age (if possible), address, and occupation?

2. How long has the interviewee lived and worked in the city?

3. In what neighborhood does the interviewee live now? Where has he or she lived in the past?

4. What aspects of neighborhood life have changed most in the past 25-plus years, according to the interviewee?

5. To what does the interviewee attribute these changes?

6. What was the best thing about living in the community in the past?

7. How have community services in the neighborhood changed?

8. How would the interviewee rate community services at present?

9. What needs are not being met in the neighborhood?

10. What does the community need in the future in order to thrive?

11. Does the interviewee plan to continue to reside in the neighborhood?
    Why or why not?

DISCUSSION

1. What is the most difficult part of this assignment?

2. What questions would you ask the instructor to clarify the assignment?

3. How would you handle the work?

4. How long would it take you to do the work?

5. What do you think you could do to get an "A" on this assignment?

6. How could the remembering skills you practiced in this chapter help you with this assignment?

WRITING ASSIGNMENT

Imagine that you are a student in the Community Service class. Write a *memorandum* (a short, formal note) to your professor asking for an appointment to talk about the assignment. You may want to specify which parts of the assignment are unclear to you. Be sure to give your name and tell which times and days you could meet with him or her. Use the format below.

_____ _____, 199_

MEMORANDUM

To: [Your Professor's Name]

From: [Your Name]

_____

_____

_____

_____

_____

Thank you.

Describing

Major, Undecided

GOALS

WRITING
◆ develop and practice describing
  skills

GRAMMAR
◆ examine and practice features of
  informational and academic writing: *present tense and other verbs,*
  passive voice verbs, and *nouns and*
  noun phrases

CONTENT
◆ learn more about U.S. colleges and
  universities

ACADEMIC FIELD
Education

Sample Authentic College/University Describing Assignments

In a college or university classroom, you will use the skills you learn in this chapter to complete assignments like the ones below.

Operating Systems/Mainframe Programming

Assignment: Business Profile

Write a profile of two area businesses that describes what type of computer system they are using and how they are using it. Your profile will inform students of the prevalence of certain types of computer systems or networks in today's business world.

Technical Writing for Engineers

Assignment: Field Report

Describe the typical writing tasks that an engineer performs. For this assignment, you will interview one local engineer (preferably a graduate of this college) to find out what types of writing he or she does on a daily basis. Your three- to five-page report will describe to prospective engineering majors the daily writing demands placed on a professional in the field.

CNN video support is available for this chapter.

Turner Le@rning
A Time Warner Company

GETTING READY

LEARNER'S NOTEBOOK

Warm-up Activity

What is the perfect job for you? In your notebook, write about your dream job (or jobs). What does a person do in this job? Where does he/she work? With whom? Why does this job appeal to you?

Grammar Preview

In previous chapters, you have read and produced informational writing that *informs* an audience about a subject. This type of writing appears not only in academic course work, but also in publications that describe a college or university and its programs: course catalogs, brochures, application forms, for example.

In the grammar activities in this chapter, you will examine and practice several of the important grammatical features of informational writing in the context of college publications so that you can better read and write these types of informational texts.

The Grammar of Nouns and Noun Phrases in Informational Writing: Learning and Using Key Terms

In college and university courses, you learn key terms in academic areas. In addition, you must learn the terminology of education so that you can operate within the college system to achieve your academic goals. You need to be able to register for appropriate courses, communicate well with advisors, administrators, and staff in various offices, and understand college catalogs and department and program brochures. In all of these settings, the terminology uses the same basic grammar. If you understand that grammar, you can learn these new words more easily and use them more accurately in your academic life.

Activity 5-1   Understanding Key Terms in Education

The following activity contains key terms taken from college catalogs and brochures. Notice that key terms may consist of a single *noun* or a *noun phrase* (*noun* + other word or words). With a partner, discuss the differences in meanings between these pairs of words. Discuss your ideas with your class.

1. a college major   *and*   a college course

2. an academic department   *and*   an academic discipline or field

3. a credit hour   *and*   a course

4. a required course   *and*   a prerequisite course

5. a core course   *and*   an elective course

6. a degree plan   *and*   a degree

7. an associate's degree   *and*   a bachelor's degree

8. admission   *and*   transfer

9. a college catalog   *and*   a program or department brochure

Introduction to Describing

Describing is one of the most common types of academic writing. As a student, you describe influential persons in a history course. In other university and college courses, you may use description in a chemistry laboratory report, a computer-aided design report, or a sociology case study.

In fact, the University of California at Los Angeles' history department ranks the word *describe* as one of the most frequently used words in essay examinations in U.S. colleges. To describe, according to a UCLA brochure developed to help students answer essay examination questions, means to "give an account of; tell about; give a word picture of," as in this typical essay exam question: "Describe the pyramids of Giza."

Types of Descriptive Details

In Chapter 2, you learned that descriptive details are often *sensory*—they enable the audience to "touch," "see," "hear," "feel," or "smell" the subject. When you describe the sights, sounds, and smells of a favorite place in an English composition course, you are using the senses to explain a subject to a reader.

Description is used in a variety of academic settings. For example, in an essay question on a history examination, you use descriptive details and past narration to demonstrate the accuracy and depth of your knowledge. In describing a course, a program, a job, or a field of study, you describe the characteristics of the subject: the range and sequence of skills, entrance and exit requirements, career opportunities, etc.

In all description, you must write accurately and clearly. In this chapter, you will see how description appears in a variety of academic situations. You can apply the describing skills you learn here to many college and university courses.

Activity 5-2   Identifying Descriptive Details

Read the following paragraphs describing various academic topics. In the list that follows each paragraph, put a check mark next to the descriptive detail in the paragraph. Be prepared to explain which sentences contain which types of descriptive information from the list.

1.   **Freshman Composition**

Freshman Composition is a challenging English course that most students take as part of their degree program. Basically, students write essays about readings. The course is called *Freshman Composition* because it is usually taken by freshmen and the main activity is writing. To enroll, students must first pass a placement essay examination. If their writing skills are weak, then students take either ESL courses or remedial English courses first. Freshman Composition students read different types of texts: essays, newspaper or magazine articles, and literature such as short stories, poems, or novels. Often, textbooks contain collections of readings. Most of the course work involves writing essay-length compositions about a reading. Students learn to summarize, paraphrase, analyze, and evaluate reading. Strong organizational and grammatical skills are needed to pass the course. In addition, many Freshman Composition courses have a standardized exit examination, which students must pass to pass the course. Many students consider the class one of the most challenging college courses because of the volume and difficulty of the writing and reading.

Check the Descriptive Details in the Reading

☐ work that you do in the course

☐ the textbook

☐ the length of the course

☐ entry requirements

☐ the skills you learn

☐ exit requirements

2.

The Student Academic Computing Center

The Student Academic Computing Center (SACC) is a busy facility that offers students access to computers. It is located in room B2-33. The facility consists of a main room with about 140 computers and two glass-walled side rooms with 60 computers that may be used by an entire class. The IBM computers are equipped with various software that is required in all disciplines at the college. Microsoft Word and WordPerfect are the word processing applications used in SACC and throughout the college. Technical aides are available to assist students who have trouble. Students may use the lab between 8 a.m. and 10 p.m. weekdays and 8 a.m. and 5 p.m. Saturdays. It's a busy facility, so there are rules to keep it running smoothly. Students may only use the computers for their class work, not for personal business. A time limit of 90 minutes per student may be enforced when students are waiting for a workstation. Students must present their college identification cards to be admitted to the lab. There's also a rule about being quiet in the lab, but it's still a bustling center of activity on campus.

Check the Descriptive Details in the Reading

☐ contents of the place

☐ location

☐ size

☐ description of features of the place

☐ people at the place

☐ time of activity at the place

☐ smells at the place

☐ sounds at the place

3.

A Teacher's Favorite Reading Place

A year ago, I didn't have a favorite place to read on campus, but when our library was renovated, it soon became my most relaxing place to read. The Educational Resource Center was refurbished from top to bottom. The falling ceiling tiles were replaced by bright white ones, and the peeling white walls were repainted in soft beiges and pale green. Even the cold tile floors were redone with multi-colored carpet tiles arranged in patterns. The best improvement to the library, however, was the seating. The old, torn cloth chairs and beaten-up wooden tables were discarded. Now there are modern stuffed chairs covered in earth-colored woolen fabrics and reddish wood tables that gleam with polish. Instead of the industrial lamps that used to hang over the tables, there are long, black metal fluorescent lamps with bulbs just bright enough to read by, but not overpowering. Under one of these lamps, seated in a comfortable stuffed chair at a quiet back table, you will often find me reading a novel or a magazine.

Check the Descriptive Details in the Reading

☐ contents of the place

☐ location

☐ size

☐ description of features of the place

☐ people at the place

☐ colors of the place

☐ smells at the place

☐ sounds at the place

FOCUSING

Activity 5-3　Pre-reading Discussion

Reading 1 in Activity 5-2 tells about college degree and career planning. In a small group, discuss what degree you might like to get and how you think you could get it.

LEARNER'S NOTEBOOK

Looking Ahead to Your Future

Think back about the job that you wrote about previously in your notebook. Add another entry to describe the education and skills you will need to get this job. What skills, training, or degree will you need? How do you plan to get those skills? If you are undecided, write about an educational program and job you may want to pursue.

READING 1   THE COUNSELING CENTER (DESCRIPTION OF A COLLEGE OFFICE)

Activity 5-4   Focused Reading

Read the following description of an academic office in a college. As you read, think about your own college. Does your college have a place similar to "The Counseling Center" where students receive academic, career, and psychological counseling? What useful information might you find there?

THE COUNSELING CENTER

The Counseling Center is a busy place that has experts and information about college degrees and careers. Outside the center are job postings and posters in glass cabinets announcing workshops and job fairs. As I walked through the door last week, I saw racks of brochures on both sides of the entrance. Students were sitting in chairs waiting to see a counselor. A receptionist asked what I needed and sent me in the right direction. Counselors 5 were talking to students in small offices lining the wall of the main counseling room. The main room is cut in half by a glass wall behind which are rows of computers on tables. Our class went to the Career and Transfer office inside the center to learn how to use the computers to find college and career information. This office has information about four-year colleges and universities, college catalogs, computerized college and scholarship search 10 programs, and national directories of colleges. The transfer counselor told us about the agreements that our college has with many four-year universities. Since many of my class-mates want to attend Temple University, he gave us papers explaining the specific courses that Temple will accept from our college. We also learned how to use the computers to find the costs and the entrance requirements of other universities. I learned a lot about colleges 15 at the Counseling Center. I will return there.

Activity 5-5   Post-reading Questions

With a group of classmates, answer the following questions about Reading 1:

1. What is the main idea of the reading? Write "*main idea*" in the margin next to the sentence that best expresses it.

2. Discuss whether your college has such a center. If anyone has visited the center, compare your counseling center with the one described above.

3. Does the reading contain descriptive detail? Underline words and phrases that describe the center.

4. Informational writing such as this contains many nouns and noun phrases. Circle the nouns and noun phrases.

5. What have you learned from this paragraph?

LEARNER'S NOTEBOOK

Reflecting on a Reading

In your notebook, write answers to these questions related to Reading 1: What specific questions do you have about your own future college or career choices? Can a counseling center help you? If so, what kind of information do you think a counseling center can give you? How would you feel about talking to a college counselor?

The Grammar of Describing: Using Present and Past Tense Verbs

In describing a place, writers often mix present tense and past tense verbs. Simple present tense verbs describe the contents and features of a place. Past tense verbs tell about past actions at the place.

Notice the verbs in these sentences from Reading 1:

present tense   present tense

The Counseling Center *is* a busy place that *contains* experts and information

present tense

about college degrees and careers. Outside the center, there *are* glass cabinets with

present tense   past tense

job postings and posters that *announce* workshops and job fairs. As I *walked*

past tense

through the door last week, I *saw* racks of brochures on both sides of the entrance.

past tense

Many students *were sitting* in chairs and waiting to see a counselor.

> **GLR**   See pages 250 of the GLR for more information on verb tenses.

Activity 5-6   Examining Verb Tenses in a Reading

With a partner, reread the rest of Reading 1. Underline the verbs. Mark them as "*present tense*" or "*past tense.*" Discuss with your class why each verb tense was used.

Activity 5-7   Examining Verb Tenses in a Paragraph

With your partner, underline and mark the tense of the verbs in paragraph 3 in Activity 5-2 on pages 119–120. Which verb tense is used more often? Why? Discuss with your class why each verb tense was used.

Activity 5-8   Writing Assignment 1: Description of a College Office

Write a paragraph to describe an office at your college, such as a department office, computer laboratory, or learning laboratory. Use Reading 1, "The Counseling Center," as a model. In the topic sentence, identify the specific name of the place and its function. You may also include an important characteristic of the place, as in the main idea sentence of Reading 1:

> specific name   characteristic   function
> The Counseling Center is a busy place where you can get information about college
> degrees and careers.

In the body of the paragraph, include descriptive details about the contents and features of the place: what you see, hear, smell, and feel. Also include information about the people and activities that take place there.

Your concluding sentence should restate the main idea of your topic sentence and may also include your comment or opinion about the place.

Activity 5-9   Peer Response

Exchange paragraphs with a partner. If possible, go with your partner to the place that he or she describes. Read your partner's paragraphs and share your answers to the following questions:

1. Does the topic sentence include the appropriate information? If not, what is missing?

2. Does the body contain specific details about the contents, activities, and people at the place? Are sensory details included? Mark places in the paragraph where more details are needed.

3. Does the paragraph have a concluding sentence?

4. Does the description accurately and clearly depict the place? Point out any places where the description is inaccurate or unclear.

5. What do you like best about your partner's paragraph?

READING 2   AMERICAN DEGREE PROGRAMS
(ESSAY ABOUT COLLEGE DEGREES)

| Activity 5-10   Focused Reading |

As you read Reading 2, think about these questions: How does a person choose a major? Where can a person get advice?

AMERICAN DEGREE PROGRAMS

The American system of college degree requirements may cause you to puzzle over the first college catalog you open.

There are so many choices of majors and courses! The system of credit hours may seem strange and confusing. In the United States, getting a college degree requires making many decisions. Which major will you choose? Which option, or specialty, within the major will 5 you focus on? Which core courses must you take? Which courses are prerequisites to other courses? What electives should you choose? How many credit hours will you need to take in order to graduate? How many will you take in each semester? When and to whom do you submit your degree plan?

First, consult the catalogs of the colleges that interest you. Browse through each to learn 10 which different subjects are offered at each institution. Consider the tuition of each school and the availability of programs of interest.

Nowadays, many students attend a two-year community college, obtain an associate's degree, and then transfer to a four-year university to get a bachelor of arts or science degree (BA or BS). Students may pursue further education after their initial degree and go on to 15 earn a master's degree (MA or MS), or a doctorate (Ph.D.).

As you read and think about majors and types of degree, talk to as many people as possible: friends, family members, counselors, advisers, instructors, department heads, and working professionals. Also, talk to yourself. "What are my interests? In what subjects do I get my highest marks? What are my skills? What do I want to do? What do I like to do?" 20 Take time to make your decision. The more people you talk to, the more information you can get, so that you can make a good decision about your future.

Activity 5-11   Post-reading Research and Discussion

With a partner, locate a college catalog from your college registrar's office or counseling center or visit the counseling center or library and ask a staff person how to view catalogs on microfilm or computer databases. When you have found a catalog of a college that interests you, complete the following tasks:

1. Read the descriptions of academic programs and majors that sound appealing. These descriptions will introduce you to academic disciplines (fields of study). The programs will be administered by an academic department, where you may have more than one choice of major (main area of study) within the discipline. The descriptions of each program usually include a set of core courses that you should take in a recommended sequence. Required general education courses, electives (optional courses), and total credits required to graduate are also listed.

2. Choose one academic major that interests you. Read the description and fill out the following chart with important information about the major or program.

   Note: In your catalog, the names of types of courses may differ from the terms used in the list. Check with your instructor if you need assistance.

   Major/Program Requirements   _____
                                           Name of Major or Program

   Number of Program Core Courses*   _____

   Course Recommended to Take First   _____

   Number of General Education Courses** _____

   Math Credit Hours Required   _____

   English Courses Required   _____

   Social Science Credit Hours Required _____

   Science Courses Required   _____

   Number of Electives Required   _____

   Total Credits Required to Graduate _____

   *Courses that are specific to this major or program

   **General courses that are required for graduation by many majors or programs

3. After you have filled out the chart, share your information with another pair of classmates. Discuss which major appeals to you the most. In your group, choose two majors that you will describe in your class.

4. Have group members make notes about each major, using information from the chart. Find areas of comparison and contrast between the two majors. Which major requires more total credit hours? More courses? More electives? Which does your group prefer? Explain why.

5. To prepare an oral group presentation about the college majors, divide the speaking tasks among group members. One group member can introduce the majors you describe. Other group members can tell about each major and another person can give a conclusion in which you compare and contrast the majors and give your opinions about which is the best choice. Organize your oral presentation as you would a paragraph: with an introduction, body, and conclusion.

6. Be prepared to answer questions about the majors you describe.

7. Take notes about at least one other group presentation, using the chart below. Ask questions about other groups' presentations.

Major Program Requirements
_____
Name of Major or Program

Number of Core Courses*   _____

Course Recommended to Take First   _____

Number of General Education Courses**   _____

Math Credit Hours Required   _____

English Credit Hours Required   _____

Social Science Credit Hours Required   _____

Science Credit Hours Required   _____

Number of Electives Required   _____

Total Credits Required to Graduate   _____

*Courses that are specific to this major or program

**General courses that are required for graduation by many majors or programs

The Grammar of Informational Writing: Passive Voice and Active Voice Verbs

College catalogs and brochures that describe programs, majors, and courses typically use present tense verbs, as in this example:

The Department of Electronics Engineering Technology *offers* a specialized option of Communication Electronics Technology. This option *is designed* to prepare the graduate for employment as a communication technician.

Often, the verbs occur in the active voice, as in Sentence 1. Here, the subject of the sentence, "the Department," performs the action—it "offers" the program.

In addition, college catalogs use verbs in the passive voice, as in Sentence 2. These sentences may focus on a program, a course, or a major. Thus, the subject of the sentence (in Sentence 2, "This option") is the receiver of the action ("is designed"). The doer of the action, the faculty who designed the program, is not mentioned in the sentence.

> **GLR** See pages 222 and 223 of the GLR for more information on present tense verbs and passive verbs.

Activity 5-12   Identifying Voice in Present Tense Verbs

Read the following passage from a college catalog. With a partner, identify the subjects and verbs in each sentence. Mark the verbs as passive voice verbs (PV) or active voice verbs (AV).

EXAMPLE

         S   PV
New students *are required* to take college placement tests.

PHOTOGRAPHY

The Photography Curriculum emphasizes several professional areas. Classroom, lecture, and laboratory assignments lead to the development of technical and artistic skills and knowledge students need to qualify for jobs in photography and allied occupations. Students may add filmmaking, television, and reprographics courses. Extensive darkroom work is required, using chemicals, films, and papers, and film and paper processing techniques in both black-and-white and color.

Outside and studio assignments are required in all courses. Professional practices and production are emphasized, and students are encouraged to develop artistic appreciation and imagination in their work. The second year emphasizes working with color materials and portfolio preparation.

The Grammar of Informational Writing: Present and Other Tense Verbs

Present tense and other tense verbs also appear in informational writing about colleges. In college catalogs, present tense verbs are used in general truth statements. Past tense verbs may be included to tell about generalizations that are no longer true. The past tense may also be used in passages that tell about past events, such as the history of a college.

Examine the verbs used in these sentences from a college catalog:

present tense

Community College of Philadelphia *is* an open admission, associate's

present tense

degree-granting institution which *provides* access to higher education for

past tense

all who may benefit. CCP *was created* April 28, 1964, by legislation in
Harrisburg and Philadelphia.

present perfect tense

More than 400,000 students *have passed* through CCP's classrooms since

past tense

the College *opened* its doors.

Activity 5-13   Identifying Verb Tenses in a Reading

With a partner, look through the college catalog you used in your oral report for Activity 5-11. Find and copy a passage that contains present tense and other tense verbs. Underline each verb and mark the tense. Compare your markings with your partner's. Share your passages with your class.

The Grammar of Informational Writing: Nouns and Noun Phrases

Informational writing in college catalogs and brochures also contains many specific nouns and noun phrases to describe departments, majors, programs, courses, requirements, and activities.

Examine the noun phrases in these sentences from a college publication:

noun phrase

Here are *some suggested introductory courses* which will help you get

noun phrase   noun phrase

started: CS 113 (*Introduction to Computer Science 1*) and MTH 141 (*College*

noun phrase

Calculus). With *a degree in Biochemical Pharmacology,* you could become

noun phrase

a biochemist.

noun phrase   noun phrase   noun phrase

Art History examines *visual art—painting, sculpture, and architecture—*

noun phrase   noun phrase   noun phrase

from *man's earliest times* to the *present day,* with *the aim of both appreciat-*

noun phrase

ing works of art and understanding them as *a form of cultural expression.*

The Rainbow Book: UB's Undergraduate Majors, Minors,
and Programs, State University of New York at Buffalo.

The noun phrases in the examples function as a variety of sentence parts: *subject, object,* or *complement.*

> **GLR**   See pages 244, 246, and 249 of the GLR for more information on noun phrases and sentence parts.

Activity 5-14   Identifying Noun Phrases and Sentence Parts

In the following passage, the noun phrases have been underlined. With a partner, use the charts on pages 245–246 in the GLR **GLR** to identify how each noun phrase is used in the sentences: as *subject, direct object, object of preposition,* or *complement of **be**.* Above each noun phrase, write the name of its sentence part.

The Justice Curriculum provides a sound educational foundation for the performance of professional activity within the justice arena. A sequence of courses is offered which will accomplish the following objectives: (1) establish a knowledge base about justice, (2) transmit a set of professional values and (3) facilitate the development of skills related to professional activity. Whether the setting is a police department, prosecutor's office, court or corrections agency, the Curriculum starts with the assumption that the need for knowledge, values and skills is critical for the performance of professional activity.

Activity 5-15   Finding Noun Phrases and Structures

Work with a partner to find the noun phrases in this passage. Then write each of them in the following chart. You may find more than one example of some structure types. The nouns in the first sentence have been put in the chart as an example.

An anticipated outcome of the Justice Curriculum is that students will be prepared for transfer to a four-year institution or to enter a justice setting at a beginning professional level. Another anticipated outcome is that persons already working in the justice setting will substantially enhance their knowledge, values and skills.

Admission to the Justice curriculum requires that a student attend a group orientation session or individual interview with a faculty member before he or she is accepted.

Simple noun	*students, transfer*
Article + noun	
Article + adjective(s) + noun	*an anticipated outcome*
Noun + noun	
Adjective(s) + noun	*the Justice Curriculum, a justice setting*
Article + noun + noun	
Article + adjective + noun + noun	*a four-year institution*
Article + noun + adjective + noun	*a beginning professional level*
Noun phrase + prepositional phrase	*an anticipated outline of the Justice Curriculum*
Noun phrase + relative clause	

Activity 5-16   Analyzing Noun Phrases in Academic Vocabulary

The following is a vocabulary list from a course entitled *Introduction to Art History*. The words are taken from *Art through the Ages* by Helen Gardner (Harcourt Brace). Students in this course will be expected to know these words—and to use them on tests to answer questions and solve problems. Analyze the noun phrases that make up these important words. Identify the types of structures you find by completing the chart that follows.

period styles   *stylistic features*   *Cave Art*
Doric columns   *general historical context*   *relief sculpture*
the Ancient Near East   *the High Renaissance*   *Baroque Art*
Forum of Pompeii   *the Dutch Masters*   *Impressionism*
tonal spread   *point of view*   *still life*
the Bauhaus   *complementary colors*   *Old Stone Age*

Simple noun
Article + noun
Article + adjective + noun
Noun + noun
Adjective + noun
Article + noun + noun
Article + adjective + noun + noun
Noun phrase + prepositional phrase
Noun phrase + relative clause

READING 3   MY GOALS AND MY MAJOR (SAMPLE STUDENT PARAGRAPH)

Activity 5-17   Focused Reading

In the following paragraph, a student describes the academic major he wishes to pursue. Read the paragraph and think about how his goals compare with your own.

MY GOALS AND MY MAJOR

I am here at the Community College of Philadelphia to study English. When my English is very good, I will study biology, chemistry, physics, sociology, physiology, and calculus. I will study all of these courses because I want to transfer to a four-year university to attain my major and goal. My major requires me to take the courses above and courses in medical pharmacology, toxicology, chemical pharmacology, medical biochemistry, medical physiol- 5 ogy, and cardiovascular pharmacology. My goal is to become a pharmacologist. Pharmacology is the science of detection and measurement of the effects of drugs or other chemicals on biological systems. I especially wish to study the therapeutic and toxic actions of drugs in humans. Also, I plan to study how to design and discover new agents and to test and improve old ones. Finally, I wish to work in a hospital as a clinical pharmacologist to 10 help people. I will be glad to become a pharmacologist. I will gain more self-confidence, knowledge and experience. I will be able to help people by using my knowledge.

Phon Quan Son
Vietnam

Activity 5-18   Post-reading Discussion

Answer these questions with a partner or small group of classmates.

1. Does the student writer include information about the following areas in his description?

   _____ name of major, program, or field

   _____ types of courses a student takes in the major

   _____ career opportunities

   _____ program entry requirements

   _____ graduation requirements

   _____ other: _____

2. Does the description introduce the program in the first sentence?

3. Does the writer use his own words?

4. Does the writer include his opinion?

Activity 5-19   Writing Assignment 2: Description of an Academic Major

Using the information you have learned from your speaking assignment and the sample student paragraph, write a descriptive paragraph about an academic major that interests you. In your introduction, include the name and a brief description of the major. In the body of your paragraph, include some of the most important information about two of the areas listed in Activity 5-18, number 1. In writing about each area, try to use your own words. If you use a catalog, do not copy directly from it. Do not include every idea about each area—only the most important ideas. In a conclusion, give your opinion about the major. Do you recommend the major? Why or why not? Will you choose it? Why or why not?

Activity 5-20   Self-editing

1. Read your paragraph again. Does it say what you want it to say? Is it organized in the best way for your meaning and this particular writing task? Make any changes needed to improve the meaning of your writing. You are writing to describe an academic major, so check for the language of informational writing.

2. Edit your individual sentences for the following and correct any errors that you find. After you have edited for each of these features, check (✓) the box to remind yourself that you have done that task.

   ☐ complete sentences

   ☐ correct punctuation

☐ correct verb tenses

☐ correct use of materials from other written sources—quoting, summarizing, and giving information to identify your source

☐ use of vocabulary appropriate for academic writing rather than speaking

☐ correct use of logical organizers

3. Rewrite your paragraph to make the corrections you decided on while editing your sentences.

Activity 5-21   Peer Response

With a partner, exchange your paragraphs about an academic major. Read each other's paragraphs and answer these questions. Discuss your answers with your partner.

1. Does the first paragraph introduce the academic major? Where is the topic sentence?

2. Is the description complete? In other words, does it describe the major areas that are listed in Activity 5-11, number 1? If not, make notes in the margins of the paragraph where information is missing.

3. Is the description clear? If not, put question marks in the margin by sentences or phrases you do not understand. Tell your partner which places need improvement.

4. Does the writer use his or her own words? If not, point out to your partner the places which seem to be copied from a catalog.

5. What did you learn from your partner's paragraph? Share that information with him or her.

LEARNER'S NOTEBOOK

Responding to a Reading

Answer these questions in your learner's notebook:

What was the most interesting part of your partner's paragraph? What did you learn from the paragraph?

What is your reaction to the academic major that your partner wrote about? Does it sound interesting? Does it sound difficult? Explain why or why not.

Does it change your mind about your own academic goals?

More About Interviewing

In Chapter 4, you used information from an interview to write a past time narrative. Interviewing is also a useful way to gather support for informational writing assignments. For the Final Writing Assignment, you and a partner will interview a college staff person to gather information about an academic topic. You may want to talk to someone about a major, a department, a program, or a career that interests you, or you may want to know more about financial aid, transferring to a four-year university, scholarships, work-study jobs, or other services or programs at your college. By interviewing the appropriate person, you can find useful information related to your academic or career goals.

Activity 5-22   Planning an Interview

College departments and offices offer even more information about specific majors and programs than you find in a catalog. It's always a good idea to talk to faculty, administrators, or staff, or read departmental brochures to find out more details about college majors, careers, or other areas of interest.

With a partner, plan to interview one faculty member, administrator, or staff member to learn more about an academic subject that interests you both. Your purpose will be not only to inform yourselves but also to inform other classmates about your topic.

Begin by reading the appropriate section of your catalog again, discussing other questions you have about the topic with your partner. Decide on a general focus for your interview. For instance, if you interview a career counselor, focus your questions on one career. If you interview a department head, concentrate on one specific major within his or her department.

Write five to seven questions. Here are a few suggestions:

1. What are the possible jobs that I can get with a degree in this major?

2. Are any required courses in the major considered especially difficult? Why?

3. How long does it usually take a student to get a degree?

4. What if a student works and goes to school at the same time? Is it possible to take courses at night or on weekends?

5. Which local four-year universities offer similar majors in this field (if you attend a two-year college)?

6. What are the requirements to get a work-study position at the college?

7. How does a student apply for financial aid?

With a partner, write questions that will interest you and your classmates.

The Grammar of Interviewing: Asking Questions

As you learned in earlier chapters, interviewing requires you to ask and answer questions. To make the best possible impression on your interviewee, your questions should be grammatically accurate.

Pay attention to the structure of your questions, keeping in mind the order of subjects and verbs in questions such as these:

What is your title?
How many students are studying this major at the college?

Activity 5-23   Question Formation

1. Review the forms of questions on page 235 in the GLR. Check the grammatical accuracy of these sample questions. Mark each as correct or incorrect. Edit the incorrect sentences to make them correct.

   a. How many majors your department has?

   b. Can a student get an associate's degree from your department in two years?

   c. Is this a popular field of study?

   d. Is the core courses in your department difficult?

2. Role-play a practice interview with your partner. Ask the questions that you and your partner have written and have your partner respond as the interviewee. Then change roles. Be careful to listen to the questions: Are they formulated correctly?

Activity 5-24   The Etiquette of Interviewing

As you learned in Chapter 4, in interviewing, you should observe certain rules or etiquette in setting an appointment, introducing yourself, and thanking the interviewee. Review the rules that you practiced in Chapter 4 before conducting the interview.

With a small group of classmates, practice proper interviewing etiquette. One or two students can act as the interviewers, another as a department receptionist, and another as the interviewee. Act out what each person says: (1) when the request is made to conduct an interview, (2) when the interview begins, and (3) at the end of the interview.

Final Steps Before the Interview

Finish your preparation by deciding who will conduct each part of the interview, how the information will be recorded, and how you will ask for clarification.

Turn-taking: As you did in Chapter 4, decide on a system of turn-taking. Decide who will speak to the receptionist, who will first speak to the interviewee, and who will ask question one, who will ask question two, and so forth.

Note-taking: In previous interviews, you may have found that if both you and your partner take notes, you will get a more accurate account of what was said. You may also have tape recorded the information. Decide which method you will use to record the interview. Remember that if you want to use a tape recorder, you should first ask the interviewee if he or she feels comfortable with that.

Clarification: Finally, discuss the questions that you and your partner might use to ask the interviewee to repeat an answer or to spell an unfamiliar word.

When you have completed these tasks, you are ready to visit the department office. Remember, be prepared either to conduct the interview immediately or ask for an appointment.

Activity 5-25   Post-interview Activities

Immediately after the interview, look over your notes and discuss them with your partner. Check to see if your facts are the same. Listen to your tape recording, if you have one, to verify your written notes. If you have serious problems with the information, return to the department office to ask your interviewee to clarify his or her answers.

LEARNER'S NOTEBOOK

Interviewing Experience

In your notebook, answer these questions about your interview experience: Was the interview successful? Were you comfortable speaking and listening to English? Did you have any difficulties? Do you wish that you had said or done anything differently? What did you learn about interviewing?

The Grammar of Informational Writing: Using Reported Speech

As you learned in summarizing in Chapter 1, reporting other people's words often requires you to introduce statements with *said* or other reporting verbs such as those on page 23. Notice how these verbs are used to change direct speech into reported speech.

EXAMPLES

Direct Speech	Reported Speech
"My department has 1,000 students."	The department chair said his department had 1,000 students.
"It's hard to study accounting and work at the same time."	Dr. Russell stated that it was hard to study accounting and work at the same time.

> **GLR** See pages 228–229 of the GLR for more information on verb tense rules for changing direct speech to reported speech.

Activity 5-26   Reported Speech

With a partner, change the following direct speech statements into reported speech statements. Use the phrase "the department chair" as the name of the speaker.

1. "The major requires 60 credit hours to graduate."

2. "Data Processing 103 is a difficult course."

3. "My department had 25 full-time faculty members in Fall 1996."

4. "Many students take Music 103 as an elective."

5. "You shouldn't take more than 12 hours in one semester."

PUTTING IT ALL TOGETHER

FINAL WRITING ASSIGNMENT: PARAGRAPH BASED ON AN INTERVIEW

On your own, write a paragraph describing the academic topic you investigated in your interview. Keep in mind your audience and your purpose: to inform your class about an academic aspect of the college.

In the topic sentence, include the name and title of the person whom you interviewed and the general subject of your interview. In the body, report the information that you learned during the interview, using reported speech. In the conclusion, comment and give your opinion about the major, program, department, or other aspect of your college that you wrote about.

Self-editing

1. Read your paragraph again. Does it say what you want it to say? Is it organized in the best way for your meaning and this particular writing task? Make any changes needed to improve the meaning of your writing. You are writing to describe an academic major, so check for the language of informational writing.

2. Edit your individual sentences for the following and correct any errors that you find. After you have edited for each of these features, check (✓) the box to remind yourself that you have done that task.

    ☐ complete sentences

    ☐ correct punctuation

    ☐ correct verb tenses

    ☐ correct subject-verb agreement

    ☐ correct use of reporting verbs

    ☐ use of vocabulary appropriate for academic writing rather than speaking

    ☐ appropriate changes of notes from interview into written academic English

3. Rewrite your paragraph to make the corrections you decided on while you were editing your sentences.

Peer Response Groups

Work with another pair of students to respond to each other's paragraphs about an academic topic. Exchange your paragraphs with other group members. Read both paragraphs of the partners who worked together. Focus on these questions and discuss your answers afterwards.

1. Does the topic sentence of the paragraph identify the person interviewed and his or her title? Does it also present the general topic of the interview?

2. Is the information in both partners' paragraphs the same? Are there factual differences? If so, point them out to the writers.

4. Do you have additional questions about the academic subject that the writers describe? If so, write them in the margins of the paragraph.

5. What appeals to you the most about the paragraphs? Why?

Revise

Make any necessary revisions in your paragraph and turn it in to your instructor.

LEARNER'S NOTEBOOK

Reflecting on Your Learning

In your learner's notebook, answer these questions: What have you learned about your college that you did not know about before you began this chapter? What is the most useful information you learned? Have your ideas about your academic future changed?

Create a Portfolio

A *portfolio* is a collection of writing, charts, or other information on a single subject. Portfolios may be required in college and university courses, in job interviews, and in careers.

In Chapter 5, you have gathered a great deal of academic information related to your college. Gather all the writing and interesting outside reading that you wish to share with classmates and put them in a folder. Label the folder with the name of your college, your name, and an appropriate title that reflects the type of information you have included. Bring the portfolio to class and share it with your classmates.

LOOKING AHEAD

Authentic Academic Description Assignments

With a partner or a small group of classmates, carefully read the academic description assignments that follow. Then do the discussion exercise after each assignment.

Criminal Justice Administration

Assignment 1: A Description of Courtroom Procedures

In this course, the professor seeks to achieve three objectives: 1) to familiarize students with courtroom processes, 2) to help them identify problem areas in the court's administration, and 3) to help them develop solutions to these problems.

Writing Assignment: As a candidate for judicial office, you are speaking to members of a local professional club, most of whom have a passing knowledge of courtroom processes. Describe two reforms you would initiate to reduce courtroom delays at a trial. Explain how each measure will achieve that purpose. Also explain potential side effects, either beneficial or detrimental, to the courtroom process. You are speaking to the professional club in an effort to secure their endorsement of your campaign.

Requirements: In order to write the assignment, you must (1) be familiar with book and lecture material on the subject of courtroom trial procedure, (2) be familiar with the issue of delays in court, and (3) be able to integrate any proposed solutions you are familiar with into the context of the question.

Evaluative Criteria: Your instructor will evaluate your essay with these criteria in mind: (1) Did you clearly understand the issue addressed? (2) Did you clearly describe the reforms you suggested? (3) Did you present the potential side effects in an effective and logical manner? (4) Did you state the ways in which your suggested reform would alleviate courtroom delays?

Adapted from Improving Student Writing by Andrew Moss and Carol Holder
(Pomona, CA: California State Polytechnic University, 1988).

DISCUSSION

With a small group of classmates, answer these questions relating to Assignment 1:

1. What is the purpose of this assignment? State the purpose in a sentence.

2. What is not clear about this assignment? Make a list of what you will need to know in order to complete the assignment successfully.

Community Involvement

Assignment 2: Description of a Community Center

In this course, the professor wants her students to visit a community service organization office or site and describe the activities that take place there. The purpose of the assignment is for students to become better acquainted with the types of community organizations in the area and with the kinds of services provided.

Writing Assignment: Write a two- to four-page description of one community organization office or site in the city or region. Possible sites include women's centers, homeless shelters, city service offices, county service offices, and religious or nonprofit service organizations. For a list of possible sites, check the local telephone directory under "Community Organizations."

Audience: You are contributing to a directory of local community organizations that will soon be published by your college. Your audience will be college students, many of whom are lower-income, working parents in need of community support.

Pre-Writing Tasks

1. Decide on a community site to visit. Have your choice approved by your instructor. Then call to arrange an appointment.
2. Visit the site for at least one hour. In your journal, record what you see, hear, touch, and feel, including your impressions. Do this before class on September 30 so we can discuss it in class.
3. In class, understand the following major concepts or ideas:
   a. the function of community service organizations
   b. the nature of community service funding and staffing
   c. the relationship between community service groups and clients
4. Visit the site again. On your second visit, try to organize your observations around certain categories of description and analysis. I suggest:
   a. organizational structure of the site
   b. interaction among staff and clients
   c. goals and perceived accomplishments of the site
   d. effect upon you as an observer.
5. From all your observations, formulate a *thesis*—a single idea which can serve as a focal point for the entire paper. As you write your first draft, the thesis can be modified. The idea may come from major ideas presented in class (see 2.).

Writing the Paper

1. State your thesis clearly, positively, and persuasively.
2. Be able to support your thesis with specific descriptions of the characteristics of the community site.

Evaluation: I will evaluate your essay with these criteria in mind:

1. Did you provide a clear and accurate description?
2. Were you able to organize your description into meaningful categories?
3. Were you able to relate your knowledge and experience to what you saw, tasted, smelled, heard. and felt at the place?
4. Were you able to present your experience clearly and persuasively, supporting your conclusion with convincing evidence?

DISCUSSION

In a small group, answer these questions about Assignment 2:

1. What is the purpose of this assignment? State the purpose in a sentence.

2. What questions might you ask the professor about this assignment? Write three questions.

Observing

Scientific Method

GOALS

WRITING
◆ develop and use observing skills in writing

GRAMMAR
◆ examine and practice several of the features of informational writing: *nouns and noun phrases, generic nouns, present tense verbs, passive voice verbs,* and *logical organizers*

CONTENT
◆ learn and apply the scientific method

ACADEMIC FIELDS
Chemistry
Physics
Environmental Science

Sample Authentic College/University Assignments that Require Observing

In a college or university classroom, you will use the skills you learn in this chapter to complete assignments like this:

Introduction to Chemistry
Writing Assignment: Lab Report

Make a model of the following elements to demonstrate how they combine in chemical reactions: N, H, Cu, O, K, and Cl. Following the procedure outlined in your textbook for creating the models, observe how many molecules of N, H, and O are produced, and draw conclusions based on your experiment. Write a two- to four-page report to describe each step in your investigation.

Microcomputer Applications
Writing Assignment: Lab Report

Design an experiment to determine how an abacus works as a counting machine. Following the procedure for using an abacus outlined in your handout, observe and record data on trial calculations to determine the number system on which the operation of the abacus is based. Compare this system with the operation of a computer. Record your observations and conclusions in a report of three to five typed pages.

 CNN video support is available for this chapter.

GETTING READY

LEARNER'S NOTEBOOK

Warm-up Activity

Have you ever wondered why certain things happen or how something works? Think about an action you have observed in nature but did not understand, such as lightning, thunder, a rainbow, a hurricane, or a storm. List what you saw, heard, tasted, smelled, or felt. Write down a possible explanation for the action. Discuss your ideas with your class.

Grammar Preview

In science courses, you will read and write predominantly informational texts. Chemistry, physics, environmental science, biology, and biochemistry textbooks contain informational writing such as reports of laboratory experiments and explanations of scientific facts. You will find similar types of writing in sociology, psychology, or anthropology and other social sciences.

Scientific informational writing is characterized by the frequent use of passive voice verbs, in addition to other features of informational writing you have previously studied. In the grammar activities in this chapter, you will examine and practice several of these important grammatical features in order to be better prepared for reading and writing in the sciences.

Introduction to Observing

When you observe a rainbow to try to understand how it occurred, you are acting like a scientist. You are using all of your senses and paying close attention to everything that happens.

Scientists do more than simply observe. They also question what they see and they try to find answers to their questions. College science students do the same. Chemistry students observe, describe, and report on chemical reactions. Biology students observe, examine, and analyze living nature or microorganisms in a laboratory. Geology students observe and draw conclusions from rock formations. In the social sciences, sociology students observe, record data, and interpret data about human behavior in different situations, such as in elevators, in airports, or in family or work settings.

In order to perform well on writing assignments involving observation, students can learn and apply the scientific method. This method will also serve you outside the laboratory. For example, in an English composition course, you may use factual observations to support ideas in an essay.

Before you examine the scientific method, think about questions like those below that scientists may ask themselves before they conduct an experiment that involves observation.

QUESTIONS ABOUT OBSERVING

- *What* am I going to observe?
- *Where* is the best place to observe?
- *When* is the best time to observe?
- *How long* will I need to observe?
- *How* am I going to measure what I observe?
- *How* am I going to record what I observe?
- *How* can I evaluate what I observe?

Applying Questions about Observing

Imagine you are taking a sociology course in which the professor assigns a project involving observation of behavior on your college campus. The assignment is to choose a topic, observe and record data, and write a report based on the observation. Your first steps are to choose a topic and decide *what, where, when,* etc. to observe.

Choosing a topic is similar to a scientist making a *hypothesis*, defined as a "working theory" or "unproved assumption" about a topic in *The Newbury House Dictionary of American English*. Imagine that you choose the topic of smoking on campus. You *hypothesize* that there are few smokers on your campus. Your hypothesis helps you to decide *what you will observe*: the numbers of smokers and nonsmokers on campus. You must answer additional questions before you observe, as the notes in the following chart illustrate.

OBSERVING ASSIGNMENT

Topic:	Smoking on campus
Hypothesis:	The majority of people on my college campus do not smoke.

Notes about Observing Questions:

What to observe	The numbers of smokers and nonsmokers on campus
Where	Courtyard outside main entrance to Bonnell Building (main campus building)

When	Monday, Wednesday, or Friday mornings (times with most students/staff present)
How Long to Record	Five separate observations of two hours each
How to Measure	Count total number of nonsmoking and smoking students outside entrance.
How to Record	Mark two columns on a notebook page labeled "Smokers" and "Nonsmokers." Make a mark for each smoker/nonsmoker observed.
How to Evaluate	Using numbers from observations, calculate the average percentage of smokers on campus.

Activity 6-1   Brainstorming about Observing Questions

With a small group of classmates, discuss the following possible topics for an observation assignment on a college campus. Fill in the charts by answering each of the questions and by completing a hypothesis statement for Topic 3. Share your group's ideas with the rest of the class.

1.   **Observing Assignment**

| Topic: | Study Habits at College |
| Hypothesis: | Most students study in groups on campus. |

Notes about Observing Questions:

| *What to observe:* | Numbers of students studying alone versus in groups |

Where: _____

When: _____

How Long to Record: _____

How to Measure: _____

How to Record: _____

How to Evaluate: _____

2.   **Observing Assignment**

Topic: Eating Habits of College Students

Hypothesis: More college students eat junk food rather than healthy food.

Notes about Observing Questions:

What: _____

Where: _____

When: _____

How Long to Record: _____

How to Measure: _____

How to Record: _____

How to Evaluate: _____

3.   **Observing Assignment**

Topic: Clothing of Male/Female College Students

Hypothesis: Most male/female students _____

Notes about Observing Questions:

What: _____

Where: _____

When: _____

How Long to Record: _____

How to Measure: _____

How to Record: _____

How to Evaluate: _____

LEARNER'S NOTEBOOK

Reflecting on Observation Topics

In your learner's notebook, write about the observation from Activity 6-1 that you would most like to conduct and write about. Why do you like this topic? How would you conduct an observation based on the topic? Would you change the hypothesis statement? If so, how? What do you think your observation might tell you? Do you think observing would be difficult? Why or why not?

The Grammar of Nouns and Noun Phrases in Informational Writing: Learning and Using Key Terms

In college and university courses, you may learn key scientific terms such as *hypothesis* in freshman courses and continue to encounter them in a variety of courses throughout your college career. In all of these courses, the terminology uses the same basic grammar: a single *noun* or a *noun phrase* (noun + other word or words).

Activity 6-2   Understanding Key Terms Before You Read

1. The following is a list of key terms commonly used in science from Reading 1, "Scientific Observation." Use each word in the blank where it belongs to complete the paragraphs.

   - hypotheses
   - phenomenon
   - recorded
   - data
   - analyze
   - theory
   - observe

   A college biology professor walked into class and placed a fish on a student's lab table. "_____ this. I'll return in three hours after you have _____ some data," the professor ordered. At first, the student was not interested, but later she started to look at the fish and took a few notes. When the professor returned, he looked at her _____, and told her to keep looking. Frustrated, she took more notes and she tried to _____ what she had seen, smelled, and felt. After another three hours, the professor finally returned. Reading the student's notes, the professor declared, "Now you are beginning to observe!" This student practiced what many scientists do when they study a problem or a _____ in nature. Scientists, like this student, gather information about a problem and use observation to test their theories, or _____, about why they think the problem occurs. After they have tested their hypothesis many times, they can then call it a _____ or law of science.

2. After you complete the paragraph, discuss these questions with a small group of classmates or with a partner:

What does each of the science words in the list mean?

What would you do to complete the observation of the fish if you were in this biology class?

3. Record the words and definitions on notecards or in your learner's notebook.

FOCUSING

Activity 6-3   Brainstorming for an Observation Topic

With a partner, choose a topic for an observation on your college campus. Use one of the observing assignments in Activity 6-1 or a topic from the following list. Discuss your topic ideas with your class.

SUGGESTED OBSERVATION TOPICS

1. courses or departments with more male than female students

2. transportation methods of college students

3. writing habits of college students

4. test-taking behavior of college students

5. talkativeness of ESL students

Activity 6-4   Deciding on a Hypothesis

Writing a hypothesis that you test when you observe helps limit what you observe. For example, if you want to research *the clothing of female college students,* you may wish to observe *the percentage of female students who wear pants or skirts.*

Use the following chart to record some general aspects of college life that interest you and your partner and write specific hypothesis statements that you might test by observation. Share your ideas with a group of classmates and your instructor. Write hypothesis statements that tell specifically what you will research in your observations.

General Aspect of College Life	Hypothesis
smoking habits	Most college smokers are male.
eating habits	Most college students buy food instead of bringing it from home.

Activity 6-5   Writing Questions for Observation

With your partner, fill in this chart and give it to your instructor before you conduct your observation:

Observing Assignment

Topic: _____

Hypothesis: _____

Notes about Observing Questions:

What: _____

Where: _____

When: _____

How Long to Record: _____

How to Measure: _____

How to Record: _____

How to Evaluate: _____

Activity 6-6   Writing Assignment 1: Campus Observation

With your partner, conduct an observation, using your Observing Assignment chart from Activity 6-5 as a guideline. Each of you should conduct the observation at the same time and take careful and accurate notes. Check each other's notes after you observe. Then, individually, write a paragraph that contains the following information:

ORGANIZATION OF CAMPUS OBSERVATION WRITING ASSIGNMENT

Introduction and Main Idea
Describe the observation that you conducted and state your hypothesis.

Support
Explain in detail what, when, where, how long, and how you conducted the observation.

Conclusion
Describe the results. Was your hypothesis proven true or false?

Activity 6-7 Peer Response

Share your paragraph with your partner and answer these questions:

1. Does your partner's paragraphs contain the same basic information as yours?

2. Are any of the points in the organizational chart in Activity 6-5 missing from your partner's paragraph? If so, mark which ones your partner needs to add.

3. What part of your partner's paragraph do you like the best? Why?

LEARNER'S NOTEBOOK

Reflecting on Your Writing

After you have written and revised your paragraph using your partner's suggestions, answer these questions in your learner's notebook:

Was this assignment difficult? If so, what was the most difficult part?
Did you get useful guidance from your instructor about how to do this assignment?
What did you learn about the process of observing?
What did you learn about your college or university campus?

READING 1 SCIENTIFIC OBSERVATION (ACADEMIC ESSAY)

Activity 6-8 Previewing and Focused Reading

Preview Reading 1 as you have in previous chapters. As you read, focus on these questions: What is the importance of the bold-faced words? What type of information is represented in each of the bold-faced "bulleted" headings in the text?

SCIENTIFIC OBSERVATION

Science represents knowledge, not simply belief or feeling. When you have scientific knowledge about a phenomenon, it means that you "know," or at least you think you know, the explanation of that phenomenon. You do not just "feel in your heart" that you are right. You think you have logical proof that you are right and that the proof is available for everyone to see and test. For example, "1 + 1 = 2" is true no matter what your religion or nationality, whether you are young or old, healthy or sick, in China or on the moon, whether it is cold or hot, night or day, in the 20th century or 10,000 BC, etc. Any other scientist can test this fact and find that it is true.

There are, of course, many fields of scientific study, but they all rely on the scientific method. Scientists in general use the following simplified guidelines to acquire scientific knowledge:

- Identify a problem or phenomenon to be studied.
- Gather information about it.
- Make observations.
- Analyze them (that is, break them down into their simplest elements and examine them).
- Form a hypothesis.
- Gather information to support your hypothesis.
- Test the hypothesis to see if it is true.
- Draw a conclusion.
- Report that conclusion.

The phenomenon of rain can be used as a very simple example to illustrate the scientific and nonscientific methods. Some nonscientific explanations of rain could be:

1. The gods of rain bring rain whenever they feel like it.
2. There is a hole in the sky through which rain falls.
3. When God is happy with people He or She gives them the right amount of rain; if not, He or She gives them too much or none at all.
4. Extra-terrestrials spray Earth with a giant rubber hose.

To follow the guidelines for the scientific method stated above, explaining what rain is and how it falls would occur as follows:

- **Identify the problem.** Rain occasionally falls from the sky onto the earth. What is it and 30 how does it happen?
- **Gather information.** Read what other people have said about rain and about when, where, and how much it falls.
- **Make observations.**

1. Look at, touch, smell, and taste some rain. Experiment with it, such as by pouring it into 35 or out of a receptacle, heating it, etc., as if you had never seen rain in your life.
2. Observe the movement of rain; describe the action.
3. Notice what seems to always precede, accompany, or follow rain.

- **Analyze.** You may conclude that rain occurs when a certain set of conditions exists, but you must state the results of your analyses in a hypothesis that you will test.   40
- **Formulate a hypothesis.** For example, "rain occurs when clouds are present. Clouds seem to be huge masses of steam that are probably the result of the sun heating the ocean waters. The wind must blow the clouds over the lands, and when the temperatures high in the sky are cooler than the clouds themselves, condensation occurs, and, consequently, rain falls."
- **Test the hypothesis.** Naturally, one cannot go and heat the ocean waters, etc., but a mini- 45 replication of this phenomenon can be made with a pot of water and a lid. Put some water in the pot and heat it to the boiling point. When steam starts to rise, warm the lid on another stove burner until it's too hot for you to touch. Then using a pot holder immediately put the lid over the steam. Notice that no *condensation* occurs (meaning no water forms on the underside of the lid). Let the lid cool off or cool it under cold water. Wipe off the lid, put 50 it back over the steam, and remove it quickly. Notice how quickly there is condensation.
- **Conclusion.** Now you can conclude that you have proved your hypothesis and you can report a scientific explanation of rain.

Activity 6-9   Post-reading Discussion

1. Each of the following statements summarizes one of the steps in Reading 1's description of the scientific method. These steps occur in correct order in the reading. Put a number beside each of the phrases below so that they occur in the order in which they appear in the reading.

   _____ Learn what people know already about the subject.

   _____ Write a conclusion about what you found.

   _____ Make a sentence that you think may explain what is happening.

   _____ Think about your observation.

   _____ Watch and note what you observe.

_____ Ask a question about something you see and don't understand.

_____ See if your suggested solution is correct.

2. Mark the following statements as *True* or *False* according to the reading. Show your answers to a partner and then discuss them with your class.

_____ Science is a belief or a feeling.

_____ A phenomenon is something that you cannot explain.

_____ The scientific method is used only in some fields of science.

_____ To analyze means to study something by looking at its parts.

_____ A hole in the sky is a scientific explanation of rain.

_____ The boiling water test proved the writer's hypothesis about rain.

LEARNER'S NOTEBOOK

Comparing Observation Assignments

Think about the observation that you conducted for Activity 6-6 and the rain experiment explained in Reading 1. How are the two observation assignments different? How are they similar? How would you feel about conducting a scientific experiment and writing the results? Would it be easy or difficult? Why? Write your answers in your notebook.

The Grammar of Informational Writing: Generic Nouns

Academic texts that *inform* you about subjects commonly contain generic (general) nouns that represent a whole class of people or things.

For example, the following sentence from "Scientific Observation" contains two generic nouns, italicized below.

Scientists in general use the following simplified guidelines to acquire scientific *knowledge*.

Notice that neither of these nouns is preceded by an article. The first generic noun is plural; the second one is a noncount noun.

GLR   See pages 240 and 244 of the GLR for more explanations on nouns and articles.

Activity 6-10   Recognizing Generic Nouns

Reread the first paragraph of "Scientific Observation." Underline all of the nouns. Make a list of the nouns that do not have articles (*a, an, the*) or determiners (*this, that, these, those, your, no, any,* etc.). Divide that list into the plural nouns and the noncount nouns. For example, *knowledge* is a noncount noun and *scientists* is a plural noun. Compare and discuss your answers with your class.

Activity 6-11   Choosing Articles for Generic Nouns

As you saw in Activity 6-10, many nouns are used in generalizations without an article (*a, an, the*). In the following paragraph, underline all the nouns. Then decide if each noun can be used without an article. Write a note about each noun to explain your decision. Remember that plural nouns and noncount nouns can be used without articles for generic (general) meaning. The first two sentences have been done as an example.

THE ORIGIN OF JUDO

Scientific observation can be applied to fields other than science. For example, it is reported that judo originated as a result of observation. A great master was meditating one day about snow falling on a branch. Instead of letting the accumulating snow's weight get so big that it would break it, the branch "yielded" and let the snow fall on the ground. The conclusion? The branch uses the snow's own strength against itself. The master developed a technique for using that principle in wrestling: judo.

Word	Notes
observation	noncount, no article needed, means the process of observation
fields	plural, all fields, general, no article needed
science	noncount, all science as a whole, no article needed
example	idiom, always used this way, no article
judo	name of a sport, no article used
result	singular noun (1 result, 2 results), must have an article—add *a*
observation	noncount, no article needed, means the process of observation
_____	_____
_____	_____
_____	_____
_____	_____

READING 2   WHAT IS A RAINBOW? (LABORATORY REPORT)

Activity 6-12   Pre-reading Discussion

With a small group of students, discuss these questions in preparation for Reading 2.

1. What is a rainbow?

2. Can you explain why these aspects of nature and science occur? (Use a dictionary to look up unfamiliar words.)

   a. rain   c. crystals

   b. gravity   d. volcanoes

3. Do you think the explanation for any of these aspects of nature and science could be tested in a laboratory? If so, how?

WHAT IS A RAINBOW?

Problem. What is a rainbow? Where do its colors come from?

Information. Textbooks such as *Concepts and Challenges in Physical Science* explain that sunlight seems to be colorless, but in fact contains a spectrum of colors. The colors do not appear unless they are refracted (bent) through water. Theories explain that, as sunlight is reflected through raindrops, it is refracted, and its spectrum of colors, in the form of a 5 rainbow, is reflected in the sky. Related theories about sunlight say that sunlight is more easily reflected on light-colored surfaces rather than dark.

    Analysis. In order to prove what a rainbow is and where its colors come from, the student-scientist needs to reproduce the conditions in which a rainbow appears. Sunlight must be viewed through water and reflected onto a surface. But it will be difficult to make a rain- 10 bow in the sky. The same effect must be produced in a more controlled environment. The sunlight should be reflected through water, bent, and shone onto a light-colored surface such as a piece of white paper. A glass of water could be used, and a way to block all of the light except for a band of light (like a rainbow) should be devised.

    Hypothesis. Sunlight is made of a spectrum of colors that can be seen when light is 15 refracted through water, which explains what a rainbow is and why it has colors.

Test. The experiment will attempt to show sunlight reflected through water (and therefore bent) and projected onto a piece of paper so that a spectrum or rainbow is created. The materials needed are a small, clear water glass, a 5- × 7-inch index card, a sheet of white paper, and adhesive tape.   20

First, in the center of the long side of the card, cut a one-half-inch wide slit. Extend the slit to about one-quarter inch from the top and the bottom of the card. Next, fill the glass with water and tape the card onto its side so that the slit runs vertically. Place the white paper on a table close to a window and place the glass on it.

When the sunlight passes through the slit in the paper, the light is bent, or refracted, by 25 the water in the glass. This produces a spectrum, or rainbow of colors, on the paper. Beginning at the end of the beam of light farthest from the glass, the following colors are reflected onto the paper: red, orange, yellow, green, blue, and purple.

Conclusion. The colors that are reflected onto the paper in this experiment are the same as a rainbow's colors. Therefore, this experiment proves that the colors of sunlight are pres- 30 ent all the time, but the presence of water (raindrops) and sunlight combine to make them visible in the form of a rainbow.

Activity 6-13   Post-reading Discussion

With a small group of classmates, answer these questions about the reading, "What Is a Rainbow?"

1. Is the problem to be studied clear to you? If not, what questions do you have?

2. Do the steps clearly explain what the writer did? If any places are not clear, mark them and discuss them with your groupmates.

3. Is the conclusion of the experiment clearly written? If not, what do you not understand?

4. How does the writer organize his or her writing? What is the function of the title? What is the topic sentence of the report?

LEARNER'S NOTEBOOK

Looking Ahead to College Science Courses

In your learner's notebook, answer these questions: How do you feel about science courses? How do you feel about writing in English about scientific experiments? Have you done it before? What is easy about doing scientific experiments? What is difficult? Why?

The Grammar of Informational Writing: Present Tense and Other Verbs

In science writing and reading, as in other types of informational writing, present tense verbs predominate. Science texts inform students of theories, laws, facts, and general truths; they also instruct students in how to test theories. In addition, science writing sometimes uses past tense verbs (simple past, past progressive, past perfect) to report on past scientific studies. Typically, past verbs are used to present the history of scientific developments and famous scientists.

Notice that in the readings, "Scientific Observation" and "What Is a Rainbow?", the simple present tense is typically used to report scientific experiments. This makes the information seem relevant and timely.

> **GLR**   See pages 214–215 and 223 of the GLR for the primary verbs used in English to express present and past time.

Activity 6-14   Identifying Present Tense Verbs

1. Reread paragraphs 1 and 2 of "What Is a Rainbow?" Underline the main verbs. What verb tenses are used? Why? Does the use of the verb tenses in the paragraphs make sense? Why or why not?

> **GLR**   See page 250 of the GLR for the names of different verbs.

2. Reread paragraphs 3–5 of "What Is a Rainbow?" What is the predominant verb time here? What verb tense is used to express this time? Why is this tense used?

The Grammar of Informational Writing: Passive Voice Verbs

Since science texts often inform you about *actions* or *results*, rather than *people* or *things* that *perform* the action, they contain passive voice verbs. This sentence from "What Is a Rainbow?" illustrates this verb:

passive verb
Sunlight <u>is made</u> of a spectrum of colors ...

Here, the sentence emphasizes *sunlight*, rather than the *person* or *thing* that performs the making of *sunlight*.

The passive voice verb lets the writer focus on the object in an action, rather than the doer. Refer to the Appendix of Irregular Verbs, pages 251–254, as reference for a list of irregular past participles.

> **GLR**   See the GLR pages 222–223 for more information on passive voice verbs.

Activity 6-15   Identifying Passive Voice Verbs

Read the following passage from Reading 2, "What Is a Rainbow?" With a partner, find and underline all the verbs. Which ones are passive? Which ones are active? Mark the passive verbs (P) and active verbs (A).

> When the sunlight passes through the slit in the paper, the light is bent, or refracted, by the water in the glass. This produces a spectrum, or rainbow of colors, on the paper. Beginning at end of the beam of light farthest from the glass, the following colors are reflected onto the paper: red, orange, yellow, green, blue, and purple.

Activity 6-16   Identifying Passive and Active Verbs in Your Writing

With your partner, exchange the paragraphs you wrote for the writing assignment about campus observation. Mark the verbs in your partner's paragraph as passive (P) or active (A). Does your partner use mostly active or passive verbs? How does his or her usage of passive/active verbs compare with your own?

READING 3   DESCRIPTIONS OF SCIENTIFIC EXPERIMENTS

The following are brief descriptions of scientific experiments that can be conducted to demonstrate laws of nature or simple machines. Read each one and discuss the questions that follow with a partner or a small group of classmates.

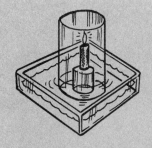

1. *Problem*   How much oxygen is in the air?

   Hypothesis   One-fifth of the atmosphere is oxygen.

   Test   Put a candle on an object (a small can or jar). Place the object in the middle of a shallow, flat glass plate filled about three-quarters full with water. Light the candle. Put a large glass jar over the candle. As the candle burns, the water will rise in the jar. Measure how high the water level rises when the candle goes out.

Materials	A candle, a small can or jar, a flat glass plate, matches.

2. *Problem*	Is water pressure stronger in deep water or in shallow water?
Hypothesis	The pressure of any liquid increases with depth.
Test	Cut off the top of a liter cola bottle. Make holes with nails at four different levels. Put the bottle in a dish. Cover the holes with your fingers. Have someone fill the bottle with water. Observe how the lower and higher holes shoot out jets of water.
Materials	A liter cola bottle, a knife, nails, a dish.

3. *Problem*	Do gases take up more space than solids or liquids?
Hypothesis	Gases take up more space than equal amounts of solids or liquids.

Test   Fill a small, narrow-necked bottle about one-fourth full of warmed vinegar. Put a small plastic funnel into the end of a balloon. Pour a large spoonful of bicarbonate of soda into the balloon. Stretch the neck of the balloon over the bottle neck. Don't let the soda spill out. When the balloon is tight on the bottle, let the soda fall into the vinegar. Shake the bottle. Watch what happens to the balloon when carbon dioxide gas is released when the soda and the vinegar meet.

Materials   A small, narrow-necked bottle, vinegar, a plastic funnel, a balloon, bicarbonate of soda.

4. *Problem*   Does the sun reflect some colors and absorb other colors?

Hypothesis   Light-colored surfaces reflect more of the sun's heat rays away. Dark surfaces absorb the rays and get much warmer.

Test   Take three jars with lids (all the same size) and prepare them as follows. Make a small hole in each lid. Wrap the first jar with aluminum foil. Paint the second jar with black paint. Leave the third jar plain. Fill all three jars with water of the same temperature. Put a little clay over each hole in the lids. Put all the lids on the jars. Place the jars in full sunshine. Use a glass candy thermometer or other type of thermometer to take their temperatures every three minutes. Observe which jar's water heats up the fastest. Which jar's water heats up the least?

Materials   3 jars of the same size with lids, aluminum foil, black paint, clay, glass candy thermometer.

5. *Problem*   What causes a volcano to erupt?

   Hypothesis   Chemical reactions cause volcanic eruptions.

   Test   Add some red food coloring to a cup of vinegar. Half-fill a plastic bot-tle with bicarbonate of soda. Place the bottle in the center of a plastic tub, dishpan, or tray. Pile gravel and then sand in the plastic tub around the bottle. Don't let the sand go inside the bottle. Cover the bottle up, leaving just the opening of the bottle uncovered. Make the sand into a volcano shape. Quickly pour all the red vinegar into the bottle. Observe what happens.

   Materials   Plastic bottle, vinegar, bicarbonate of soda, plastic tub, gravel, sand.

Activity 6-17   Post-reading Discussion

With a small group, discuss these questions about Reading 3:

1. Which of these experiments are you familiar with?

2. Have you conducted any of the tests before? If so, tell about your experience.

3. Which of the experiments interests you the most? Why?

4. Some people say, "A picture is worth 1,000 words." Do you agree or disagree? Do the drawings that accompany these experiments help you?

The Grammar of Informational Writing:
Chronological Organization in Scientific Writing

Scientific and technical writing is usually organized logically. For example, informational writing in the sciences often discusses cause and effect relationships. However, sometimes scientific reports organize the writing in a chronological pattern so the story of the scientific process is told.

A good example of this type of chronological writing is found in laboratory reports that follow the sequence of events or actions in the lab. The lab reports in science courses present the steps in a scientific test in the order in which they were performed. These reports also past tense verbs for past time actions along with present tense verbs for generalizations.

Common Chronological Organizers

First actions	Subsequent actions	Final actions
first	*next*	*finally*
to begin	*then*	*final*
	later	*in the end*

GLR See pages 215 of the GLR to find meanings and uses of chronological organizers.

Activity 6-18   Identifying Chronological Organizers

Identify and underline the chronological organizers in paragraph 5 of "What Is a Rainbow?" Check your answers with a classmate. The paragraph is repeated here.

First, in the center of the long side of the card, cut a one-half-inch wide slit. Extend the slit to about one-quarter inch from the top and the bottom of the card. Next, fill the glass with water and tape the card onto its side so that the slit runs vertically. Place the white paper on a table close to a window and place the glass on it.

Activity 6-19   Adding Chronological Organizers

With a partner, choose one of the brief descriptions of scientific tests from pages 159–162. Add appropriate chronological organizers to some of the sentences in the description. Compare your word choices with another set of partners.

PUTTING IT ALL TOGETHER

FINAL WRITING ASSIGNMENT: REPORT ON A SCIENTIFIC EXPERIMENT

Conduct a scientific experiment and write a report on your actions and observations. Your audience will be your classmates. Your purpose is to demonstrate your knowledge of a scientific topic as well as your ability to express your ideas clearly in English. You will also be informing your classmates about your scientific topic.

First, with one or two other classmates, choose one problem from "Descriptions of Scientific Experiments" (see pages 159–162) that interests you. Select a topic that you or your classmates have some knowledge about.

You will conduct the experiment together. In your report, write the steps a person must take to conduct the test and what he or she will observe. Then write a conclusion based on the experiment. Each of you will write an individual report about this experiment. Your reports should describe in chronological order each step you took. Use Reading 1, "Scientific Observation" (page 152–153), Reading 2, "What Is a Rainbow?" (pages 156–157), and the steps that follow to guide you.

Steps in Observing

Test the hypothesis. You and your group members must conduct the test together. Share responsibilities for the work. Gather materials you will need. Discuss methods you will use.

Record your observations. As you perform the experiment, make careful notes of what you observe, hear, smell, taste, etc. Write everything that you and your classmates do. Write what happens as you observe the experiment.

Draw a conclusion. Based on the experiment, what can you conclude? Write a statement that summarizes what the experiment showed.

Pre-experiment Discussion

1. Before you conduct your experiment, discuss these details within your group and then with your whole class:

    a. What specific materials will you need to conduct the test?

    b. Where can the test be conducted?

    c. By what methods can you record your actions and observations?

    d. Should you do the test more than one time?

2. You may want use this outline to take notes before and as you conduct the experiment.

Title of Experiment _____

Hypothesis _____

_____

Materials _____

_____

Methods _____

_____

Observations _____

_____

Conclusion(s) _____

_____

LEARNER'S NOTEBOOK

Reflecting on the Experiment

After you complete the experiment, answer these questions in your notebook: Was the experiment successful? Why or why not? Did you and your group members work well together? Did you have any trouble taking notes? What will be most difficult about writing your report?

Pre-writing Discussion

With your classmates, discuss these questions before you each write your reports:

1. Look over the notes each of you took. Do you have questions about the steps in your experiment?

2. Do you have questions about how to express your ideas in English?

3. Consider the audience for your report. What will you need to do in your writing to satisfy your instructor? What will you need to do to interest other classmate readers?

Self-editing

1. Read your paragraph again. Does it say what you want it to say? Is it organized in the best way for your meaning and this particular writing task? Make any changes needed to improve the meaning of your writing. You are writing scientific information, so check for the language of informational writing.

2. Edit your individual sentences for the following, and correct any errors you find. After you have edited for each of these features, check (✓) the box to remind yourself that you have done that task.

☐ complete sentences

☐ correct punctuation

☐ correct verb tenses

☐ correct subject-verb agreement

☐ use of vocabulary appropriate for academic writing rather than speaking

☐ clearly organized, using appropriate chronological organizers

☐ if you use any passive verbs, check the form and spelling carefully. You might show these sentences to your instructor to be sure that you have used this sentence type correctly

3. Rewrite your paragraph to make the corrections you decided on while you were editing your sentences.

Peer Response

Share your paragraph with a classmate. Discuss the following questions.

1. Does the writer introduce one of the five experiments from Reading 3? Does he or she explain the experiment clearly? Underline this sentence.

2. Does the writer explain the steps in the test and what he or she observed? Circle the sentences.

3. Does the writer use details about the steps and the observations? Underline the details.

4. Does the paragraph have a conclusion?

5. What do you like most about the paragraph? Tell your partner.

Revise your paragraph and submit it to your instructor.

LEARNER'S NOTEBOOK

Evaluating Your Writing

After you have turned in a revision of your paragraph to your instructor, write about your writing experiences so far in this course. Which assignments have been the most difficult? Which have been the easiest? What is the most difficult part about writing? Do you edit and revise your writing more now than you did before you started the course? Is it easier to write now than when you first began the course?

Authentic Academic Assignments

With a partner or a small group of classmates, carefully read the following academic assignment, which requires observing. Then do the discussion activity after the assignment.

Principles of Electronics

Writing Assignment: Laboratory Report on Job 1: The Electric Circuit

Objectives:

1. To wire a series lamp circuit
2. To measure the total current flow
3. To calculate operating resistance of the load
4. To calculate power dissipated by the lamp

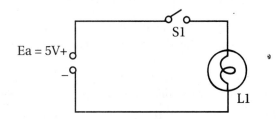

Procedures

1. Adjust the DC power supply (2–10 volt range) for 5 volts DC.
2. Wire the circuit shown above.
3. Close switch one (S1). The lamp is on/off.
4. Measure the voltage drop across the lamp. Voltage lamp (VL) = _____.
5. Open switch one (S1). The lamp is now on/off.
6. Set the DC meter to measure current.
7. Wire the circuit shown on the next page.

Note: Insert the DC meter in series with the lamp.

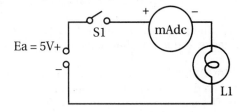

8. Close switch one (S1). The lamp is now on/off. Observe and record the total current flow.
   Total current (IT) = _____.
9. What is the voltage drop across the lamp? VL = _____. (See step 4.)
10. The current drawn by the lamp (step 8) is equal to _____.
11. Using test data from steps 4 and 10, calculate the resistance of the lamp (RL).
    RL = VL/IL

12. Using test data from steps 10 and 11, calculate power dissipated by the lamp.
    Watts lamp = IL × RL.

Conclusion

Write a brief report describing the fundamentals of an electric circuit. Explain how to connect meters in a circuit.

DISCUSSION

In a group, discuss these questions about the writing assignment above:

1. What information do you need in order to complete the assignment?

2. How can you get this information?

3. Do you think the experiment is difficult or easy to conduct? Why or why not?

Guidelines for Writing Assignment 1: Students in this course are given the following guidelines for writing laboratory reports. Read the guide and answer the discussion questions that follow.

Guidelines and Rules Concerning the Format of the Laboratory Report

Baltimore City Community College

The complete laboratory report may be either neatly handwritten in ink (black or blue) or typewritten. The point here is that neatness and legibility are important. If the instructor cannot read a sloppily written or typed report, then the effort and time taken in its preparation has been wasted. In our courses, ample time is given from the date the experiment was performed until the report is due.

1. TITLE. The title of the experiment at the beginning of the report should be a descriptive phrase that identifies the experiment. As an example, "The Common-Emitter Amplifier" is more descriptive than "Experiment 4," as it may not be apparent what Experiment 4 actually is. In addition, the name of the person submitting the report should be included, along with the names of other laboratory partners. Finally, the date the experiment was performed must be included.

2. PURPOSE OR OBJECTIVE. The particular experiment is to be performed for some definite reason. A brief, 1–3 sentence statement that explains why the experiment is being performed is included.

3. WIRING (SCHEMATIC) DIAGRAM. A schematic diagram of the circuit(s) used in the experiment must be included. The diagram must be neatly drawn and properly labeled with all component values used. The use of templates to draw electronic symbols is not mandatory, and the symbols can be drawn freehand. However, all connecting lines must be drawn with a straightedge.

4. PROCEDURE. This contains short comments in chronological order about the measurements, instruments used, and any special techniques used. Such comments are usually sufficient to explain what was done during the experiment. Long explanations are generally not necessary and usually not desirable. The comments nevertheless should be complete enough to allow another person to perform the experiment for verification.

5. DATA TABLES. In almost all experiments, a number of measured values should be recorded in ink. Charts are the most convenient method of recording these data, since all values are readily available for analysis.

   The student should also understand that all erasures and changes in data are observed by others with great suspicion. Recording errors should not be erased. They should be indicated as errors by drawing a single line through incorrect data and writing the correct value beside it. Many industrial firms also require that the employee initial the change along with the date. Indicating the error by the single-line method retains the original measurement for future analysis if it should be found to be important. In some experiments, the possible error is the only interesting part of the experiment, and the measurement would be completely lost if it were erased, scratched our, or otherwise defaced.

6. CALCULATIONS. All experiments require a certain number of calculations before final results are obtained. Sample calculations that are completely identified should be included. It is not necessary to show repeated calculations.

7. RESULTS AND CONCLUSIONS. The results and conclusions are probably the most important part of the experiment. The entire experiment is considered a failure if the student does not understand the results and cannot decide how to express the conclusion. Many instructors read this part of the report first and then refer to the other items for supporting information. The conclusion should be as brief as possible (less than one written page). Long conclusions often tend to bury the actual results of the experiment and instead become a procedure sheet. One statement that should be avoided is "Everything went as expected."

DISCUSSION

Answer these questions about the "Guidelines and Rules Concerning the Format of the Laboratory Report" in your group.

1. What is your general reaction to the guidelines and rules? Explain.

2. Which parts of the guidelines and rules do you find very strict? Which parts seem less strict? Point out these parts in your group.

3. Which parts of the requirements would be the hardest for you to meet? Why?

4. Which parts would be the easiest to meet? Why?

5. How does this assignment compare with the writing assignments that you completed in this chapter?

6. What is the most valuable information you learned from the guidelines sheet?

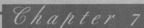

Chapter 7

Analyzing

Why Advertising Sells

GOALS

WRITING
◆ develop analyzing skills

GRAMMAR
◆ examine and practice several of the features of interactive communication and persuasion: *you* and *we, questions, contractions,* and *if sentences*

CONTENT
◆ learn about and examine advertising techniques

ACADEMIC FIELDS
Advertising
Marketing

Sample Authentic College/University Analyzing Assignments

In a college/university classroom, you will use the skills you learn in this chapter to complete assignments like the ones below.

Infrastructure Engineering and Management, 4th year

Assignment: Analysis of Company Privatization

In countries with a high degree of government control of the economy, the use of state companies as authorities for infrastructure management is common. One example of this is state ownership of electric companies such as Electricité de France or Eletrobras (Brazil). Analyze briefly the potential advantages and disadvantages of privatizing these companies.

Nutrition, 2nd year

Assignment: Risk-Benefit Analysis

Analyze the risk-benefit ratio of food additives or red meat in the diet.

Business, 2nd year

Assignment: Essay Examination Question

Consider the issue of comparable pay for comparable work. Analyze the issue; support your analysis.

 CNN video support is available for this chapter. Turner Le@rning

GETTING READY

LEARNER'S NOTEBOOK

Warm-up Activity

In your notebook, write about a time when you successfully persuaded someone to change his or her mind or to do something. How did you persuade the person?

Grammar Preview

Interactive communication communicates personally with an audience. In other words, it is writing that "talks" to the reader. Often, this type of writing tries to persuade the reader to do something. For example, an advertisement communicates personally to the reader to persuade him or her to purchase a product or service. (*Dillard's. We fit your life.*)

In college and university courses, you encounter interactive communication in various disciplines. In an English composition course, you analyze essays to see how the writing communicates personally to the reader. In advertising and marketing courses, you examine the techniques used in advertisements to involve and persuade consumers.

Interactive communication contains grammatical features such as questions and pronouns, especially *we* and *you* (*What's **your** idea of fun?*—cruise vacation ad). Writing that tries to persuade uses conditional sentences with *if* (***If** it's out there, it's on CompuServe*—commercial). Modal auxiliary verbs are also used to shift meanings and power relationships in different situations (*The one product you **should use** to style your hair*—hair product ad).

In this chapter, you will focus on several important features of interactive communication and writing that tries to persuade so that you will be a better reader and writer of these types of writing.

Introduction to Analyzing

In your college/university work, you will discover that analysis is very important. For example, when you look at a bicycle, you see the result of many small parts working together. If you wanted to know how that bicycle worked, you could take it apart and then put it back together, observing how each part fits into the whole. Then you could make some statements about how the parts fit together, and how the whole bicycle works. Your observations and conclusions would result in an *analysis*. Or, if you go to a party at your friend's house, and the party is not a success, you might analyze the parts of the party in order to discover what did not work by asking questions, and you might then summarize your thoughts and recommend changes to your friend for the next party.

In college courses, you might analyze a biology experiment, a poem, or a case study in business. For a biology experiment, you might dissect a frog, taking its organs from its body and studying each of them, observing the process of dissection, asking questions (where was the kidney? how did the heart work?), taking notes on the results, and drawing conclusions about your observations. If you were studying a poem, you might discuss the theme of the poem, look carefully at the writer's images or symbols and analyze its other poetic qualities, then evaluate why you think the poem was successful or unsuccessful. To analyze a business case study, you could break the situation into its parts (for example, the business organization, the clients, the problem, and the evaluation processes), ask questions about them, and study the answers to the questions, perhaps analyzing the advantages and disadvantages of several solutions to the problem. You might then draw conclusions and make recommendations based on your analysis.

The processes of analysis can also be applied to writing and reading. When you write a paragraph, you analyze your audience by asking questions about the audience (age? interests? what do they know?) so that you know better what to write and how to write it. When you read a textbook, you select the important parts to remember and ask questions about the content. When you read a classmate's paragraph, you notice its parts: the introduction, the body, and the conclusion.

Activity 7-1   Analyzing Student Problems

With a small group of classmates, read the following descriptions of problems that face typical college students. How would you "divide up" the problem in order to examine it? Which areas of the problem could you examine? What questions could you ask? What possible conclusion(s) might you reach after your analysis? The first problem has been filled in as an example.

1. *Problem:* Obed works 30 hours per week and takes four college classes, so he feels he never has time for fun.

   Questions to ask Obed: Do you have to work 30 hours per week? Do you have to take four classes at the same time?

   Possible Conclusion: Maybe Obed can take fewer classes or work fewer hours.

2. *Problem:* Olga has a nursing degree from her native country. She would like to work as a nurse in the United States, but she must first pass an English language examination and a nursing examination.

   Questions to ask Olga: _____

   Possible Conclusion: _____

3. *Problem:* Smita wants to purchase a personal computer.

   Questions to ask Smita: _____

   Possible Conclusion: _____

4. *Problem:* Ryo's parents constantly ask him where he goes and what he does. He feels that they treat him like an child.

   Questions to ask Ryo: _____

   Possible Conclusion: _____

The Grammar of Nouns and Noun Phrases in Academic Writing: Learning and Using Key Terms

In this chapter, you will analyze advertisements ("ads") by looking carefully at how each is put together and dividing each ad into its design parts. You will decide which advertisements are successful and which are not, and you will be able to explain why you have made that decision.

Notice that the key terms in advertising and marketing in this chapter consist of a single *noun* or a *noun phrase* (noun + other word or words).

- target
- appeal
- femininity
- idealized
- mood
- image
- portray
- ad
- discretionary spending money

Activity 7-2   Using Key Terms in Advertising and Marketing

To prepare for readings in the fields of advertising and marketing, learn the vocabulary that relates to these fields by completing the following sentences with the vocabulary words in the list above.

1. Advertisers _____ certain groups in their ads. For instance, they think about children when they develop advertisements for toys.

2. _____ is an abbreviation for advertisement.

3. Ads show _____, perfect people rather than real people.

4. Some ads are aimed at teenagers who have _____. In other words, teens sometimes have money to spend as they want.

5. Ads often _____ happy people having fun.

6. These ads _____ to us because we want to have fun, too.

7. The _____ of a man in an ad is one of manliness.

8. Women in ads often represent _____ and beauty.

9. Ads try to create a positive _____ that will lead us to buy the products.

FOCUSING

READING 1   ADVERTISING TECHNIQUES (ESSAY ON ADVERTISING)

ADVERTISING TECHNIQUES

Like all forms of communication, effective and successful advertisements have clear purposes and carefully targeted audiences. No one "ad" appeals to every person, just as no one product is appealing to every person. Some ads are focused on white, middle-aged males whose economic status is high; others target teenage girls with large amounts of discretionary spending money.

The major purpose of advertisements is to sell products. However, advertising is also a reflection of society—of behaviors, expressions, cultural expectations, and assumptions. Advertising attracts us because it demonstrates how we would like to act, feel, and be in many situations.

Generally, ads are idealized rather than real. We can identify the idealized values of a culture by studying its advertisements. For example, in the United States, idealized ads about happy families on vacation show people who never seem to get dirty or angry or sick, who are never frustrated by travel, whose children behave in remarkably generous and loving ways. Selling a product happens more easily if the ad portrays happy people having fun.

Many ads use this "feel good" approach to sell their products: not perfume, but femininity and quiet beauty, not sports cars, but images of manliness and womanliness that appeal to our ideal selves (the people we would like to be). If the product is linked in our

minds with those images, the mood and the message will lead us to department store shelves
or car dealerships.

In the United States, idealized women are often used in advertisements. Observing how 5
these women are used—their looks, gestures, body postures, expressions, and physical
placement—demonstrates several aspects of U.S. culture. For example, the culture of youth
in the United States is demonstrated by the overwhelming majority of women in ads being
under the age of 20. They often pout or coo in childlike ways, tuck their heads down and
look up immaturely, and have very slender, almost childlike bodies that are physically flaw- 10
less. In contrast, the idealized men in ads have often been portrayed as independent, adven-
turesome, competitive, and "cool."

Marketing Approaches

College and university marketing majors study techniques that help them present idealized culture. Here are some examples of these techniques.   15

Bandwagon: groups of happy, relatively ordinary (but really ideal) people (just like us) all
especially happy about the product, all "jumping on the bandwagon."

Testimonial: single rather ordinary (but really ideal) people (just like us) testifying to the
worth of a product, demonstrating how happy we will all be with that product.

Authority: a person of authority advises us to buy a product. For example, a doctor (or 20
someone portraying a doctor), looking authoritative and kind, testifies to the worth of a
medical product.

False authority: a person who is famous in one area advises us to buy a product in another
area. For example, a popular football player advertises the worth of women's hosiery, or a
famous movie star advertises a medical product.   25

Sex: an ideal mate is seen as the object of the ad. For example, beer ads may picture mini-
mally clothed women having fun with beer-drinking men; the underlying message is that the
beer helps the men "win" the women. Similarly, women are encouraged to buy products by
watching ideally beautiful women: if you buy this product, he will notice you because you
will become like the model.   30

Status: ideal people model expensive clothing or use elite-sounding products. The message
is that the product will lead its user to success and status.

Humor: some advertisements promote products with cartoons, amusing stories, computer
animations, and humorous characters. If the viewer of the ad is happy, that person will be
more likely to remember and to purchase that product.   35

Fear: sometimes frightening the viewer can be a powerful selling tool. For example, a burn-
ing house and a terrified family can sell smoke detectors.

Facts, statistics: usually used in combination with another technique. For example, if view-
ers understand and appreciate the facts they are smart enough to buy the product (a form of
status).   40

Often an advertisement will mix its messages in order to widen the appeal. For example,
a car ad might show a sexy woman lounging against the body of the car, while a man's voice
speaks about the car's power, performance, and precision (male terms). The driver in the ad
will probably be young and male; he will be ideally competent as he escapes the everyday

world through speed. The quality of the car reflects the quality of the owner. Eventually the 45 ad's message may link power and sex: "Pure shape, pure power, pure Z. It turns you on."

Design Techniques

In addition to the techniques for developing successful messages, designers of advertisements also focus on the "look" of the ad. The placement of pictures and words, the use of color and graphics, and the amount of white space are important in print ads. The answer 50 to the questions below is "It depends … on the audience, the purpose, and the product."

Does the ad look crowded? Should it? Why or why not?
Is a black-and-white ad as effective as a full-color ad? Why or why not?
What should the viewer see first when s/he looks at the ad? Why?
For television advertisements, music and movement are also important. 55
Should the music be quiet and subtle or loud and striking? Why?
Should the actors be loud or quiet? Why?
How much movement should there be? Why?

LEARNER'S NOTEBOOK

Analyzing Your Buying Habits

Think about a brand-name product that you usually buy (shampoo, ice cream, cola, etc.). Why do you buy that brand? Think about the ads you see for that brand. In what ways are they persuasive?

The Grammar of Interactive Communication: *You*

The purpose of interactive communication is to communicate with you, the reader. Therefore, one feature of this type of writing is the frequent use of *you* pronouns:

you   *your*   *yours*   *yourself*

Advertisers use these words to make their ads talk to you, the audience. The purpose is to appeal to you so that you can relate the product to your own life, and ultimately, buy it. The language of ads often includes *you* pronouns.

EXAMPLES

*A great party can last for hours. Shouldn't **your** coffee?* (Thermos Company, advertisement for an insulated coffee pot)

*This could be **your** 10 minutes of fame.* (Lawry's Foods, Inc., advertisement for Chicken Sauté sauce)

*When was the last time **you** dreamed in color?* (Flexsteel Furniture advertisement for sofas)

*Imagine **yourself** in a Mercury.* (Ford Corporation advertisement for a Mercury car)

The Grammar of Interactive Communication: *We*

Along with the *you* words, advertisers also use *we* pronouns:

$$we \qquad our \qquad ourselves \qquad us \qquad ours$$

These pronouns communicate to the reader that the company which made the product consists of real humans (just like you).

EXAMPLES

***We** even made the mirrors roomier.* (General Motors Corp. advertisement for a Chevrolet Blazer truck)

*Let **us** help you bring home the most important power of all. The power to be your best.* (Apple Corporation advertisement for a Macintosh computer)

> GLR   Refer to pages 217–236 in the GLR for more information on pronouns.

Activity 7-3   Identifying *You* and *We* Pronouns in Advertisements

Find five advertisements in a magazine or newspaper that contain *you* and *we* pronouns. Cut out the advertisements, paste them on sheets of paper, and circle the *you* and *we* pronouns in each ad.

Fill in the chart that follows with information about the use of pronouns in the ads that you have collected. Remember that companies use *you* and *we* pronouns to communicate that they (*we*) are human beings, just like *you*, the consumer. Discuss your answers with a partner or small group of classmates. Information about how pronouns are used in a sample advertisement has been put in the chart as an example.

Sample Advertising Text

Our restaurants are as great looking as our food. Good times you can taste and afford.
(Ruby Tuesday restaurant)

Pronoun Used	Who the Pronoun Represents	Purpose for Using Pronoun
our	Ruby Tuesday owners	To make the owners seem like humans, like the reader
our	Ruby Tuesday owners	To make the owners seem like humans, like the reader
you	the reader	To make you feel the ad is "talking" directly to you so you'll eat there
_____	_____	_____
_____	_____	_____
_____	_____	_____

The Grammar of Writing That Tries to Persuade: Using Conditional Sentences

Another feature of persuasive advertisements is the use of conditional *if* sentences. Here is an example:

If it's got to be clean, it's got to be Tide. (Procter & Gamble Company advertisement for Tide detergent)

The condition presented in this advertisement is that if you want your clothes to be clean, you must use Tide detergent. Often the condition in persuasive *if* sentences appeals to a certain audience.

> **GLR**   Refer to page 233 in the GLR for more information about *if* sentences.

Activity 7-4   Identifying Conditional Sentences

Look over the advertisements that you examined in previous activities on page 178. Identify and copy the conditional *if* sentences on another piece of paper. Then, for each *if* sentence, write a sentence that identifies the target audience for the *if* condition. Compare your analysis sentences with those of a partner or a small group of classmates.

READING 2   STUDENT-DESIGNED ADVERTISEMENTS

Advertisements can appear in a variety of places: on television or radio, in magazines or newspapers, on billboards, or on the Internet. Another common type of advertisement is the **brochure**, "a small, short, printed booklet describing a company's products or services" (*The Newbury House Dictionary of American English*). Brochures may contain multiple pages, but they commonly consist of one page of paper folded into two or more parts.

The following advertisements are examples of three-fold brochures. They were written and designed by students.

Activity 7-5   Focused Reading

With a partner or a small group of classmates, analyze the students' advertising brochures by answering these questions. Share your answers with your class.

1. Who is the audience for each ad? How do you know?
2. What is each ad's purpose? How do you know?
3. When you looked at each ad, what did you see first? Second? Why?
4. What pleases you about each ad? Why?
5. What is the most persuasive part of each ad? Why?
6. Does the ad use *you* or *we* words to appeal to the reader? Does the use of these words appeal to you?

A

For Someone You Love

Things you should know about Heart Attacks

SIGNS OF A HEART ATTACK

1. Central severe chest pain (crushing, not sharp) that is constant and lasts for several minutes
2. Chest pain moves through the chest to either arm, shoulder, neck, jaw, mid-back, or pit of stomach
3. Heavy sweating
4. Nausea and vomiting
5. Extreme weakness
6. Victim is anxious and afraid
7. Skin is pale, fingernails and lips may be blue
8. Extreme shortness of breath
9. Pain may be mistaken for indigestion
10. Any one or all of these symptoms may be present

HEART ATTACK

A heart attack occurs when there is not enough blood and oxygen reaching a portion of the heart due to a narrowing or obstruction of the coronary arteries that supply the heart muscle. If the lack of blood and oxygen is prolonged, a part of the heart muscle will die.

IF YOU SEE SOMEONE HAVING A HEART ATTACK

1. Place them in a comfortable position, but not lying down. Lying down flat makes breathing more difficult.
2. Loosen tight clothing, especially around the neck.
3. Keep the victim warm.
4. Calm and reassure the victim.
5. Call an ambulance (911 in most areas)

For more information:
American Heart Association of Wyoming
1329 Hugur Ave.
Cheyenne, Wyoming
(307) 632-1746

B

STUDENT INTERN PROGRAM

College of Business

REQUIREMENTS

- Advanced Business Standing (60 hrs. +)

  Completed or will complete prior to internship the following courses:

- Accounting 2020 (402)
- Finance 3250 (625)
- Marketing 3210 (621)
- Management 3210 (621)

  All students must submit one of the following to the Student Intern Office, Room 109A, College of Business Building by the specified deadline dates.

1. Student Intern Application signed by College of Business Academic Advising Office (Rm. 3)
2. A copy of transcript
3. Resume
4. A cover letter (addressed to the employer) for each internship

FIELDS

Accounting
Business Administration
Economics
Finance
Management
Marketing
Operations Management

INTERESTED?

Let us send you more information. Just fill out the following information and return to the address below.

Name: _____

Phone: _____

Address: _____

City: _____

State: _____ Zip: _____

Return to:

Business Assistance Center
College of Business
University of Wyoming
P.O. Box 3275
Laramie, Wyoming 82071-3275

(307) 766-2363

UNIVERSITY OF WYOMING

C

Beware of Colorado Tick Fever

What is Colorado Tick Fever?

Colorado Tick Fever is an acute viral illness characterized by fever, headache and body aches. Other symptoms may include lethargy, nausea, abdominal pain and, rarely, a skin rash. Typically, the illness lasts four to five days followed by apparent recovery, but then the fever and symptoms recur for another two to three days. Complete recovery usually takes two to three weeks. The disease is rarely life threatening, and infected persons are usually resistant to reinfection. There is currently no effective treatment or preventive vaccine available for tick fever.

What Causes It?

From 100 to 300 cases of Colorado Tick Fever are reported to the Colorado Department of Health each year Colorado Tick Fever virus, harbored in rodents, infects man through the bite of an infected Rocky Mountain wood tick. Adult ticks emerge in February or March and seek larger animal hosts including man for a blood meal that is a prerequisite for their reproduction. Illness will usually begin within six days.

Who Gets It?

Hikers are the most likely persons to acquire ticks and become infected with Colorado Tick Fever. Campers, fishermen, mountain residents, and those who work or visit the mountains during the months of March through July, or even into early fall, are at risk of exposure.

Prevention

"Tick checks" are the cheapest and most effective methods of reducing the risk of Colorado Tick Fever according to a study recently completed by the Colorado Department of Health. A tick check is simply the periodic checking and removal of attached and unattached ticks from one's body. These should be performed at two to three hour intervals while outdoors in the mountain environment. Tick checks can be done alone, but are more thorough if a companion or parent helps examine an individual's back and scalp. Tick checks are effective because ticks spend some time on an individual's body before actually transmitting the virus. An estimated 75 percent of Colorado Tick Fever cases could be prevented if everyone in the outdoor mountain environment used this method routinely.

Activity 7-6   Writing Assignment 1: Designing an Advertisement

With a partner or a small group of classmates, design a successful advertisement for a product. The product may be real or it may be imaginary.

Use a single sheet of paper.

Use some visual aid (a drawing, a photograph, etc.) and some words.

You may fold the paper in half or in thirds (like a brochure) if it makes your ad more effective.

Your audience for this advertisement is your classmates. Be persuasive!

Activity 7-7   Self-editing

1. Read your advertisement again. Does it say what you want it to say? Is it organized in the best way for your meaning and this particular writing task? Does it connect with its audience? Is it persuasive? Make any changes needed to improve the meaning of your writing.

2. Edit your individual sentences for the following, and correct any error(s) that you find. After you have edited for each of these features, check (✓) the box to remind yourself that you have done that task.

    ☐ check your vocabulary choices for words that have the most appeal to your audience

    ☐ if you used the pronouns *you, we,* or *I,* check to be sure that you used the correct form and spelling

    ☐ if you used any *if* clauses, check the verbs in both parts of the sentences

    ☐ if you used any proper names for products or organizations, check the spelling and the capitalization of the names

3. Rewrite your advertisement to make the corrections that you decided on while you were editing your sentences.

4. Prepare the advertisement in a draft format to show the style you and your partner or group plan to use in the final version. This is not the final version but a draft to show to the other members of your class to get ideas about making the advertisement as attractive as possible.

Activity 7-8   Peer Response

Exchange advertisements with another pair or group of classmates. With your partner or your group, analyze the ad designed by your classmates. Answer the following questions, and be specific in your responses.

1. What persuasive techniques did the designers use?

2. What is the most persuasive part of the advertisement? Why?

3. What suggestion(s) can you offer the designers to make their ad more persuasive?

4. Look at other advertisements designed by your classmates. Decide which ad you like best and why.

LEARNER'S NOTEBOOK

Analyzing a Classmate's Advertisement

Answer these questions in your notebook: Which advertisement designed by your classmates did you prefer? Analyze that ad. What was appealing and persuasive about the ad? Use specific details from that ad to support your ideas. Include the ad's purpose, audience, and graphics.

Analyzing Advertisements

To analyze advertisements, you can break down the content of the ads into three main areas: audience, purpose, and language.

When you consider audience, ask this question and consider these characteristics: Who is the audience for this ad?

- age
- interests
- gender
- economic status
- education
- social status

Think about the purpose of the ad by asking:

How is this ad selling its product? (More than one of the following ways may apply to each ad.)

- beauty of a person
- achieving social status
- humor
- fear/safety
- beauty of surroundings
- achieving economic status
- cultural association
- listening to an authority
- graphics (art): typeface, white space, layout, use of color, etc.

What language in each of these ads helps sell the product?

- *you* words
- questions
- modal auxiliary verbs
- informal language
- *we* words
- utterances (phrases, not complete sentences)
- *if* sentences
- contractions

Activity 7-9   Analyzing Advertisements

The designers of the following advertisements have one purpose: to sell their products. They use many of the techniques described in "Advertising Techniques" on pages 175–176.

Analyze the following ads with a partner or a small group of classmates. Look carefully at each ad so that you identify the techniques of the designers. Discuss your ideas with your partner or group.

Use the questions from page 183 to identify the audience, purpose, and language used in each of the ads.

A

B

The Grammar of Interactive Communication: Using Questions

Questions are an important feature of interactive writing such as advertisements. The question speaks directly to you, the reader, so that you will interact with the ad—and buy the product. Often the questions appeal to a common problem or desire of a certain target group. Some advertisement questions supply answers; others do not.

EXAMPLES

Have you driven a Ford lately? (Ford Motor Company advertisement for Ford Escort automobile)

Why reapply? Just press your lips. (Cover Girl advertisement for lipstick)

Activity 7-10   Analyzing Questions in Ads

With a partner, read the following questions and answers from advertisements. Identify the audience and purpose of the ad.

1. *Have you noticed the welcome mat is hardly ever out for smokers? For a great smoke, make yourself at home.* (Benson & Hedges advertisement for cigarettes)

   Audience: _____

   Purpose: _____

2. *Do you believe? Some people don't believe reduced-fat crackers and cookies can taste good.* (Keebler Company advertisement)

   Audience: _____

   Purpose: _____

3. *You promised yourself you'd be good after the holidays. Who knew it would be this easy? 60 heavenly calories.* (Kraft General Foods, Inc., advertisement for General Foods International instant coffees)

   Audience: _____

   Purpose: _____

4. *Is there a food for my older cat that's easy to digest? Absolutely.* (Ralston Purina Company advertisement for Cat Chow Mature cat food)

   Audience: _____

   Purpose: _____

The Grammar of Interactive Communication: Using Reduced Questions

Reduced, or elliptical, questions are commonly used in ads because they are more informal. The questions are written in the way that people speak, so they omit some words that would normally appear when people write the same question.

Feel like a donut? Maybe it's time for a Boost. (Mead Johnson & Co. advertisement for Boost nutritional drink)

Ever done it in the dark? (Mars Incorporated advertisement for Milky Way Dark candy bar)

Keep in mind that most academic writing is more formal than the interactive writing that appears in advertisements. Certain expressions that are used regularly in advertisements and in spoken English are not appropriate in academic writing. The GLR (GLR) explains how questions are formed in academic writing on pages 235.

Activity 7-11   Changing Reduced Question Form to Academic Form

With a partner, read the following questions from advertisements. The questions are written in informal reduced form. Rewrite them in the formal English of academic writing. The first question is answered as an example.

1. Reduced form: *Painful backache? Nothing is proven more effective or longer-lasting than Advil.* (Whitehall Laboratories, Inc., advertisement for Advil pain reliever)

   Academic form: _____ Do you have a painful backache? _____

2. Reduced form: *Remember the night you pulled this from your freezer? You could have pulled this from the refrigerator.* (Tyson advertisement for Ready-to-Eat Roasted Chicken) (Note: The advertisement contrasts the Tyson product with a photograph of a frozen TV dinner.)

   Academic form: _____

3. Reduced form: *Looking for an out-of-town home? Accurate, reliable information and pricing on out-of-town properties is right at your fingertips.* (Meredith Corporation advertisement for Better Homes and Gardens real estate guide)

   Academic form: _____

4. Reduced form: *Easy? It's in the bag.* (Reynolds Corporation advertisement for oven bags for baking meat, vegetables, etc.)

   Academic form: _____

The Grammar of Interactive Communication: Use of Contractions

Contractions are another feature of advertising language because they are more informal. Contractions make the ad sound like conversation, which is another way for the language to interact with the audience.

> **Feel like a donut? Maybe it's time for a Boost.** (Mead Johnson & Co. advertisement for Boost nutritional drink)
>
> **Don't let back pain stop you.** (Advil advertisement for pain reliever)

Be careful about using contractions in academic writing. Some teachers may not accept contractions in your academic writing because academic writing is more formal than the interactive writing that appears in advertisements. See page 238 in the GLR for more examples and information about using contractions.

Activity 7-12   Identifying Contractions in Advertisements

Look over the advertisements that you examined in Activities 7-3 and 7-9. Circle the contractions. Make a list of the contractions and next to them list the full forms of the verbs. Note the spelling and form of the contractions. Compare your lists with those of a partner.

Activity 7-13   Analyzing Advertisements

Read the following advertising texts. Which advertising techniques are used to persuade the reader? What language is persuasive? Who is the audience?

1. Golden Ideas (Source: Newspaper)

    Of course! What could be nicer than 14K gold earrings for that special lady on your Christmas list? Select from four equally attractive linen weave styles. She'll love the timeless looks. And any choice is a delightful addition to her dress or casual fine jewelry collections.

A.	**Rectangle earrings**	*orig. $115,* now **$57.50**
B.	**Shield earrings**	*orig. $105,* now **$52.50**
C.	**Circle earrings**	*orig. $125,* now **$62.50**
D.	**Drop earrings**	*orig. $85,* now **$42.50**

    > Ask about our convenient payment plan. Fine Jewelry.

Techniques: _____

Persuasive language: _____

Audience: _____

2. ALL YOU CAN EAT! (Source: Advertising brochure)

   Fresh Homemade SPAGHETTI. Fresh Homemade Spaghetti with our famous Sauce and Italian Bread. Every Monday Night—only $2.95. Carry Out, Delivery.

   Techniques: _____

   Persuasive language: _____

   Audience: _____

3. Woman Loses 85 lbs. in 171 Days with New Approach to Eating (Source: Magazine advertisement)

   Linda Boyce, a 23-year-old grocery cashier with a long-standing weight problem, is now a trim size 10 after a loss of 85 pounds within a little over five months, without resorting to drugs, injections, liquid protein, or highly restrictive diets.

   Linda now joins the thousands of Americans who have lost substantial amounts of weight thanks to a new approach to scientifically controlled natural food formulation developed by Weight Loss Medical Centers and known as Nutri/System 2000.

   After losing 85 pounds, Linda Boyce feels like a new person and is basking in the admiration of her family, friends and recently acquired husband. Formerly "shy and embarrassed" about her appearance, she now lives a full, completely normal life and is quick to give her rapid weight loss all the credit.

   Techniques: _____

   Persuasive language: _____

   Audience: _____

The Grammar of Writing That Tries to Persuade: Using Words with Positive Connotations

Another important feature of writing that tries to persuade is the careful choice of words. In advertising texts, for instance, words are carefully selected to present the product in a favorable light so that the reader or listener associates positive feelings with the product. Words are chosen for their positive *connotations*—the meanings the word carries in addition to its basic, "dictionary" meanings (*denotations*). Words with negative connotations may also be included to suggest the disadvantages of not using the product being advertised.

Examine how words with positive and negative connotations are used in the text of this ad for shampoo:

positive   negative

Neutrogena Anti-Residue Shampoo *revitalizes dull, lifeless* hair by removing residue that daily shampoos, conditioners, and styling products may leave behind.

positive   positive

Want proof? Use it once a week and your *favorite* shampoo will work *better* than ever.

Activity 7-14   Analyzing Connotations of Words in Ads

The following texts from advertisements contain words that carry either positive or negative connotations. Read the texts and, with a partner, circle words that produce positive or negative feelings. Mark the words as positive or negative. Discuss your answers with your class.

1. Wearever Air cookware

    Wearever Air cookware comes with this amazing guarantee. No more burning. No more burnt pancakes, burgers or eggs. No more sticking. No more scrubbing or scouring. Ever. Revolutionary, patented Wearever Air technology is the secret. It controls heat, so everything cooks evenly and completely, without burning. No more burning, sticking or scrubbing. Guaranteed.

2. Murphy's Oil Soap ad

    Beneath your rugs is a wood floor, filled with warmth and beauty, just waiting for Murphy Oil Soap. Murphy's gently removes the damaging, dried-on dirt that vacuuming can leave behind, helping preserve your floor's finish and its natural glow. So roll up your rugs and care for your wood the Murphy's way. You may not roll them back.

3. Toshiba Portable Computer ad

    Satellite, Satellite Pro, Portege and Tecra. Quite possibly the best reasons there are for buying a portable computer. Four distinct Toshiba notebook lines assure that whatever your needs, there's one uniquely suited to you. Toshiba portables offer uncompromised quality, and are recognized by the computer industry for technical superiority. And Toshiba has award-winning customer service and support.

LEARNER'S NOTEBOOK

Analyzing the Design of Ads

Choose an advertisement from a magazine. In your notebook, write a paragraph that analyzes the design of the ad by answering these questions: Does the ad look crowded? Should it? Why or why not? Is a black-and-white ad as effective as one in full color? Why or why not? What should the viewer see first when she or he looks at the ad? Why?

Be prepared to share your notebook entry with a small group of classmates.

READING 2   *SEVENTEEN* MAGAZINE (STUDENT SAMPLE ESSAY)

Activity 7-15   Focused Reading

The following is an essay written by a student about advertising. As you read, notice how the content of the three paragraphs is organized into a multi-paragraph essay.

SEVENTEEN MAGAZINE

Seventeen magazine is for teenagers. It is written especially for females, so it focuses on female fashion, males, and media. These are topics that males might not be interested in. The magazine features many articles about inexpensive products and pastimes, so *Seventeen* wants to attract middle-class students in junior high or high school. A lot of the advertisements present middle-class goods rather than expensive things. For example, there are ads 5 for Cover Girl mascara, Sears clothing, and Aspen perfume.

This magazine's purpose is mainly to make the life of a teenage girl easier: to make her feel better, look better, and have less stress. It tries to persuade teen girls that they are important. One of the articles talks about girls' contact sports like hockey and soccer becoming more popular. The magazine also informs girls about the latest fashions. One article 10 explains the "coolest" pajamas for a sleepover. And last, *Seventeen* tries to entertain its readers. There is a fiction story about a girl and her friend who always make fun of the people they see.

One advertisement that got my attention was for Eastpak backpacks. It was very dramatic, a picture of a skeleton lying in a desert wearing a backpack. The ad meant to grab the 15 reader's attention with something shocking—a skeleton. The words also attracted me: "Eastpak. Guaranteed for life. Maybe longer." The advertisement's message was clear. It showed that the backpacks would last a lifetime. It was appealing because of its drama.

Nadia Fellag
U.S.A.

Activity 7-16   Post-reading Discussion

1. Reread the *Seventeen* magazine essay. As you do, mark the essay by

    - circling any words that you do not understand
    - underlining (or highlighting) important ideas
    - writing your responses to the ideas in the margins
    - putting a plus (+) in the margin for ideas you agree with
    - putting a minus (-) in the margin for ideas you disagree with

2. Share your annotations with a partner. Discuss the ideas you both think are impor-
    tant.

3. With your partner, write a one-sentence summary of the essay. Be sure to include
    the main ideas of the essay in the sentence.

Activity 7-17   Analyzing the Organization of a Student Essay

With your partner, reread the student essay, *"Seventeen* Magazine." Discuss the organization of the essay by answering these questions: Is the essay organized in a logical way?
Are the paragraphs presented in a logical order? Why or why not? Share your ideas with
your class.

Activity 7-18   Writing Assignment 2: Analyzing a Magazine and Its Advertising

For this assignment, you will write a three-paragraph composition analyzing a popular
magazine and one advertisement from the magazine. Since this is multi-paragraph
composition that analyzes a magazine and not an advertisement, you will use different
grammar from that in the advertisement that you wrote earlier in this chapter.

　　　Choose a magazine. You may purchase a current popular magazine (like *Sports
Illustrated, People,* or *Elle*) or you may borrow a magazine from a library or a friend. Do
not choose an academic journal. Instead, choose a magazine that you can read, enjoy,
and understand. Bring it to class.

1. Audience Analysis:

    a. Look at the Table of Contents, the advertisements, and the cover of the magazine
        you have chosen. Using that information to identify and describe the targeted
        audience, consider

        - age
        - interests
        - gender
        - economic status
        - education
        - social status

b. Write a paragraph analyzing the audience that your magazine targets. Use details from the cover of the magazine and from three advertisements to support your opinions.

c. You may want to begin this paragraph with a sentence that introduces your magazine and its general audience:

Martha Stewart Living is a magazine for women.

Then you can provide specific details about the magazine's audience, using the magazine cover and three advertisements as support.

2. Analysis of Purpose

   a. From the Table of Contents select two or more articles in your magazine to read.

   b. Write a paragraph that analyzes the purpose of your magazine. Does your magazine

   • inform the readers? What about? _____

   • persuade the readers? Of what? _____

   • entertain the readers? How? _____

   c. Use details from the Table of Contents and the articles you read to support your opinions about the purpose of the magazine.

3. Analysis of Advertisement

   a. Choose one advertisement in your magazine that seems particularly interesting.

   b. Using the process described earlier in this chapter, analyze that advertisement.

   c. Write a paragraph presenting your analysis. To support your opinions, use specific detail to illustrate how the design and language of the advertisement make it appealing to the magazine's audience.

Activity 7-19   Self-editing

1. Read your composition again. Does it say what you want it to say? Is it organized in the best way for your meaning and this particular writing task? Make any changes needed to improve the meaning of your writing.

2. Edit your individual sentences for the following, and correct any errors that you find. After you have edited for each of these features, check (✓) the box to remind yourself that you have done that task.

☐ complete sentences

☐ correct punctuation

☐ correct verb tenses

☐ correct subject-verb agreement

☐ use of vocabulary appropriate for academic writing rather than speaking

☐ clearly organized and using appropriate logical organizers

3. Rewrite your composition, making the corrections you decided on while you were editing your sentences.

Activity 7-20   Peer Response

1. Work with a partner. Exchange compositions. Read all three of your partner's paragraphs. Then write in your learner's notebook about the paragraph you liked best. Use details from that paragraph to support your opinion.

2. Choose the paragraph you liked least. In your learner's notebook, list three questions or three suggestions that will help your partner improve his or her paragraph. Be polite and specific.

3. Discuss your opinions about those two paragraphs with your partner.

LEARNER'S NOTEBOOK

Writing a Composition

In your notebook, write about your experience writing a multi-paragraph composition. Was it more difficult to write a longer composition? Why or why not? How do you feel about your writing skills now? Is it easier to write now than when you began the course? Why or why not?

PUTTING IT ALL TOGETHER

FINAL WRITING ASSIGNMENT: ANALYZING A TV AD

For this assignment, you will write about an advertisement (known as a "commercial") on television.

Watch two advertisements on television. View each one several times and take careful notes about the ads. Then, choose one ad for the writing assignment that follows.

You will write three paragraphs about this commercial.

- Write a paragraph that identifies the audience for the ad.

- Write a paragraph that describes the advertisement. Remember that your audience has not seen the ad, so you need to be specific. Use details to describe the product and the way the product is presented.

- Write a paragraph that analyzes the purpose(s) of the ad. Does the ad

    inform the readers? What about? _____

    persuade the readers? Of what? _____

    entertain the readers? How? _____

LEARNER'S NOTEBOOK

Recording Notes

Write your notes about the two television advertisements. Begin writing your first draft of your paragraph.

Self-editing

1. Read your composition again. Does it say what you want it to say? Is it organized in the best way for your meaning and this particular writing task? Make any changes needed to improve the meaning of your writing.

2. Edit your individual sentences for the following, and correct any errors that you find. After you have edited for each of these features, check (✓) the box to remind yourself that you have done that task.

  ☐ complete sentences

  ☐ correct punctuation

  ☐ correct verb tenses

  ☐ correct subject-verb agreement

  ☐ use of vocabulary appropriate for academic writing rather than speaking

  ☐ clearly organized, using appropriate logical organizers

3. Rewrite your paragraph to make the corrections that you decided on while you were editing.

Peer Response

For this activity, gather all the writing that you have done for this course.

1. Choose your favorite paragraph. At the end of that paragraph, write a short memo to your teacher that describes why you like this paragraph. Be specific!

2. Exchange your favorite paragraph with a partner. Read your partner's paragraph and memo. Do you agree with the memo? Below the author's memo, write why you liked or disliked this paragraph.

3. Discuss the best parts of your paragraph and your partner's paragraph with your partner.

• •

Authentic Academic Assignments

L O O K I N G   A H E A D

With a partner or a small group of classmates, carefully read the following academic analysis assignments. Then do the exercises that follow.

Agricultural Economics: Third-Year Major Field Course

Assignment—Analysis of Articles: Four general subject areas will be addressed during this semester. These areas are:

1. industrial organization
2. product marketing

3. international trade
4. marketing in developing countries

You are to analyze five articles on the reading list not previously assigned. Not more than two articles should be selected from one subject area. Articles from popular publications are generally not acceptable.

The analysis should be only one page, typed, and single-spaced. It should contain the author, title, and source of the articles, including the library call number (if applicable). Give a brief summary of the content and analyze the article by presenting your evaluation of its strengths and weaknesses.

DISCUSSION

Answer these questions with a small group of classmates.

1. What is the purpose of this assignment? State the purpose in a sentence.

2. Write three questions might you ask the professor about this assignment.

Ecological Plant Morphology: Senior-Level Major Field Course

Assignment—Take-Home Examination: A plant species that you are studying appears to you to vary quite a bit in some set of morphological characters. Furthermore, this variation seems to parallel an environmental gradient.

1. Outline the differences you have observed.
2. Describe a simple set of experiments you could perform in order to distinguish the variations and analyze those differences (i.e., whether the variation is ecotypic or phenotypic).
3. If the variation is due to phenotypic plasticity, analyze the range of phenotypic flexibility in the characters.
4. If the variation is ecotypic, analyze the ecological significance of the variation.

DISCUSSION

Answer these questions with a small group of classmates.

1. What is the purpose of this analysis?

2. What are the advantages of this take-home analysis question over an in-class exam?

3. What is not clear about this assignment? Make a list of what you will need to know in order to complete the assignment successfully.

Marketing: Sophomore Year Introductory Course

Assignment—Case Study Analysis: Write a three-page summary of your analysis of macro environmental trends. This means you should analyze all of the macro environmental issues (government, technology, etc.) and the past, present, and future trends in each category. Evaluate the relative importance and interdependence of each category for the resulting complexity dimension in the Duncan model. Also evaluate the level of instability in the macro environment. You may obtain data from the case and outside library research for the same time period as the case.

Suggestions:

Do your own work. The assignment is an opportunity for you to demonstrate individual knowledge of theory. You will have plenty of other opportunities throughout the semester to demonstrate joint work.

Do not waste space. Typical space-wasters are introductory and ending paragraphs similar to those normally used in English writing courses. In other words, there is no need to tell the reader what you are going to do before you begin doing it. Just do it so clearly that it is a "no-brainer" for the reader.

- Edit your work several times.
- Edit for grammatical accuracy.
- Edit several times for readability.
- Edit each sentence to guarantee it communicates what you mean to say.

Make sure each sentence is worth saying—does it lead the reader logically to the next point you are making?

Write simple sentences using a first person mind-set. Many people write structures such as "Jack was hit by Bob," when the simple structure is "Bob hit Jack."

Analyze information using theories from lectures and the text readings. I am not asking you to "manage" the firm, so you need not indicate what the firm should do. The information you analyze will include both factual data as well as theory-based judgments about trends. In general, avoid value-based opinions, which are not a substitute for analysis.

Staple your pages together. There is no need for plastic covers. I stop reading at the designated page limit. Follow the format instructions on your syllabus. Do not try to get around this rule by using tiny print.

DISCUSSION

1. Is the purpose of this assignment clear? What questions might you ask the professor about this assignment? List them.

2. In what ways will this analysis differ from typical academic analysis papers? Describe these types of differences.

3. This assignment has many informal words and idioms. Discuss the unfamiliar idioms with your teacher.

4. What can you learn about the professor and his expectations by reading his suggestions for this assignment? Be specific in this audience analysis.

5. What problems do you anticipate the writer of this report will have? List three to five potential problems.

6. How might that student solve those problems? Take notes about possible solutions.

Grammar and Language Reference

The examples in this GLR come from the readings in the book, from academic text-books used in U.S. colleges and universities, and from other sources. They are authentic uses of English rather than "made-up" examples.

CONTENTS

Section 1 Grammar Common to All Types of Writing

1A   Sentence Types: Basic Terminology

In your academic work, you will read and write a variety of sentence types. Understanding how to use these sentence types will help you express your ideas and the relationships among your ideas clearly and logically. Correct sentence punctuation will help your readers understand your writing.

There are three important terms to use to talk about sentence structure:

A **sentence** contains a subject and a verb. Sentences must have correct punctuation so that readers can easily tell when one sentence ends and the next begins.

An **independent clause** is a complete sentence. It can stand alone.

A **dependent clause** is not a complete sentence. It must be attached to an independent clause to make a complete sentence.

1B   Simple Sentences

A simple sentence must have at least a subject and a verb. Another name for a simple sentence is **independent clause.**	<u>Every person</u> <u>has</u> two types of self. <u>I</u> <u>don't understand</u> the meanings and the pronunciations of words. <u>Practice</u> <u>is</u> the basis of all effective methods of improving self-esteem.
Notice that the subject and verb can be more than one word long. Simple sentences can be long and complicated, but they have only **one subject and one verb.**	<u>Every reader</u> <u>uses</u> different strategies to help him or her read more effectively. <u>Psychologists</u> <u>have offered</u> a number of different explanations about the concept of self. <u>Both men and women</u> <u>are expected</u> to wear head coverings.
Adverbial phrases are sometimes moved to the beginning of simple sentences to give them variety.	**This semester,** <u>I</u> <u>have to take</u> English 072 *(Speaking),* English 082/092 *(Reading and Writing),* and Data Processing 103 *(Computer Applications).* **Last month** <u>I</u> <u>took</u> my English 092 midterm. **In North America,** <u>the most common type</u> <u>was</u> the bark canoe.

Continued

| Sometimes writers use short simple sentences for **dramatic effect.** | I come to class very often, except when I am sick or get lost. I always <u>get</u> lost. |

1C   Compound Sentences

To make a compound sentence, you combine two or more simple sentences using a comma and a coordinating conjunction or you can use a semicolon to make the combination.

| The subjects are underlined once and the verbs are underlined twice in these examples of **compound sentences.** | <u>The teacher</u> <u>explains</u> very clearly, and <u>she</u> also <u>helps</u> all the students to work on the computer to correct their assignments.

<u>It</u> <u>was used</u> until the 6th century, and <u>some of its bridges</u> still <u>carry</u> traffic today.

<u>It</u> <u>was used</u> mostly by local traffic, so <u>little effort</u> <u>was made</u> to keep it repaired. |
| There are only seven **coordinating conjunctions.** Some students remember these words by using the word "FANBOYS." It is important to notice that the coordinating conjunctions need to have a comma when they are used to make compound sentences. The comma is written at the end of the first sentence. | F = *for*
A = *and*
N = *nor*
B = *but*
O = *or*
Y = *yet*
S = *so* |

Semicolons can be used in place of the *comma + coordinating conjunction*. However, semicolons are not used as much in academic writing as the *comma + coordinating conjunction*. You should avoid using large numbers of semicolons in your writing.

Compound sentences are not used much in academic writing. They are used when the writer wants to emphasize a **balance or parallelism** between two ideas or pieces of information.

| Notice how the writers of the examples use parallel structure for **dramatic effect.** | It would be disrespectful, **and** we would feel ashamed.

Now, some or all of these delicacies may not be your cup of tea, **but** they are not tabu to you. |

1D   Complex Sentences

Complex sentences are frequently used in academic writing. Most academic writing is made up of complex sentences with a few simple, compound, or compound-complex sentences used for special purposes. The basic sentence of academic writing is the complex sentence. A **complex sentence combines a simple sentence with a dependent clause.** Another term for a dependent clause is subordinate clause. There are three major types of dependent clauses—**adverbial clauses, relative clauses,** and **noun clauses.**	Example of a complex sentence simple sentence I have to try now dependent clause or subordinate clause because ESL is the basis for my later English studies.
Adverbial Clauses are like adverbs. They give information about *when, where, why, how,* and other adverbial information. Notice that the adverbial clause (underlined in the following example sentences) can come either at the beginning or the end of the sentence.	You slowly build an opinion of yourself adverbial clause <u>as you interact with other people.</u> adverbial clause <u>When I stop at the words I don't understand and look their meanings up in the dictionary,</u> I forget everything. adverbial clause The project was a large one <u>because the road was to extend the length of Italy.</u>
Relative Clauses combine with nouns to make complex noun phrases. They are underlined in the example sentences. Relative clauses (underlined below) begin with relative pronouns like *which, that, who,* or *whom.* See page 9 for more information about these noun phrases.	European engineers built roads from broken stone <u>which they placed in layers and packed into the soil.</u> These canoes, <u>which were "dug out" of large logs,</u> were most commonly used in South America and Asia. Old Order Amish people, <u>who live in small communities in New York, Pennsylvania, the Midwest, and a few parts of Canada,</u> cannot wear clothing <u>that is pretty, fashionable, vain or proud.</u> Continued

Noun clauses work like nouns in sentences. They are often used as direct objects and sometimes as subjects of sentences, as the underlined noun clause in the example sentences show. See page 227 for more information about noun clauses used with reporting verbs.	Lahey reports <u>that a recent study by Timothy Straman (1992) at the University of Wisconsin proved Rogers' ideas.</u> Some psychologists believe <u>that our cultural circumstances have a powerful impact on many fundamental aspects of intelligence.</u>

IE Compound-Complex Sentences

Compound-complex sentences are not used as often as complex sentences. They are probably used more than basic compound sentences because academic writers like the style that uses dependent clauses. A compound-complex sentence is a compound sentence that also has a dependent clause. There are **three clauses—two independent clauses and one or more dependent clauses.** Analyze the second example yourself.	When someone was sick, a family member rode by horse to call the doctor, and the doctor came by buggy. independent clause #1: complex sentence with adverbial clause When someone was sick, a family member rode by horse to call the doctor. adverbial clause when someone was sick independent clause #2 The doctor came by buggy.

1F Punctuation of Sentences: Basic Rules and Common Problems

Writers must understand six basic punctuation marks: the **period,** the **question mark,** the **comma,** the **semicolon,** the **apostrophe,** and **quotation marks.** Other punctuation marks are used but not as often. These six are used repeatedly in academic writing.

Periods and question marks indicate the end of sentences and questions. The reader expects these to be used to mark complete units. A sentence is presented as a unit that starts with a capital letter and stops with either a period or a question mark. Notice the punctuation in the example sentences:	Can you live with two selves inside you, the self and the ideal self? You can, but it may be difficult at times. What do you think about space travel? Of course, there are both advantages and disadvantages. <div align="right">Continued</div>

Commas, semicolons, apostrophes, and quotation marks are internal markers. They are used inside sentences for several different purposes: • A comma is used to separate parts of a sentence. • A semicolon is used to combine two or more sentences to make a compound or compound-complex sentence. • An apostrophe is used to make contractions and to mark possessive forms. • Quotation marks mark the exact words of sources and also mark words used for special meanings. The examples illustrate uses of all of these internal punctuation marks. Can you find all of them?	I remember a long time ago, when I was four years old, every morning I got up and asked my aunt, "Where is my mom?" At 2 o'clock, she closed the store, and she went to work at another place, which was a tailor school. My family and my friend's family came to the United States on the same day. Change is almost continuous; standing still is rare in human lives.

1G Basic Uses of Commas

Sometimes students have been told that commas are used to indicate a place where a speaker would "take a breath." Actually, in the United States, comma use is based on a group of rules about sentence punctuation. Six of these **basic uses of commas** in academic writing are given here.

Commas can be used to create compound and compound-complex sentences.	It was used in the 6th century, and some of its bridges still carry traffic today.
Commas can be used to mark the end of introductory phrases and clauses.	In bad weather, travelers sometimes leave their automobiles at home.
	If I don't try now, I think I can't try when I start to study English 101.
Commas can be used to separate items in a series.	Fifth Avenue in New York City is an interesting street filled with people, shops, and museums.
Commas can be used to separate parts in dates and addresses.	By 1839, the road had reached Vandalia, Illinois, where lack of money and political disputes stopped it.
Commas can be used to indicate transition words and expressions.	The name that stuck, however, was the National Road.
	Moreover, when rain falls so heavily that roads and cars are covered in water, people travel by boat.

Continued

Commas can be used to separate nonrestrictive relative clauses from the rest of the sentence.	One time a good friend of mine, who is a Muslim, and I were having a delicious dinner at some people's house.

1H   Basic Uses of Semicolons

Semicolons can be used to create a compound sentence or a compound-complex sentence without using a coordinating conjunction.	When God is happy with people He or She gives them the right amount of rain; if not, He or She gives them too much or none at all.

1I   Basic Uses of Apostrophes

Apostrophes are used to form **contractions** and to make the **possessive form** of nouns and pronouns.

You need to be careful about the use of contractions in academic writing. Some teachers will accept them in papers; other teachers require the full form. Generally, very formal writing does not use contractions. Compare these two passages. The first is very formal and the second less formal. Differences in audience and purpose lead to different formality levels—and to different decisions about using contractions.	formal scientific essay When you have scientific knowledge about a phenomenon, it means that you know, or at least you think you know, the explanation of that phenomenon. You **do not** just "feel in your heart" that **you are** right. informal academic writing from a personal past time narrative When my parents brought me to the hospital, the doctors said that I had pneumonia, and maybe I wouldn't survive.
Writing that gives advice often uses contractions.	By telling us what we shouldn't do, tabu helps us to know what we ought to do.
Apostrophes can be used to indicate possessive forms of nouns.	But the area was a long way from the Eastern cities and towns where most of the **nation's** business took place. Most of **America's** pioneers followed its six hundred miles across six states.

Continued

Its vs. It's. These two words are pronounced the same but they are grammatically different. Its is the possessive form of it. It's means "it is" or "it has."	**It's** really just not possible to pass on all math-related tasks to someone else. (It's = it is) Inns, taverns, and towns grew up along **its** length. (Its = belonging to it)

1J   Basic Uses of Quotation Marks

There are always two sets of quotation marks. They are put at the beginning and the end of the words being marked.

Quotation marks tell the reader that you are writing the **exact words someone else said or wrote.**	"Let us, then, bind the republic together with a perfect system of roads and canals. Let us conquer space," Senator John C. Calhoun told Congress in 1816. In 1805, a proposal was put before Congress for a road to connect East with West—"a road from Cumberland… within the state of Maryland, to the river Ohio."
Quotation marks are also used to mark words that are given **special meaning** or used in some unusual way. Sometimes the author has actually created a new word and marks it with quotation marks.	Captain Cook brought the word home with him, and it has become part of the English language as "tabu" or "taboo." They know what is "proper" behavior—what is kosher.

1K Punctuation Problems: Recognizing and Correcting Comma Splices

A comma splice is a compound sentence that has a comma but does not have a coordinating conjunction. A comma cannot be used alone to make a compound sentence. This example shows a comma splice incorrect punctuation:	I went places with her, she read stories to me before I went to bed.
To correct a comma splice, you can separate the clauses and make independent sentences.	I went places with her. She read stories to me before I went to bed.
You can add a semicolon.	I went places with her; she read stories to me before I went to bed.
You can add a coordinating conjunction.	I went places with her, and she read stories to me before I went to bed.
You can use subordination. This method might require other changes in the sentence to get exactly the right meaning.	After I went places with her, she read stories to me before I went to bed.

1L Punctuation Problems: Recognizing and Correcting Fragments

A fragment is a piece of a sentence—not a complete sentence. However, a fragment may *look* like a complete sentence because it begins with a capital letter and ends with a period. Using fragments is a feature of spoken English. Academic writing requires complete sentences. You need to learn the differences between the grammar of speaking and the grammar of academic writing.

The use of adverbial clauses as sentences is a common error in student writing.	Example of a fragment (incorrect) My father let me play, and my mother didn't like that. Because my punishment was too easy.
The simplest solution is to join the fragment to its related independent clause and to correct the punctuation.	My father let me play, and my mother didn't like that because my punishment was too easy. *Continued*

Sometimes it is possible to create two independent sentences by removing the subordinating word and making other changes to create a complete sentence of the fragment.	My father let me play, and my mother didn't like that. My punishment was too easy.

1M Prepositional Phrases: Adverbials, Complex Noun Phrases, and Prepositional Verbs

Prepositions are used in three ways in English. Recognizing these different uses can help in learning to use prepositions more accurately. For more proficient writers, knowing the uses of prepositional phrases is more important than learning the definitions of individual words.

Prepositions are often used to make adverbial phrases. These adverbial phrases tell *where, when,* and *how.* The adverbial prepositional phrases are underlined in the following examples:	But none of us would ever cuss like that <u>in a synagogue, church, mosque, temple, or shrine.</u> I would like to introduce to you one big tabu that existed <u>during the Communist system in the Soviet Union.</u> They love the land and feel a sacred obligation to work it <u>with their hands.</u>
Prepositions are very frequently found attached to a noun in a complex noun phrase. These examples are from the reading "What Is a Rainbow?" in Chapter 6. You might try finding some more examples of prepositional phrases in the reading "Scientific Method" from the same chapter.	*a spectrum of colors* *a glass of water* *a band of light* *the long side of the card* *the paper in this experiment*
Prepositions are also closely tied to some verbs and need to be learned as part of the structure of particular verbs. A few of the ones used in the reading on "Tabu: Hey Don't Do That" are listed here. (See the following WWW site for a list of these and other prepositional verbs: http://www.gsu.edu/~wwwesl/egw/index1.htm).	*refer to*: Tabu also can indirectly <u>refer</u> **to** what one should eat. *talk about*: Tongans <u>were talking</u> **about** marriage and other social relations, *look at, talk to*: and they listed people one should not <u>look</u> **at**, <u>talk</u> **to,** or wed.

1N   Noun Phrases and Relative Clauses

One of the basic features of academic writing is the use of long, complicated noun phrases. Many of these noun phrases are created by adding a relative clause to the basic noun. These noun phrases give detailed and exact information about the basic noun. Many of these phrases are technical language that must be learned and used in exactly the way expected in a particular academic field.

Relative clauses are sometimes called **adjective clauses** because they are like adjectives. They add more information to a noun to make it more exact and detailed. In the example, the noun phrase is underlined.	The Student Academic Computer Center is <u>a busy facility that offers students access to computers.</u>
Relative clauses are sentences that have been changed to make clauses. A relative pronoun is added; sometimes the word order is changed; and then the relative clause is attached to a noun. Notice that the relative pronoun has two jobs: (1) it connects the clause to the noun phrase and (2) it has a grammatical function inside the relative clause as the subject, object, etc. of the relative clause. The word *that* connects the relative clause to the noun strategies; the word *that* is also the subject of the relative clause.	Basic sentence: The Student Academic Computer Center is a busy facility. Sentence becomes a relative clause: The Student Academic Computer Center offers students access to computers. Subject of the second sentence replaced with relative pronoun: that offers students access to computers Relative clause to the noun added to make the complex noun phrase: a busy facility that offers students access to computers
Here are some examples of definitions from a physical science textbook. The relative clauses are in bold. It will be easier to memorize such terminology and use it on tests and in problems if you understand how the definitions are structured.	Light is a form of electromagnetic energy **that can be changed into heat, electricity, and other forms of energy.** A prism is a triangular piece of glass **that breaks up white light into a band of colors.** Chlorophyll is a green substance **that gives leaves their color.**

Section 2 Past Time Narrative

OVERVIEW OF PAST TIME NARRATIVE GRAMMAR

Past time narrative is writing that tells a story of something that happened in the past. Past time narrative is used to write personal **stories in the past.** It is also used in academic writing to tell about the history of a discipline, such as the history of medicine, or the history of a period of time, such as the Stone Age.

Past time narrative writing requires you to use several grammatical features that are frequently found in this type of writing. These features include:

- *past tense verbs*
- *chronological organizers*
- *proper nouns, and*
- *personal pronouns.*

Academic writing always includes features common to all writing, including complete sentences and proper punctuation. This passage from "My First Day at School" in Chapter 4 is an example of past time narrative. It shows how these grammatical features interact with each other in this type of writing.	At that time, I was living in Vietnam. My mother brought me to school when I was five years old. The name of my school was Phu Dong. The first day of school, I wore a white shirt with blue shorts. I also carried a new book bag. I was joyful when I saw many children my same age standing with their parents in front of the school.

2A   Past Tense Verbs

The **simple past tense** is the most frequently used verb in part time narratives. It is used to tell the basic story of the narrative. It is also used to give facts about the past and about things that happened in the past. In these sample sentences from "My First Day at School," all the verbs are in simple past tense.	When the bell **rang,** I and all my little classmates **came** into the classroom. I **was** afraid when I saw my teacher. She **was** a severe woman, about 36 years old.
Past progressive is used to emphasize the ongoing nature of some past event—that it happened over a period of time. Past progressive can also be used to write about two past time events that happened at the same time. Remember that this verb combines *was* or *were* with the *ing* form of the verb.	My mother **was standing** outside of the class.

Continued

Past perfect. Remember that this verb combines *had* with the past participle of the verb. See Appendix 1 for a list of the past participles of irregular verbs.	When my brother ran home to look in on me, I **had wet** my diapers.

2B   Chronological Organizers

An important features of narratives is the use of chronological organization. This means that the story is told in the sequence in which it occurred—following the chronology of the events. Chronological organizers are various types of adverbial words, phrases, and clauses that can be used to help the reader understand the sequence of events and how they relate to each other in time.

Words can be used such as *first, next, then.*	The *first* day of school, I wore a white shirt with blue shorts.
	The Old Pike *soon* became part of a national network of roads.
	My friend Phong helped me home, and *then,* my parents were scared, so they took me to the hospital.
Chronological organizers can be phrases such as *after that at first* *before that one day* *during the war ever since* *at that time 100 years ago* *in/before/after (a date or time)* *since the beginning of the century* *last week/month/year*	**Early in the 1900s,** however, another new vehicle—the automobile—brought the road back to life. Then, **in May 1978,** my mom became sick. **From the beginning of that day,** I really became a well-behaved student.
Clauses can be used such as: *until you graduate from college* *when he was young* *while they are in school* *before they began* *after it was introduced*	**When I was ten years old,** I spent one year in a resettlement camp in Thailand **after I had left my country, Vietnam.** Settlers had been moving west **since the early 1700s.** One day a boy on the other team kicked my leg **while I was running next to him.**

2C   Proper Nouns

Narratives of all sorts use proper nouns to give the **names of the people, countries, companies, events,** and so forth that were involved in the story. Learning about the forms of names and how they are used in writing can be a big challenge for writers from other countries and cultures that have different ways of forming and using names. The emphasis here is on learning about using the names of the people who are discussed in academic materials.

Generally, a person's **full name** is used first.	For example, psychologist **Judith Kearins** (1986) hypothesized that Australian aboriginal people possess better visual memory skills for objects than white Australian children.
Later in the passage, the person is often referred to by a **shorter form** of the full name. When the name combines a first (or given) name with a last (or family) name, the last or family name is used for the short version.	**Kearins** found that aboriginal and white Australian subjects used different memory strategies to approach the task.
Of course, people are also referred to by the **appropriate personal pronoun.**	She reasoned that excellent visual memory skills have allowed the aboriginal people to thrive in the different physical desert environments in which many of **them** live.
Many other forms of names can be found in academic materials, especially in history materials. You will need to notice carefully how these names are used so that you can use them accurately in your own writing, especially on tests that cover the material. Here are some examples of names from a physics textbook.	**Full Name** **Short Version** Stephen Hawking Hawking Albert Einstein Einstein Marie Sklodowska Curie Curie Sir Isaac Newton Newton

2D   Personal Pronouns

Because narratives can use numerous proper nouns to refer to particular people, places, events, companies, countries, and so forth, personal pronouns are another feature of this type of writing. The most difficult task for the writer is to be sure the reader knows exactly what the pronoun is referring to. If you are writing about an event that involves two or more people, keeping the pronoun reference straight can be a challenging task.

Personal pronouns have a **subject form,** an **objective form,** and one or more **possessive forms.**
    subject forms: *I, you, he, she, it, we, they*
    objective forms: *me, you, him, her, it, us, them*
    possessive forms: *my/mine, your/yours, his, her/hers, its, our/ours*

Pronouns must **match nouns in number**—singular with singular and plural with plural. This applies equally to proper and common nouns.	**White adolescents** performed better when the task material was manufactured objects than **they** did when the objects were natural. Finally, has your **ethnic community** influenced your approach to memorization and other intellectual skills—and, if so, how has **it** done so?
Pronouns must also **match the noun in gender.**	Also, **Phong** does not live near me although I sometimes visit **him** in Maryland.
Because academic writing so often refers to concepts and processes, the pronoun *it* is frequently used.	**The course** is called Freshman Composition because **it** is usually taken by freshmen and the main activity is writing.

Section 3 Informational Writing

OVERVIEW OF INFORMATIONAL WRITING

Informational writing is found throughout the textbooks used in your academic courses. This type of writing is used to state facts, data, theories, and definitions.

All of these features work together to make up the informational writing style, as you can see in the short sample below from "The Student Academic Computing Center" in Chapter 5.

- The most important feature of informational writing is the use of long, complicated noun phrases.
- Generic nouns are used to talk about groups rather than about individuals.
- Many pieces of informational writing use logical organizers to show the relationships among sentences, since this writing is organized by logical methods rather than in time sequence.
- Passive sentences are often used because this style focuses on processes and theories rather than on people and actions.
- Finally, present tense verbs are frequently used to make general truth statements. Since present tense is used, subject-verb agreement is a feature of informational writing.

The Student Academic Computing Center (SACC) is a busy facility that offers students access to computers. It is located in room B2-33. The facility consists of a main room with about 140 computers and two glass-walled side rooms with 60 computers that may be used for an entire class. The IBM computers are equipped with various software that is required in all disciplines at the college. Microsoft Word™ and WordPerfect™ are the word processing applications used in SACC and throughout the college. Technical aides are available to assist students who have difficulties.

3A   Complex Noun Phrases

Complex noun phrases put a lot of information into a sentence, so they are the most common characteristic of academic writing. These complicated noun phrases take several forms, but each complex noun phrase contains a main or core noun. Other words can come either before or after this central noun. The central noun in the first four phrases is given in bold type. Try finding the central noun in the last two phrases yourself.

Complex noun phrases from the sample of informational writing, "The Student Academic Computing Center":
1.   a busy **facility** that offers students access to computers
2.   a main **room** with about 140 computers
3.   two glass-walled side **rooms** with 60 computers
4.   **computers** that may be used for an entire class
5.   software that is required in all disciplines at the college
6.   students who have difficulties

OVERVIEW OF NOUN PHRASE STRUCTURES
noun + prepositional phrase   a main room with about 140 computers
noun + relative clause   a busy facility that offers students access to computers
noun + a combination of several other features   two glass-walled side rooms with 60 computers that may be used for an entire class
Another noun phrase type is often used in academic writing combines two or more nouns into a single phrase. For example, in the phrase *the Student Academic Computing Center,* the noun *Student* is being used like an adjective, but it remains a noun in form. Usually a noun that is used as an adjective will be singular in form.
Notice the nouns used as adjectives from the previous example of informational writing: side rooms   the IBM computers   word processing applications
Here are other examples of nouns used as adjectives from the same paragraph: a time limit   class work   college identification cards

3B   Generic Nouns

In informational writing, we often communicate about groups of people or classes of things rather than about particular objects or people. We do this when we are making generalizations or giving definitions. Generic nouns have four major types, illustrated in this chart.

• Plural noun without an article	**Scientists** in general use the following guidelines.
• Singular noun with the article *a* or *an*	**A picture** is worth 1,000 words.
• Singular noun with the article *the*	All fields of scientific study rely on **the scientific** method.
• Noncount noun without an article	**Science** represents **knowledge,** not simple **belief** or **feeling.**

EXAMPLES OF GENERIC NOUNS FROM ACADEMIC READING MATERIAL

Plural nouns without articles can be used to refer to classes or groups.	The negative and positive poles of a wet cell are called **electrodes**.
The with a singular noun is often used in technical writing.	**The electrolyte** is a moist paste inside the cell. **The telegraph** is still used today, but the technology has changed.
A or *an* with a singular noun is used to refer to one member of one example of a type. The meaning is about general types and not about particular instances. It means something like "one of this kind of thing."	In 1946, two American scientists were the first to build **a working computer.** **An electrician** is a person who is trained to install and repair electrical equipment.
A or *an* with a singular noun is often used in definitions. This definition of a battery is from an electronics textbook.	**A battery** is a source of direct current.
Noncount nouns are commonly used in informational writing. Remember that no article is used for this type of generalization.	In the future, **artificial intelligence research** may result in computers that can "think" like humans.

3C Logical Organizers

In contrast to past time narrative writing with its chronological organization, informational writing is organized in some logical manner. Recognizing the logic behind particular writing is a challenge for writers who come from different cultural and linguistic backgrounds. This chart provides a reminder of the vocabulary you can use to indicate the logical relationships among sentences, and the ideas within sentences, in your writing.

Meaning	Coordinating Conjunctions	Subordinating Conjunctions	Transition Words
adding	and		also in addition additionally moreover furthermore
cause/result	so	if when	as a consequence thus as a result therefore
choice	or nor		instead on the other hand
comparison (similarities)			by comparison also as well as similarly both ... and likewise
concession	yet	although even though	nevertheless in spite of despite
condition		if even if unless	
contrast (opposites)	but	whereas while	however instead on the other hand in contrast to nevertheless on the contrary
emphasis			as a matter of fact indeed in fact
example			for example for instance as an example as an illustration
reason/cause	for	because since as	

Continued

summary or conclusion			after all all in all finally overall	in conclusion in closing in summary in sum
time		then when before while after since until		

3D   Passive Sentences

Passive voice is a common feature of academic writing, especially in scientific and technical fields.

Passive sentences can be used when you write about:

- **things**—rather than the people who use them
- **processes**—rather than the people who do them
- **history of a discipline or a period of time**—rather than the people who were involved

Many verbs can have either an **active** or a **passive** form. The **active form** is used when the writers wants to focus on the actor or actors. Here are the two passive sentences from the reading "Scientific Observation" in Chapter 6. Sentences 1 and 2 are passive sentences. Sentences 3 and 4 are active sentences using the same information. Although they have many words in common, active and passive sentences are very different. Sentence 1 is focused on "rain"; sentence 3 is focused on "one." Sentence 2 focuses on a mini-replication of a phenomenon while sentence 4 is about the person who does the experiment. The writer of the original passage chose passive sentences to convey his desired meaning.

1. Passive	Rain **can be used** as a very simple example to illustrate the scientific and non-scientific methods.
2. Passive	But a mini-replication of this phenomenon **can be made** with a pot of boiling water and a lid.
3. Active	One **can use** rain as a very simple example to illustrate the scientific and non-scientific methods.
4. Active	A person **can make** a mini-replication of this phenomenon with a pot of boiling water and a lid.

In the first example, the writer is interested in rain rather than in the people who use it to illustrate the scientific method. So, *rain* is the subject and the verb is a passive form. In the second example, the focus is on the mini-replication of the phenomenon rather than on the person who might make that experiment.

PASSIVE SENTENCES IN ACADEMIC WRITING	
Passive sentences occur in different academic disciplines. Science and social science textbooks ~~contain~~ have many uses of the passive, as in the following passages.	A shiny plastic balloon **is taken** into a warm room and filled with helium. It **is** then **taken** into a cold room. When the balloon **is moved** from the warm room into the cold room it becomes smaller. This happens because when helium **is cooled** it contracts, or shrinks.
	Isaac Newton **was born** in England in 1652. During his extensive career in science, he made scientific discoveries in areas such as light, color, and planetary orbits, in addition to gravity. Newton **is** also **credited** with the invention of the mathematical branch called calculus. His most famous book **was called** Principia. Because of his many contributions to science and mathematics, Newton **was knighted** in 1705. He died in 1727.
	For example, we **are** all **shaped** by our culture and **must be understood** in that context. Culture **is defined** as the patterns of behavior, beliefs, and values that **are shared** by a group of people.

3E   Present Tense Verbs

Present tense verbs can be used in many different settings. They can even refer to future time in sentences such as "Also, I **plan** to study how to design and discover new agents and to test and improve old ones." In academic writing, present tense verbs are frequently used in the following ways:

Simple present tense verbs are often used for generalizations. These generalizations can be made both about personal and non-personal information.	I like my writing class a lot. Pharmacology is the science of detection and measurement of the effects of drugs or other chemicals on biological systems.
Present progressive verbs are used with action verbs to show that something is ongoing at the present moment. While this form is frequent in conversational English, it can also be found in writing about things that are happening now.	The United States **is** rapidly **becoming** a multicultural and multiethnic country.

3F   Present Perfect Tense

Present perfect verbs are not nearly as common in academic writing as the simple present tense. Present perfect verbs are used to make a connection between the past and the present. The present perfect is often used to introduce a topic and to show how the past is related to the present, as in these examples from *Psychology: An Introduction* by Benjamin B. Lahey:	The sociocultural perspective **has become** important in psychology in recent years. Many psychologists **have come** to believe that the basic course in psychology overemphasizes the ways in which people are the same and neglects the important message that the human race comes in a rainbow of varieties.

3G   Subject-Verb Agreement

Because present tense verbs are so common in academic writing, student writers have many opportunities to apply the rules involved in "subject-verb agreement." Subject-verb agreement is a relationship between a subject and a verb. The subject requires a particular form of the verb. Plural subjects require a simple form of the verb. Singular and noncount subjects require changes in the verb. In these examples, the subject is underlined one time and the verb two times.	Seventeen magazine is for teenagers. The magazine features many articles about inexpensive products and pastimes, so Seventeen wants to attract middle class students in junior high or high school. A lot of the advertisements present middle-class goods rather than expensive things.

STRATEGIES FOR SUBJECT-VERB AGREEMENT

Strategy 1. Learn to find the main subject word. You must know if the main subject noun is singular, plural, or noncount.

Strategy 2. Remember that subject-verb agreement occurs with

- simple present tense
- present and past of *be* (*am/is/are* and *was/were*)
- present perfect verbs (*has/have*)
- present and past progressive verbs (*am/is/are* and *was/were* with the present participle) and present perfect verbs (*has/have* with the past participle).

Strategy 3. Generally, if the subject has *s*, it is a plural subject, and the verb will **not** have *s*. A singular or noncount subject requires *s* for the verb.

Strategy 4. Generally, any subject that is not clearly plural is treated as singular. Infinitives are treated as singular: "To study is to learn." Clauses are treated as singular: "That he studied hard was shown in his high grades."

Strategy 5. Remember that some nouns end with *s* but are not plural. These include words such as *mathematics, economics,* and a few others.

<u>Nuclear physics is</u> the study of the nucleus of the atom and its changes.

3H   Subjects That Require Verbs with *+s*

Singular count nouns	<u>The quality of the car reflects</u> the quality of the owner.
Singular pronoun: *he, it, she*	"Pure shape, pure power, pure Z. <u>It turns</u> you on."
Singular proper noun	<u>Seventeen magazine is</u> for teenagers.
Noncount Noun	<u>Advertising attracts</u> us because it demonstrates how we would like to act, feel, and be in many situations.
Infinitives	
Gerunds	<u>Observing</u> how these women are used—their looks, gestures, body postures, expressions, and physical placement—<u>demonstrates</u> several aspects of U.S. culture.
False Plurals	<u>Mechanics is</u> the motion of objects.
linguistics *mathematics*	
news *physics*	

31   Verbs That Require *s*

Simple Present Tense	Some advertisement <u>promotes</u> products with cartoons, amusing stories, computer animations, and humorous characters.
Be	If <u>the viewer of the ad</u> <u>is</u> happy, that person will be more likely to remember and to purchase that product.
Progressive and Passive. Because *be* requires subject-verb agreement, progressive and passive verbs change to agree with their subjects.	<u>I</u> <u>am listening</u> to the sound upstairs. <u>Somebody</u> <u>is shouting.</u> In the U.S., <u>women</u> <u>are</u> often <u>used</u> in advertisements.
Present Perfect	In contrast, <u>ideal men in ads</u> <u>have</u> often <u>been portrayed</u> as independent, adventuresome, competitive, and "cool."

Section 4 Writing Definitions

OVERVIEW OF DEFINITIONS IN ACADEMIC WRITING
Academic writing includes many definitions for terms that students are expected to understand and to use in their own writing. Your textbooks in many university courses will contain numerous key terms must be learned and used exactly in your writing on tests, in reports, and in research papers.
Textbooks will often mark this important vocabulary in special print. Sometimes the words will be given **in bold type** or *in italic type*. Vocabulary you need to know is also sometimes listed in special sections at the beginning or end of each chapter.

| These examples are from textbooks widely used in the United States. | Hydrogen, oxygen, carbon, sodium, and chlorine cannot be broken down. All of these substances are **elements**. An element is a simple substance that cannot be broken down into simpler substances. |
| | The term **behavior** refers to all of a person's actions that others can directly observe. |

4A   Understanding the Grammar of Definitions

X is Y.	*Kinetic energy* is energy of motion.
X means Y.	*Amnesia* means the loss of long-term memory.
X refers to Y.	The term *behavior* refers to all of a person's actions that others can directly observe.
Y is called X.	A device called a *thermograph* turns the invisible heat energy into a visible picture.
Someone calls Y X.	This "heat picture" is called a *thermogram.*

4B   Complex Noun Phrases in Definitions

A common pattern for a definition is	A tabu is something that we shouldn't do.
noun to be defined +	noun to be defined: a tabu
verb (often a form of *be*)	verb: a form of *be:* is
the category (classifying noun phrase) with details that separate the noun from other nouns in the same category.	classifying noun phrase: that we shouldn't do core nouns: tabu = something

Section 5 Reporting Other People's Words and Ideas

OVERVIEW OF REPORTING
One of your basic tasks as a student is to report the words and ideas of other people in your own writing. In summaries, research papers, and other types of writing, you are expected to use words and ideas taken from other people's writing. To do this, you must understand and use the verbs of reporting and other related grammar.

5A   Verbs of Reporting

The following words can be used to report the words or ideas of a person or a research report. While in spoken language we just use the verb say/said, in academic writing we have a wider range of choices for more exact meanings and for stylistic variety.

admit	*confirm*	*insist*	*report*	*tell*
anticipate	*consider*	*mention*	*say*	*think*
argue	*deny*	*point out*	*state*	*understand*
believe	*doubt*	*recall*	*stress*	*warn*
claim	*find*	*recommend*	*suggest*	*write*

5B   Noun Clauses with Verbs of Reporting

The basic grammar for verbs of reporting requires a noun clause as the direct object.
    Notice that the formality of academic writing requires the use of "sequence of tense." The noun clause is in bold.

She said **that she was an accounting major.**

Sequence of tense means that the verb in the clause changes to match the verb in the main verb phrase. Also, pronouns have to be changed to fit the new context. Generally, verb changes happen in the following patterns:

- simple present tense becomes simple past tense
- simple past tense becomes past perfect
- *will* becomes *would*
- *can* becomes *could*

Continued

Direct Speech (Actual Words)	Reported Speech
"My department **had** 25 full-time faculty members in Fall 1996."	She **said** that her department **had had** 25 full-time faculty members in Fall 1996.
"I **didn't know** how to use a computer before coming to the U.S."	He told us that he **had not known** how to use a computer before coming to the U.S.
"I **will** transfer to Drexel University next year."	She reported that she **would transfer** to Drexel University next year.
However, sequence of tense is often not followed if the writer thinks the change would alter the meaning of the reported words. For example, simple present tense is often kept in statements of generalizations, and *will* is often kept for future time meanings since the change to *would* could imply that the meaning is conditional.	The department chair **said** that his department **has** 1,000 students. She **said** that it **will take** her four years to graduate.

5C   Punctuation for Exact Quotations

Quotation marks are used to tell your reader that you are writing **the exact words** someone else said or wrote. Notice the capitalization and the commas in the examples.	Russell says, "It's hard to study accounting and work at the same time." "It's hard to study accounting and work at the same time," Russell says. "It's hard to study accounting," Russell says, "and work at the same time."

Section 6 Stating Opinions and Trying to Persuade

OVERVIEW OF WRITING THAT TRIES TO PERSUADE

All writing can be called "persuasive," since the writer wants to **persuade** the reader that the information in his or her writing is accurate. However, some kinds of writing have persuasion as their main purpose. For example, *advertisements* try to persuade a reader or viewer to buy a product or service.

Writing, such as advertising, that tries to persuade typically contains several features. It uses structures to control the strength of generalizations so that the claims being presented are not seen as too strong. Writing to persuade also uses conditional *(if)* sentences.	So if you want the ultimate PC experience, just remember one little number, www.intel.com.

6A   Adverbs of Frequency Used to Limit the Strength of Generalizations

Adverbs of frequency are those words that are used to indicate **how often something happens.** They range from *always* at the top of the scale to *never* at the bottom of the scale.

always	*sometimes*
frequently	*seldom*
often	*never*
usually	
generally	
rarely	

Academic writers often use one of the adverbs of frequency to **limit the strength** of a generalization. You will seldom find words as strong as *always* or *never* in academic writing. If such strong words are used, the writer must have very strong evidence to support such a statement. Here are some examples to show how these words are used. Think about what the sentences would mean without the adverb. Surely they would be much too strong and would not persuade a careful reader.	*Often,* the textbooks contain collections of readings. *Sometimes* I look at my classmates' assignments.

6B   Quantifiers and Other Words of Measurement Used to Limit the Strength of Generalizations

Academic writers seldom use words like *all, none* or *no* because they make such **strong generalizations.** If these words are used, the writer must have very strong evidence to support the statements. Otherwise, the reader will not be persuaded by what is called "overgeneralization."

many	*a lot of*	*a few*
most	*a great deal of*	*few*
some	*a number of*	*a little*

Analyze the ways that these words are used in the examples. How would the sentences change if they were removed?	In *many* states in the United States, *some* stores have a sign on the door in summer that says, "No shirt, no shoes, no service."
	In *almost all* societies, covering certain areas of the body is considered essential. In *most* groups, publicly baring of the reproductive organs is tabu, and they must be covered.

6C   Modal Auxiliaries Used to Limit the Strength of Generalizations

Academic writing often includes general statements to explain events or situations. Writers use modal auxiliary verbs in such statements to show that the explanation is **possible** or **reasonable.**

could *may* *might* The writer presents **reasonable explanations.** However, other explanations are possible.	As you gaze spellbound at the largest home in America, you *may* find yourself able to utter but a single word: "Wow."
can The writer expresses a **possibility.** *Can* also means that an action is allowed or is within the capacity of a person or machine or system. These statements show a **stronger certainty** than statements using *could, may,* or *might.*	You *can't* buy love and happiness. But you *can* rent it for a weekend.
should *ought to* The writer gives a good explanation and expects that it is **highly likely** to be true.	You *should* see a difference in 10 days. Continued

must *have to* The writers give a very strong explanation with **little room for doubt.**	Quite simply, you no longer *have* to go out for food that's out of this world.
will The writer has almost no doubt. This is a statement of **certainty.** This use of *will* is **not about future** time but **about every time.**	On an American cruise, you*'ll* spend seven days exploring five ports of call on four islands.

6D   Other Uses of Modal Auxiliaries in Academic Writing: Giving Advice to Readers

Academic writing can include **recommendations and advice.** In this type of writing, the writer selects modals to show the strength of the advice. Also, the strength of the advice depends on the power relationship between the writer and the reader: the writer needs to have high enough status or appropriate academic standing to give advice to the reader.

can *could* This is the **weakest level** of advice. The writer means only that these are the possible choices.	Blankets of fiberglass *can be* inserted between beams in floors and ceilings.
may *might* These modals suggest **choices** and options. Readers may choose to accept the advice or to reject it.	Why *might* cryogenic surgery *be* preferable to ordinary surgery?
should *ought to* The writer believes that this is **very good advice** or, that this action is the responsibility of the reader.	How *should* the windows in a house *be* positioned if you want to heat the house using passive solar heating?
must *have to* The writer means that the action is required and that **no choices** are given. The writer implies that the punishment for not taking the advice is severe.	The engine of a car *must be* kept from getting too hot. <div align="right">Continued</div>

will This is the **strongest possible advice.** In fact, it is so strong that few people can use this modal to give advice.	
command forms of verbs The next higher step in strength is the **command.** The writer tells the reader what to do.	*Describe* how heat travels through empty space.

6E   Conditional *(If)* Sentences

Conditional sentences contain an *if*-clause and a main clause. The *if*-clause gives the cause. The main clause gives the result. Various verbs can be used depending on the meaning. Conditional sentences can be used to give advice. The main clause is a command.	**If** you want better living at real-life prices, come to IKEA.
The main clause can have different modals depending on the strength of the information. *Must* means that the rules for doing statistical studies require a random sample. *Will* means that the writer's evidence strongly predicts the result.	If you love unspoiled beaches, unhurried golf, and landing the "big" one, we've got your number. If you're looking for a durable chair that looks great, you've come to the right place. I hang my bicycle on the wall. If anyone asks, I just tell them it's modern art.

6F   Connotations of Words

Writers who try to persuade choose their words carefully in order to present the exact meaning that will relate their desired message. They choose a word because of its **connotation,** or the **meaning** that the word carries in addition to its basic "dictionary" meaning. Some words have *positive* connotations; they make you think of good things. Other words have *negative* connotations; they make you think of bad things. This careful choice of words is found in academic and other writing that presents an opinion, a view, or a message.

Examine how words with positive and negative connotations are used in the text of these advertisements:

Sheer without fear. Beautifully sheer, deceptively strong.
                    —advertisement for women's hosiery

The experience is simply immeasurable. Your first glance of Biltmore House is, quite literally, breathtaking.
                    —advertisement for a hotel

Section 7 Interactive Communication in Writing

AN OVERVIEW OF INTERACTIVE COMMUNICATION: SPEAKING VS. WRITING

In conversations, we often ask questions, refer to the other people in the conversation as *you*, and talk about *I* and *we*. There are many other characteristics that make a conversation different from writing—fragments, informal vocabulary, and more.

Writers sometimes use features of conversational grammar in academic writing. This style reaches out to, and attempts to interact with, the reader. Very frequently you will find academic writers using questions and the pronouns *you*, *we*, and *I*.

Notice how this writer combines questions and personal pronouns with otherwise formal academic writing.

Can you live with two selves inside you, the self and the ideal self? You can, but it may be difficult at times. First, you may feel uncomfortable if there is a great difference between the person you are and the person you wish to be.

Note: Use of contractions is a frequent feature of "interactive" writing. See Section 1B on the use of apostrophes for more information and for examples.

7A   Using Questions

In writing, the use of questions differs from their use in speaking in three ways: (1) the writer both asks and answers the questions; (2) the purpose of the questions is often to help structure or organize the writing; and (3) the questions often signal key points or key pieces of information.

> What will you do today? NewCom and the Internet make it easy.
>
> What's on TV? Or should that be "What is your TV on?"

Questions can be used to structure an entire piece of writing. After the question, the author gives an answer.	How long has it been since you had a big, hot, steaming bowl of Wolf brand chili? Well, that's too long. What does it mean to be conscious? Clearly it has something to do with being in a state of awareness.
Sometimes questions in informal writing appear in reduced form, as they do in conversations.	Looking for a data compression utility for Windows? There's only one choice. Tight space? This drop-leaf table folds in half. Hard to believe? The price for this dining set is only $99.
In formal writing, the same questions would read this way.	Are you looking for a data compression utility for Windows? Do you have tight space? Is it hard to believe?

7B   *You, We,* and *I*

You, we, and *I* are used in academic and other types of writing to give some of the **flavor of conversation** to the written material. Examples are given here to show how writers have used these pronouns effectively.

When giving advice, writers often speak directly to the reader as *you.*	How *you* look at things can profoundly affect what *you* see.
Writers sometimes combine questions with *you.*	*You* use a word processor every day. Shouldn't *you* use the best?
In writing that tries to persuade, the pronouns *you, I,* and *we* are used to catch the reader's attention, as in these advertising statements aimed at persuading the reader to purchase a product or service.	Try it. See what it can do for *you.* You'll find that the best thing about the LTE-5000 is what *you* make of it. At Compex, *we* take the extra step in quality assurance—testing every product *we* ship. *I* lost 89 pounds in just 10 months, and *I* have kept the weight off for a year now.

7C   Using *I* in Academic Writing

Some writers think that they should never use the pronoun *I* (and its forms, including *me, my,* and *mine*) in academic writing, but this is not always true. Personal narratives require the use of personal opinions and personal evidence which feature the use of *I* pronouns.

Here is a passage taken from Chapter 5 to show how a writer uses *I* in academic writing.

> The Counseling Center is a busy place that contains experts and information about college degrees and careers. Outside the center, there are glass cabinets with job postings and posters that announce workshops and job fairs. As *I* walked through the door last week, *I* saw racks of brochures on both sides of the entrance.

7D   Informal Vocabulary

Vocabulary in writing is generally more formal than the vocabulary we use in speaking. However, interactive writing may include less formal vocabulary when its purpose is to get readers **to interact** with the writing, as in these examples of advertising texts: Notice that in the first sentence, the writer uses the informal verb form *Got* rather than the more formal *Do you have.* What are more formal equivalents of the bold-faced words in the second and third examples?

Got a lot of empty wall space to fill up, but can't quite afford any Van Gogh originals? No problem.

Teachers, and students, for that matter, like the Macintosh because it makes learning more interactive and fun. We all know that the more engaged *kids* are, the more likely they are to be learning.

Choosing a computer can be *tough.* So do what your *kids* do when they have a *tough* question: Ask a teacher?

Student writers should be careful not to use spoken, slang expressions in formal academic writing, except in writing that includes quotations of direct speech.

INFORMAL VOCABULARY THAT IS GENERALLY INAPPROPRIATE IN ACADEMIC WRITING

Spoken Vocabulary	Possible Written Equivalents
kid	*child*
mom	*mother*
dad	*father*
stuff	*things, items*
great	*good, pleasant*
lots of	*many*
okay	*acceptable, appropriate*
got	*have, bought*
guy	*man*
tough	*difficult, strong*
pretty (as an adverb)	*very, relatively*
neat, nice, fun	*enjoyable*
a little bit	*a little*
you know, well (as connectors)	*(none—leave them out)*
really, real (as an adverb)	*very*

7E   Using Contractions

Contractions are commonly used in interactive writing because the writer wants the writing **to "speak" personally** to the reader. In this example, an advertiser uses contractions to make the writing sound informal and conversational.	Text from a magazine advertisement: There's so much to see and do in Texas, you'll need plenty of fuel to keep you going.
You need to be careful about the use of contractions in academic writing, however. Some teachers will accept them in papers; other teachers require the full form. Generally, very formal writing does not use contractions. Compare these two passages. The first is very formal and the second less formal. Differences in audience and purpose lead to different formality levels—and to different decisions about using contractions. Notice that the writer of "Tabu: Hey Don't Do That" in Chapter 3 did not use contractions in every sentence but mixed contractions with full forms.	Formal academic writing from a textbook: Density does not depend on the size or shape of a substance. Informal academic writing from a paragraph about tabus: According to this tabu, people **couldn't** say and think bad things about the political system in the Soviet Union. The government was afraid of people's criticisms.
Writing that gives advice often uses contractions in commands as in the second example.	**Don't** take things too seriously.
Its vs. *It's*. These two words are pronounced the same but they are grammatically different. *Its* is the possessive form of "it" (as in second example). *It's* means "it is" or "it has" (as in first example).	**It's** all the clean sensitive skin needs. **Its** native seascape is magnificent, featuring wide flat stretches of sand and soaring dunes.

Section 8 Basic Grammar Terminology: Learning How to Talk About Your Sentences

These are words that students and teachers use often when they talk with each other about the grammar of student writing. These charts provide an overview of the uses of these grammar structures in sentences. The charts do not teach you how to use the grammar, but provide examples of the uses of the basic vocabulary for talking about English grammar. The topics are presented in alphabetical order. Only the terms most likely to be used by teachers or textbooks are given here.

8A   Adjectives

Adjectives are words like *happy, important,* and *colorful.* Adjectives are used in sentences in two ways: They combine with nouns in noun phrases, and they can be in the third position in a sentence to give information about the subject of the sentence.

Adjectives in **noun phrases**	a **new** book bag a **well-behaved** student **savory** herbs **raw** fish
Adjectives in the **complement** of a sentence	At this time, I was **afraid** when I saw my teacher.
Most adjectives have **comparative** forms.	These are words like *happier* and *happiest* or *more important* and *most important.*

8B　Adverbs and Adverbials

Adverbs are words that give **information about time and place.** They answer questions such as *when, where, why,* and *how.*

Single words that have this grammar are called **adverbs** *(sometimes).* 　　Groups of words that have this grammar are called **adverbials.** 　　There are adverbial phrases and adverbial clauses *(in class, when the bell rang).*	*Sometimes* I get lost. Prepositional phrase used as an adverbial phrase: I obeyed the teacher, and I did not do anything wrong *in class.* adverbial clause *When the bell rang,* I and all my little classmates came into the classroom.

8C　Articles and Determiners

Articles—*a, an,* and *the*—are often used in noun phrases. Sometimes the articles are described as determiners. The **determiners** are a larger group that also includes *this/that, these/those, each, much, no, another, some,* and several other words. The personal pronouns can also be used as determiners.

some	students
this	tabu
my	son
another	thing
a	child
a	decision
the	self
her	exam

8D   Auxiliary Verbs

English verbs are either simple single words, or they combine two or more words to make the verb. For example, present and past progressive verb tenses combine a form of *be* with the *-ing* form of the verb. In this situation *be* is called the **auxiliary verb.** Sometimes you will hear the term **helping verb.** This just another name for the auxiliary verb.	simple present tense **study or studies** auxiliary verb + main verb (present perfect) **has studied** simple past tense **studied** auxiliary verb + auxiliary verb + main verb (present perfect + progressive) **has been studying** auxiliary verb + main verb (present progressive) **is studying** auxiliary verb + main verb (a passive verb) **is required**
Questions and negatives can also require *do, does,* or *did* as an auxiliary verb.	*Does* your mood *change* in a second? I *didn't break* my leg. I was lucky.
Modal or **modal auxiliary** is the name for the words *will, would, can, could, shall, should, may, might, must.*	*One-A-Day,* every day, *will help* keep you strong from the inside out.

8E   Comma Splices

A **comma splice** is a compound sentence that has a comma but not a coordinating conjunction. A comma cannot be used alone to make a compound sentence. Many teachers consider this a very serious error.	My aunt was married, she didn't have children. I went places with her, she read stories to me.
To correct a comma splice, you can separate the clauses and make independent sentences.	My aunt was married. She didn't have children. I went places with her. She read me stories.
You can add a **semicolon.**	My aunt was married; she didn't have children. I went places with her; she read me stories. <div align="right">Continued</div>

You can add a **coordinating conjunction.**	My aunt was married, but she didn't have children. I went places with her, and she read me stories.
You can use **subordination.** This method might require other changes in the sentences to get exactly the right meaning.	Even though my aunt was married, she didn't have children. After I went places with her, she read me stories.

8F   Complements

The complement **describes or renames** the subject. This structure is often used in definitions of terminology. Complements are often nouns, noun phrases, or adjectives.	My favorite teacher <u>was</u> **Mrs. Hedayati.** In fifth grade, I <u>was</u> **very lazy.** A tabu <u>is</u> **something we shouldn't do.**
A **linking verb** connects the complement to the subject. These are verbs like *be, become, seem, taste, look, feel* and others. (A list of linking verbs is on the WWW at http://www.gsu.edu/~wwwesl/egw/vanassch.htm).	Now that we <u>are</u> **older,** we <u>look</u> **different,** our personalities <u>are</u> **different,** and we don't dress alike. He <u>felt</u> **sorry for me.**

8G   Conjunctions

The two most frequently used kinds of conjunctions are **coordinating conjunctions** and **subordinating conjunctions.** (See http://www.gsu.edu/~wwwesl/egw/bryson.htm for more details on conjunctions.)

Coordinating conjunctions *for, and, nor, but, or, yet, so* are used to combine words and phrases. They are also used to make compound sentences and compound-complex sentences. The most common are *and, but, or,* and *so.*	*And* used to connect two nouns for the subject: My friend **and** I went to the park to play soccer. *And* and *but* used to make a compound sentence: She was angry **and** she wanted to hit me, **but** she couldn't do it.
Subordinating conjunctions are used to make complex sentences and compound-complex sentences. Subordinating conjunctions create units that are called **subordinate clauses** or **dependent clauses.**	Complex sentence with a subordinate clause using *when*: It was wonderful **when I was a child.**

8H   Fragments

A fragment is a **piece of a sentence**—not a complete sentence. However, a fragment may look a complete sentence because it begins with a capital letter and ends with a period.

Using fragments is a feature of spoken English. Academic writing requires complete sentences. Many fragments would be correct in speaking but they must be changed into complete sentences in writing. The use of adverbial clauses as sentences is a **common error** in student writing. In the examples, the fragment is an adverbial clause separate from its sentence.	I will study all of these courses. **Because I want to transfer to a four-year university to attain my major or goal.** My aunt died. **When I was 18 years old.**
The simplest solution is to **join the fragment** to its related independent clause and to correct the punctuation. See how the fragments in the first set of examples are corrected here.	I will study all of these courses because I want to transfer to a four-year university to attain my major and goal. My aunt died when I was 18 years old. <div align="right">Continued</div>

| Sometimes it is possible to **create two independent sentences** by removing the subordinating word and making other changes to create a complete sentence from the fragment. | I will study all of these courses. Then, I want to transfer to a four-year university to attain my major and goal. |

8I   Infinitives

| An **infinitive** is the combination of *to* + verb. Infinitives are used in four major ways: as direct objects, as adverbials, with nouns, and with adjectives. The examples illustrate, in order, an infinitive as the direct object, an infinitive as an adverbial to tell why, an adjective + infinitive, and a noun + infinitive. | After one year, my parents decided **to move to America.**

I am here at the Community College of Philadelphia **to study English.**

It was **difficult to tell** my twin sister Liz and me apart when we were children.

a list of instructions for the **computer to follow** |

8J   Nouns

A noun is a word like *student, computer, car, child,* or *vocabulary* used in a sentence as subject or object. The nouns in these sentences have been marked in **bold.** See page GLR 23 for more information.

A **student** needs a **computer.**	**Students** need **computers.**
A **child** should not have a **car.**	**Children** should not have **cars.**
Vocabulary is often on **tests.**	**Students** learn **vocabulary** for **tests.**

| **Count nouns** have singular or plural forms. Regular count nouns form their plurals by adding *"s"* for the spelling. Irregular count nouns have some other way to form the plural. The first three nouns are regular; the next three are irregular. (See http://www.gsu.edu/~wwwesl/egw/susan.htm and also http://www.gsu.edu/~wwwesl/egw/crump.htm for information on how to spell regular and irregular noun forms.)   Continued |

COUNT NOUNS HAVE TWO FORMS

Singular count noun	**Plural count noun**
student	*students*
computer	*computers*
car	*cars*
child	*children*
woman	*women*
knife	*knives*

Noncount nouns are neither singular nor plural. They cannot be used with *a* or *an*; *s* is not added to make a plural. (See http://www.gsu.edu/~wwwesl/egw/sansom.htm for more information on count and noncount nouns.)

NONCOUNT NOUNS HAVE ONLY ONE FORM

water	*food*	*information*
salt	*music*	*vocabulary*
money	*accounting*	*terminology*

8K   Noun Phrases

Noun phrase is the name for the combination of a noun with other words. The combination functions in a sentence just like the simple nouns do—as subject (first example), object (second example), or complement.	**My class** had finished at 11:50 a.m. I always think about **my dear father**.
A noun phrase can include several different kinds of structures. In the examples, the first phrase is article + adjective + noun. The second is article + adjective + adjective + noun.	a wonderful time the most beautiful place
A **complex noun phrase** is a noun phrase that is long and complicated, with words attached before or after the main noun. The first example shows an article + main noun + prepositional phrase (preposition + noun). The second shows an article + adjective + main noun + relative clause.	the science of detection and measurement the civil war that went on in my country

8L   Objects

The word **object** is used for two different types of grammar: verbs and prepositions.

A **transitive verb** must have a **direct object.** Sometimes this direct object is just called the object of the verb. The direct objects are in **bold** in these examples.	Many French people <u>adore</u> **horse meat.** I <u>like</u> **working with people.**
Some verbs can have another object, called the indirect object. The **indirect object** (me) "receives" the direct object (some medicine).	They <u>gave</u> **me** some medicine and <u>put</u> a cast on my arm.
Prepositions have objects. The combination of a preposition with its object is called a prepositional phrase. In the example sentences, the prepositions are *with, in,* and *to.* Their objects are underlined.	**with** onions and savory herbs **in** the stomach **to** the outside

8M   Participles

The **present participle** is used to form present (first example) and past progressive (second example) verb forms.	I <u>am</u> **studying** English now. My mother **was waiting** for me.
The **past participle** is used to form present and past perfect verb tense. It is also used to make passive verbs. The examples illustrate these three in order.	I <u>have</u> never **forgotten** this experience. My class <u>had</u> **finished** at 11:50 a.m., but I did not return home. Sunlight <u>is</u> more easily **reflected** on light-colored surfaces.

8N Phrases and Clauses

A **phrase** is a group of words that work together as a single unit. Phrases include noun phrases, verb phrases, and prepositional phrases. The examples illustrate these three in order.	The Appian Way has been called of its length
Unlike a phrase, a **clause** is built like a sentence with a subject and a verb. The most important clause types are **adverbial clauses, noun clauses,** and **relative clauses** shown in **bold** in the three examples.	I was nervous and unhappy **because everything was new and different.** I thought **that I had said** something wrong. Also, it was "crowned," **which means** the center was higher than the sides, so that rain would drain off it.

8O Prepositions

Prepositions are words like *in, on, at,* and many others. Another term that is used is **preposition phrase** or **prepositional phrase.** This terminology refers to the combination of a preposition with its object. Prepositional phrases are often used as adverbials to tell *when, where, why,* and so forth.	Prepositional phrase as an adverbial to tell where: Imagine yourself **in a Mercury.** Prepositional phrase as an adverbial to tell how: Similarly, women are encouraged to buy products **by watching ideally beautiful women.**
Prepositional phrases are also often attached to nouns in complex noun phrases. Research has shown that this combination is more common than the combination of a noun plus a relative clause.	• he culture **of youth in the U.S.** • men **in ads** • teenage girls **with large amounts of discretionary spending money**
Prepositions are also closely tied to some verbs and need to be learned as part of the structure of particular verbs. (See the following WWW site for a list of these prepositional verbs: http://www.gsu.edu/~wwwesl/egw/verbprep.htm.)	focus on — Some ads are **focused on** white, middle-class males. appeal to — No one ad **appeals to** every person.

8P   Pronouns

Pronouns are words like *I, me, you, we, us, he, him, she, her,* and *it.* These are also called personal pronouns because they refer to persons.

I was joyful when I saw many children of my age standing with their parents in front of the school.

Other words are also called pronouns. These include the following types:
1. **demonstrative** pronouns (*this/that* and *these/those*)
2. **relative** pronouns (*who, whom, that, which,* and some others)
3. **interrogative** pronouns (*who, whom, whose, why, how,* and some others) for asking questions

1. Officially, *this* road was called the Cumberland Road, but it soon was known as the National Pike, the Great Turnpike, and the Old Pike.
2. The name *that* stuck, however, was the National Road.
3. *Where* was it?
What did it look like?
Why did you like it?

8Q   Sentences

A sentence is a complete unit that contains a subject and a verb. In writing, a sentence begins with a capital letter and ends with a period, a question mark, or an exclamation mark.

I <u>had</u> fun there because there were many children to play with.
<u>Does</u> the ad <u>look</u> crowded?

Sometimes a verb requires a **direct object.** Direct objects are nouns, pronouns, and other words that complete the meaning of the verb. This kind of verb is called a **transitive verb.**	Every day <u>I</u> always <u>played</u> **soccer** with my friends after school.
Sometimes the verb requires a **complement.** Complements can be nouns, pronouns, or adjectives. This kind of verb is called a **linking verb** because it links the subject to the information in the complement.	<u>It</u> <u>was</u> very **dramatic.** <u>Advertising</u> <u>is</u> a **reflection** of society. <div align="right">Continued</div>

Sentences can also have **adverbials.** These answer questions like *when, where,* and *how.*	It <u>cooks</u> **evenly.**
This example sentence doesn't have either a direct object or a complement. The verb is called an **intransitive verb.** An intransitive verb never has an object or a complement.	<u>My arm</u> <u>was aching</u> and <u>I</u> <u>was crying.</u>

8R   Subjects of Sentences

Subjects can be single nouns, longer noun phrases, complicated complex noun phrases, pronouns, and other combinations of words that can be used as nouns. In these examples, subjects are underlined with one line. The subjects of the first two sentences are single nouns. The subject of the second is a two-word noun phrase. The fourth example shows a subject of two nouns combined with and and the last has a complex noun phrase as the subject.	<u>Partners</u> must <u>trust</u> each other. <u>You</u> may not <u>roll</u> them back. <u>Bad weather</u> <u>forces</u> people to find alternative methods for traveling when automobiles cannot <u>transport</u> them. <u>Aerobics</u> and <u>a toning workout</u> <u>burn</u> fat and <u>tone</u> muscles. <u>Stagecoaches, carriages, Conestoga wagons loaded with freight, and droves of cattle and sheep</u> <u>traveled</u> the road.

8S   Verbs in Sentences

Each English sentence must have a subject and a verb. The verb in a sentence is often called the verb phrase.

subject   verb phrase As the railroad moved West, <u>the National Road</u> <u>grew</u> quiet.

Verbs can be **active** or **passive.** In active sentences, the **subject does** the action. In passive sentences, the **subject receives** the actions that someone else does. In the active example, the mother does the sewing. In the passive example, the local travelers use the road *(it)*. Also, the road workers make little effort to repair it.	<u>My mother</u> <u>sewed</u> only one style. <u>It</u> <u>was used</u> mostly by local traffic, so little <u>effort</u> <u>was made</u> to keep it repaired.

8T   Verb Forms

Verbs like *want* or *know* are used primarily in the verb phrase in sentences and in infinitives and a few other cases.

Want and most other verbs are **regular verbs;** they form their simple past tense and past participle by adding *-ed* to the basic word.
 	
    Write and many other verbs are **irregular verbs;** they form their past tense and past participle in ways different from the regular verb.
 	
    (See the list of irregular verbs on the WWW at http://www.gsu.edu/~wwwesl/egw/jones. htm.)
	I want to study nursing for my career, and **I know** this major will require more reading in biology, history, psychology, medical language, writing, etc.

8U   Verb Tenses

simple present tense	Every person <u>has</u> two types of self.
simple past tense	The first day at school, I <u>wore</u> a white shirt with blue shorts.
present perfect tense	I <u>have had</u> long talks with Zairean friends about cheese.
past perfect tense	The individuals who <u>had "died"</u> typically reported the following sequence of events.
present progressive tense or **present continuous tense**	Cocaine <u>is</u> quickly <u>becoming</u> one of the more widely abused drugs in the United States.
past progressive tense or **past continuous tense**	My mother <u>was standing</u> outside of the class.

APPENDIX: LIST OF IRREGULAR VERBS

BASE FORM	PAST TENSE FORM	PAST PARTICIPLE FORM
awake	awoke	awoken
be	was	were/been
bear	bore	born
beat	beat	beaten
become	became	become
begin	began	begun
bend	bent	bent
bet	bet	bet
bid	bid	bid
bind	bound	bound
bite	bit	bitten
bleed	bled	bled
blow	blew	blown
break	broke	broken
breed	bred	bred
bring	brought	brought
broadcast	broadcast	broadcast
build	built	built
burn	burned/burnt	burned/burnt
burst	burst	burst
buy	bought	bought
cast	cast	cast
catch	caught	caught
choose	chose	chosen
cling	clung	clung
come	came	come
cost	cost	cost
creep	crept	crept
cut	cut	cut
deal	dealt	dealt
dig	dug	dug
dive	dived/dove	dived
do	did	done
draw	drew	drawn
dream	dreamed/dreamt	dreamed/dreamt
drive	drove	driven
drink	drunk	drunk
eat	ate	eaten

BASE FORM	PAST TENSE FORM	PAST PARTICIPLE FORM
fall	fell	fallen
feed	fed	fed
feel	felt	felt
fight	fought	fought
find	found	found
fit	fit	fit
flee	fled	fled
fling	flung	flung
fly	flew	flown
forbid	forbade	forbidden
forget	forgot	forgotten
forgive	forgave	forgiven
forsake	forsook	forsaken
freeze	froze	frozen
get	got	gotten
give	gave	given
go	went	gone
grind	ground	ground
grow	grew	grown
hang	hung	hung
have	had	had
hear	heard	heard
hide	hid	hidden
hit	hit	hit
hold	held	held
hurt	hurt	hurt
keep	kept	kept
kneel	knelt	knelt
knit	knit	knit
know	knew	known
lay	laid	laid
lead	led	led
leap	leaped/leapt	leaped/leapt
learn	learned/learnt	learned/learnt
leave	left	left
lend	lent	lent
let	let	let
lie	lay	lain
light	lit	lighted
lose	lost	lost
make	made	made
mean	meant	meant

BASE FORM	PAST TENSE FORM	PAST PARTICIPLE FORM
meet	met	met
misspell	misspelled/misspelt	misspelled/misspelt
mistake	mistook	mistaken
mow	mowed	mowed/mown
owe	owed	owed
pay	paid	paid
prove	proved	proved/proven
put	put	put
quit	quit	quit
read	read	read
rid	rid	rid
ride	rode	ridden
ring	rang	rung
rise	rose	risen
run	ran	run
saw	sawed	sawed/sawn
say	said	said
see	saw	seen
seek	sought	sought
sell	sold	sold
send	sent	sent
set	set	set
sew	sewed	sewed/sewn
shake	shook	shaken
shave	shaved	shaved/shaven
shear	sheared	sheared/shorn
shed	shed	shed
shine	shone	shone
shoot	shot	shot
show	showed	showed/shown
shrink	shrank	shrunk
shut	shut	shut
sing	sang	sung
sink	sank	sunk
sit	sat	sat
sleep	slept	slept
slide	slid	slid
sling	slung	slung
slit	slit	slit
sow	sowed	sowed/sown
speak	spoke	spoken
speed	sped	sped

BASE FORM	PAST TENSE FORM	PAST PARTICIPLE FORM
spend	spent	spent
spill	spilled/spilt	spilled/spilt
spin	spun	spun
spit	spit	spit
split	split	split
spread	spread	spread
spring	sprang	sprung
stand	stood	stood
steal	stole	stolen
stick	stuck	stuck
sting	stung	stung
strike	struck	struck
string	strung	strung
strive	strove	striven
swear	swore	sworn
sweep	swept	swept
swell	swelled	swelled/swollen
swim	swam	swum
swing	swung	swung
take	took	taken
teach	taught	taught
tear	tore	torn
tell	told	told
think	thought	thought
thrive	thrived/throve	thrived
throw	threw	thrown
thrust	thrust	thrust
tread	trod	trodden
understand	understood	understood
uphold	upheld	upheld
upset	upset	upset
wake	woke	woken
wear	wore	worn
weave	wove	woven
wed	wedded, wed	wedded, wed
weep	wept	wept
wind	wound	wound
win	won	won
withhold	withheld	withheld
withstand	withstood	withstood
wring	wrung	wrung
write	wrote	written

Credits

Chapter 1: Page 25: Jean Ann Stevens, "Building Self-Esteem," *Say Goodbye to Shy: Change Your Thinking, Change Your Life* (Newport Beach, CA: SandPiper Press, 1995).

Chapter 2: Page 39: "The National Road," *Cobblestone* magazine, June 1991, Vol. 12, No. 6, 4–5.
Pages 48–49: Excerpted from "On Down the Road," *Cobblestone* magazine, June 1991, Vol. 12, No. 6, 36–40.

Chapter 3: Pages 67–69: Allen F. Roberts, "Tabu: Hey, Don't Do That!" *FACES* magazine, fall 1996.
Page 77: Doranne Jacobson, "Clothing Do's and Don'ts," *FACES* magazine, fall 1996.
Page 83: (left) The Image Works, © Daniel Sheehan; (right) PhotoEdit, Long Beach, CA, © Bachmann; (bottom) PhotoEdit, Long Beach, CA, © Robert Brenner.

Chapter 4: Pages 93–94: Benjamin B. Lahey, "Cultural Circumstances and Memory Skills,"

excerpted from *Psychology: An Introduction* (Brown & Benchmark, 1995).

Chapter 7:
Page 184: (A) "Single Male Looking for Single Female to Share Cave and Adventures . . ." Paramount Pictures and Circuit City advertisement. (B) "What's the Scoop on Dannon Light 'n Crunchy Frozen Yogurt?" Reprinted with permission of The Dannon Company, Inc.
Page 185: (C) "Soothe Your Soul in New Jersey." Reprinted with the permission of the New Jersey Department of Commerce and Economic Development, Division of Travel and Tourism. (D) "Make a Man Remember." Longing Perfume, Coty, Inc. advertisement; (E) "Barbizon: Train to Be a Model or . . . Just Look Like One." Reprinted with permission of Barbizon, Inc. (F) "I Looked in the Mirror, and All I Could Think Was These Glasses Have to Go!" Reprinted with the permission of CBA Vision Corporation, Duluth, GA.

Index